THE ROAD TO SECESSION

NEW PERSPECTIVES IN AMERICAN HISTORY

UNDER THE EDITORSHIP OF

James P. Shenton

John M. Dobson, POLITICS IN THE GILDED AGE:
A New Perspective on Reform

Gerald Sorin, ABOLITIONISM: *A New Perspective*

The Road to Secession

A New Perspective
on the Old South

William Barney

Foreword by James P. Shenton

PRAEGER PUBLISHERS
New York • Washington • London

PRAEGER PUBLISHERS
111 Fourth Avenue, New York, N.Y. 10003, U.S.A.
5, Cromwell Place, London SW7 2JL, England

Published in the United States of America in 1972
by Praeger Publishers, Inc.

© 1972 by Praeger Publishers, Inc.

Library of Congress Catalog Card Number: 77–189902

Printed in the United States of America

For my parents,

William and Mary J. Barney

Contents

Foreword

by James P. Shenton

Nothing in history is fixed in its interpretation. The historian is forever re-examining evidence or examining new evidence to develop new understandings of past events. As his awareness of the complexity of the human condition and of its social expression deepens, the historian struggles to incorporate these added dimensions within his discipline.

The process of historical reinterpretation, which adds excitement to the task of being a historian, in some measure is a reflection of the changing needs and interests of new generations. More fundamentally, new interpretations of history reflect the profound forces that operate to bring about social change. For the historian, like any other man, is not immune to the influence of the currents that shape the experience and attitudes of his time.

In the decades since the end of World War II, historians have increasingly employed the tools and techniques of analysis developed by sociologists, political scientists, social psychologists, and anthropologists. Armed with these interdisciplinary methods, they have been better equipped to probe the complex motivations of men. Their ability to analyze the extraordinary variety of mass behavior has been vastly improved by the use of statistical analysis and computers to unravel the meaning of mountains of raw data. It now seems possible to explain not only the behavior of a handful of people but that of whole cities, classes, and even societies.

More important than the changes in methodology are the changes in historians' attitudes and approaches, reflecting the impact of vast social changes. Thus, for example, the black revolution in America and abroad has obliged historians to abandon their traditional preoccupation with governing elites to examine the interaction of whites and blacks on all levels of human experience. Americans have suddenly become aware that a vast segment of their national life, that of nonwhites, has been shrouded in neglect. And, because so much of the nonwhite experience has been that of a downtrodden and oppressed people, historians have had to begin to develop techniques of analysis that will permit an understanding of how the common man functioned. In a world growing smaller, a world in which the masses of mankind aspire to a fuller dignity, historians are faced with the demand that they probe the history of the many rather than the few. To meet this demand, they are beginning to explore not only the history of nonwhites but also that of the neglected female. Similarly, historians are beginning to look into the ways in which ethnic origin has affected American whites—for example, the attitudes and behavior of American labor.

With the new effort to understand the individual in mass society has come a desire to know more about the functioning of the institutions that affect everyman. The family, the school, the system of criminal justice, the institutions of government, to name but a few, are being subjected to deepening scrutiny by historians as well as other social scientists.

The authors of this series, well aware of these significant changes in the world and in historians' ways of interpreting it, are attempting a twofold task. They seek, first, to synthesize the most recent scholarship on a significant period or theme in American history. Second, they attempt to project contemporary relevance into past experience so as to give the student a fresh perspective on material that may be familiar to him in more conventional presentation. The consistent emphasis on changing interpretations, it is hoped, will stimulate interest in history as a dynamic discipline and will dispel any lingering vestiges of the myth that historians are somehow above the fray, uniquely capable of pure objectivity.

In this volume Professor Barney has penetratingly analyzed the antebellum South. For most Southerners, a fundamental commitment to slavery dictated a policy of economic and political expansion, which they saw as inextricably linked to the dynamic growth of slavery. Committed to equalitarian principles and natural-rights doctrine, and aware that the world increasingly viewed slavery as barbarous, Southerners struggled to reconcile their democratic ideology and moral precepts with the "peculiar institution." The Southern answer to this contradiction also was expansion. But the rise to national power of the Republican Party, determined to confine slavery, slammed shut the escape hatch of expansion. Radical Southerners seized the opportunity to force secession. The result was civil war and the emancipation of the slaves. When it was finally defeated, the South had been freed of slavery, but its racial attitudes remained rooted in a belief in black inferiority. These largely unaltered beliefs have underscored the American racial dilemma that persists until the present day.

Preface and Acknowledgments

It is easy to become confused amid the welter of interpretations concerning the coming of the Civil War. Democracy versus aristocracy, industrialism versus agrarianism, nationalism versus states' rights—these dichotomies have been the main conceptual frameworks employed by historians. Often, such sweeping generalizations have been grafted onto preconceived patterns of either a "great moral debate" culminating in an "irrepressible conflict" or of emotional blundering leading to a needless war. Recently, historians have begun to move beyond traditional confines by turning to the issues of race and class, which contemporaries intuitively placed at the center of the raging debates of the 1850's.

Eugene Genovese, in *The Political Economy of Slavery*, has given us a sophisticated Marxist analysis of a beleaguered Southern master-class opting for secession in a bold attempt to stave off both internal crisis and the external threat of the Republican party. Steven Channing's *Crisis of Fear* is a harrowing account of the racial phobias that cut across class lines in South Carolina and precluded any compromise with the Republicans. These works, among the best of recent scholarship, focus on the crucial issues of race and class but fail to integrate them into a balanced interpretation. Genovese is surely correct in stressing the class base of Southern slave society and the ideological manifestations of the planters' hegemony, but he underestimates the egalitarian racism that was the dominant public ideology. The power of the planter, as well as the act of secession itself, rested upon the loyalty of a nonslaveholding majority that feared the potential social and economic consequences of emancipation far more than they resented the actual elite status of the slaveholder. Conversely, Channing, by examining only Southern racism, fails to explain why Southerners did not take more comfort in the Jim Crowism of contemporary Northern society, which denied the free black even a semblance of equality.

The thesis offered here considers the class structure and racial attitudes of slave society in conjunction with the problem of expansion, in an effort to shed new light on the coming of the war from the Southern perspective. For all their differences in 1860, Northerners and Southerners agreed that slavery had to expand in order to survive. Herein lay the fundamental issue that precipitated civil war. Both the racial and the class accommodations of Southern society were predicated on the continual extension of slavery. Southerners were convinced that, if they acceded to the Republican demand of confining slavery to a fixed area, they would eventually run out of land on which to support plantation agriculture and space within which to disperse the black population so as to avoid socially dangerous concentrations of slaves.

Previous expansion had permitted Southerners to avoid the central ambivalence of their civilization: the eventual destiny of the blacks in a biracial society committed to white supremacy. Not only was racial discipline possible as long as the South had room for her blacks, but ultimately an all-white society was conceivable if enough slaves were carried off southward to stock future plantations in tropical America. Without this expansion, the South foresaw only racial catastrophe.

By 1860, after a decade of repeated failures to extend slavery, the leaders of the Democratic party in the cotton states decided to stake their future and that of the South on a desperate bid to win recognition of Southern rights in the territories. They split the national Democratic party and ran their own candidate, John Breckinridge of Kentucky. But they were not confident of success and, with Lincoln's election, immediately pushed for secession.

Radicals had been preaching the benefits of Southern nationalism for a generation. Although Northern efforts to keep slavery out of the territories acquired in the Mexican War and to force California into the Union as a free state had provoked a sectional crisis in 1850, Southern extremists were thwarted then and throughout the 1850's. They were social outsiders on the periphery of political leadership within their respective states and, despite their skill at propagandizing, were unable to convince the Southern masses that slavery was endangered.

"Bleeding Kansas," John Brown's raid, and the rising power of free-soil Republicanism succeeded where the radicals had failed. Once Southerners began to doubt that slavery could ever expand or be secure within the Union, the radicals were able to exploit these anxieties until confidence in the national government's ability or will to protect Southern lives and property was fatally undermined. Whether slavery was to die a slow death through restriction or a sudden one in the holocaust of a Republican-sponsored invasion became, for the Lower South, the crux of a dilemma that only Southern independence could solve. The Civil War was to prove how disastrous an illusion secession would be; but, at least in 1860, the radicals stood redeemed when the South sought room for her racism.

One of the pleasures of completing research is the opportunity it presents for acknowledging the help of those who made the finished work possible. In particular, I would like to thank Professor James P. Shenton of Columbia for being both a teacher and a friend, Gladys S. Topkis of Praeger Publishers for her confidence and advice, and my wife, Elaine, for typing the manuscript and, above all, for being herself.

WILLIAM L. BARNEY

Cold Spring, N.Y.
April, 1972

THE ROAD TO SECESSION

1. The Quest for Room

The antebellum South was a biracial society in spite of itself. Southern whites, utterly dependent upon black slave labor for their wealth and ever fearful of the consequences of emancipation, were enmeshed in an institution that was a source of both prosperity and despair. The Southern paradox appeared insoluble. In the words of Jefferson, "We have the wolf by the ears, and we can neither hold him nor safely let him go. Justice is in one scale, and self-preservation in the other." As in most such encounters, self-preservation won out, and the South geared her institutions and ideologies to minimize the manifold tensions and contradictions generated by the enslavement of large numbers of blacks in a white culture professedly committed to a Christian and egalitarian ethos.

The fundamental problem was the moral and social legitimacy of slavery. The issue of morality was met by denying the black man's humanity, by placing him in evolutionary limbo, between the ape and the white man. If one agreed with the premise of the Richmond *Examiner* that the Negro was a "totally distinct and inferior animal or species of animal from the Caucasian," it became far easier for Christian whites to accept their enslavement of blacks as part of the natural order of creation and as much an expression of God's will as was the subordination to whites of beasts of burden. On a more positive note, Southerners claimed that the Bible sanctioned slavery. This was the favorite proslavery argument of the Protestant South. It was the one with which they felt most comfortable, because it conformed to their literal reading of the Bible and did not require a fantastic, if not farcical, stretching of the Biblical story of creation into a brief for polygenesis.

The social defense of slavery rationalized the hegemony of the slaveholding elite that dominated Southern life. It was a delicate position, because elitist rule rested on the loyalty to slavery of the nonslaveholding majority. This majority, at best economically stunted by slave competition and at worst cast aside by a labor system that had no use for it, was, however, enfranchised and had the power to destroy slavery. Appeals to racial pride were always effective with this group, for many of the whites were so poor that the color of their skin was the highest badge of social status to which they could aspire. Moreover, all classes feared amalgamation, the loss of racial purity through interbreeding with an inferior race. Released from the discipline and segregation of slavery, so the argument went, the blacks would become sexual, as well as social, rivals of the white masses.

Racism, however, was not the only ideological link binding rich and poor whites together in a social acceptance of slavery. After all, the virulent racism of the North, which treated blacks as pariahs, was solid proof that emancipation need not, and probably would not, result in racial equality. Class-oriented arguments were, therefore, added to the anti-Negro rhetoric. These class appeals were plausible because of the sheer number of slaves—at least 30 per cent of the total population in a majority of the slave states. Nonslaveholders were repeatedly told that the unleashing of millions of emancipated slaves on the labor market would lead to ruinous economic competition, depress wages, and beggar the poor of both races. The menial and degrading physical labor that had to be performed in every society would no longer be confined to black slaves. The status and security of the nonslaveholder would be obliterated: To the infamy of losing his daughter to the black man next door would be added the injury of losing his privileged rank in a labor aristocracy.

Despite the legitimization of her peculiar institution, the South could never feel secure. Much as Southerners were tempted to rebel against their heritage, they were undeniably part of a Western civilization that increasingly scorned their pretensions to honor and denounced them as un-Christian hypocrites. A South Carolina congressman pointed out that the South's sensitivity on the slavery issue was perfectly understandable. "Is she not held up to ridicule and contempt, to scorn and execration, in every conceivable mode and on every possible occasion?" The elite worried that this moral flagellation of the South by the outside world would result in internal doubts, perhaps even in defeatism—the feeling that "the Institution of Slavery is doomed. That all the world is opposed to it and that we ourselves will not or cannot do any thing to avert it." The slaveholders used their control of the positions of influence and channels of communication to unite the South in a fervid defense of slavery. Dissenters were driven out or forced to remain silent, the mails were censored, and all institutions were purged of any abolitionist traces. An ideological offensive was launched that taunted the North with the moral shortcomings and class exploitations of free capitalistic society and proclaimed the necessity of slavery for the survival of republican institutions. There was much bluff and bluster in this Southern response, but, given the tenacity with which Southerners of all classes fought to preserve slavery during the Civil War, the conclusion reached in 1849 by Governor James Hammond of South Carolina on the effects of abolitionist agitation seems reasonably valid: "My opinion has long been that the discussion of the Abolition question has eased nearly every conscience in the South about holding Slaves, and that Self-interest will prompt us almost to a man to go through any Struggle and risk any change rather than emancipate them in any way, much less on our own soil."

While the South tended to unite in self-righteous defense against outside attacks, the political realities of coexisting in a Union with a growing Northern antislavery majority and the social and economic consequences of plantation agriculture had combined by 1860 to present formidable internal and external threats to the preservation of Southern society. At the heart of the crisis was the expansion of slavery. The existing class and racial arrangements of the South's biracial society were secure only as long as additional slave territory could be acquired. This belief, which was almost axiomatic in both the North and the South, resulted from the unique manner in which expansion had alleviated the most serious paradoxes and stresses of the slave South.

The history of slavery in the South was largely the story of its expansion. This expansion, from the tidewater of Virginia and the Carolinas in the late seventeenth century to the river valleys of eastern Texas by the mid-nineteenth century, enabled successive generations of Southerners to carry slavery into new territories. These surges of growth not only were converted into political power in Washington through increased representation but also satisfied two basic internal needs of the South. Additional slave territory sustained the economic viability of slavery by providing fresh land to replace the exhausted soil of the older plantation regions, creating markets for the sale of surplus and agriculturally unprofitable slaves from the Upper South, and enlarging opportunities for both the slaveholders and those striving to attain that status. Moreover, the diffusion of slaves through expansion permitted Southerners to avoid the fundamental problem of how to maintain control over a growing number of slaves confined to a closed area. The slaves had to be kept ignorant and tied to the land, because urbanization and industrialization entailed too grave a risk of slackened discipline and eventual race warfare. But a given amount of land subjected to an exploitive agriculture could support both whites and blacks for only a limited period before losing its fertility. Meanwhile, the concentration of slaves would grow ever denser until it reached unmanageable proportions. Soon—within a generation, some Southerners prophesied—the master would be fleeing his slaves. This was the Southern dilemma. The continual maturation of slavery within a fixed geographical area created class and racial stresses that could be relieved only through expansion. The extension of slavery, in turn, generated powerful opposition, capped in 1860 by the triumph of the Republican party, which was pledged to the strict containment of slavery within its existing limits. For the South, the dilemma had become a question of survival.

LAND AS THE ECONOMIC ELIXIR

Of the many myths spawned by the plantation legend of the Old South, few are as alluring, or as deceptive, as the languorous, timeless image of the white-columned plantation, the homestead of the planter—that polished aristocrat with deep ties to the land, moving with grace and ease in a milieu of wealth, stability, and refinement. In fact, most planters were grasping parvenus, and their homes were simply overgrown log cabins. But what most distorts reality in this image is the absence of a sense of time and movement. It was precisely the restlessness and dynamism of most planters that attracted the attention of contemporaries. Thomas Cobb, a leading jurist of antebellum Georgia, described the planters as a class that was "never settled. Such a population is almost nomadic." Cobb explained this mobility by noting that the prime determinant of a planter's wealth and status was not his land but his slaves. As a result, his surplus income was invested in more slaves rather than in improvements to the land.

> The homestead is valued only so long as the adjacent lands are profitable to cultivation. The planter himself having no local attachments, his children inherit none. On the contrary, he encourages in them a disposition to seek new lands. His valuable property (his slaves) are easily removed to fresh lands, much more easily than to bring the fertilizing materials to the old.

Mobility was characteristic of all Southerners and appears to have been a function of economic class. In Jefferson County, Mississippi, an alluvial planting area on the banks of the Mississippi, about 87 per cent of the nonslaveholders left the county during the 1850's. This percentage dropped among slaveholders in proportion to the number of slaves held, until it reached a low of 17 per cent for those owning 100 slaves or more. The main flow of migration was from the worn-out lands of the Southern Atlantic states to the virgin soils of the Southwest and across Louisiana into Texas. By 1860, South Carolina, an older state, had lost to emigration nearly half of all white natives born after 1800. (The annual and even seasonal movement was also quite heavy, but, because of gaps in the census returns, it cannot be measured.) Writing from the newly opened Alabama frontier in the mid-1830's, a planter's daughter noted that there were "a great many persons moving away from the place and going to the Choctaw [P]urchase and [a] great many coming in which keeps the number pretty much the same."

Whole counties were virtually depopulated by the Texas land fever, only to be refilled by a new wave of settlers. So prevalent was the wanderlust that many resorted to religious metaphor or cited positive secular values to explain their drive. In explaining his life-style, which had seen him constantly on the move, the yeoman farmer Gideon Linecum pointed to his "belief and faith in the pleasure of frequent change of country." Eli Lide, a planter's son who had moved to Alabama from South Carolina in the 1830's, rationalized his move to Texas twenty years later in terms of "something within me [that] whispers onward onward and urges me on like a prisoner who has been 58 years and idles in his Lord[']s vineyard and lived on his bounty and made no returns for the favors received."

Southern institutions were transplanted across the Appalachians with but minimal disruptions. Planters frequently sent ahead a younger son or a trusted overseer with a few field hands to stake out the new territory and clear the land. When the planter arrived with his wagons, livestock, family, and slaves, he quickly re-established the community leadership to which he was accustomed. He assumed the responsibility of meeting the frontier's rudimentary cultural needs by hiring private tutors, perhaps setting up one of the few schools, and donating land or funds for the upkeep of an imported minister. In a few years, his slaves would have carved out of the wilderness the plantation on which his economic primacy rested. Finally, as long as he catered to the democratic sensibilities of the yeoman farmers, he could be virtually assured of political influence and, even, office. No concessions of substance were required, only of style. For example, it was always politically wise to express anti-aristocratic sentiments and to show an acceptably egalitarian spirit in one's personal dealings, no matter what one's natural inclinations. These were the rules of the game, and to violate them brought opprobrium—as one Virginia planter newly arrived in Mississippi discovered. A local farmer, observing that the good gentleman disdained soiling his hands, did not hesitate to tell him that, if he had "taken hold of a plough" and worked by the farmer's side, his help would have been welcomed, but "to see him sitting up on his horse with his gloves on, directing his Negroes how to work," was not to the farmer's taste. Most planters learned the rules soon enough. Generally speaking, then, there was a remarkably successful transfer of the prior structure of institutions and leadership from the Old South of Jefferson to the newer one of Jefferson Davis.

A potential source of conflict in the spread of the plantation was class competition for the better lands. This was usually not a problem, however, because the emigrants, naturally enough, sought out a region similar in soil and climate to what they had left behind. Traditionally, the yeomanry had avoided the heavy, sticky prairie soils and the wet, marshy bottomlands. These areas were thought to be unhealthy and required a much greater initial investment to cultivate than the lighter soils in the uplands or the sandy loam back on the ridges. As a result, when the Southwest was opened up, much of the prairie and alluvial soils, the most productive and fertile in the South, were left by default to the planters. Where competition did exist, it was usually short-lived. The average farmer was a speculator. For him, it was good business to enter a new region, put up a log cabin, clear the forest and make other improvements, and then sell out for a profit after a few years. If a wealthy planter should want the land, all the better. With plenty of land to the west, one could repeat the process several times in a lifetime.

The expansion of the South meant a continual renewal of slave society. Yet, Southerners always had the nagging doubt that the process itself had not solved any problems but only perpetuated them. The doubt, akin to a fear of overdependence, can be understood by looking at the economic forces that fueled the South's search for land.

The nature of plantation agriculture and the consistently low ratio of land to labor costs explain much of the South's outward thrust. Besides initially requiring large units of land, staple-crop production on the plantations exhausted the soil at an alarming rate. Throughout most of the antebellum period, good land was so cheap and available in such quantity, especially relative to slave labor, that it was more profitable to ruin a plantation, pick up stakes, and start anew on virgin soil than to practice soil-conserving agriculture through crop rotation, deep plowing, and the use of fertilizers. Soil erosion and sterility became serious problems not only in scattered localities but in entire districts. By the early 1850's, the plantation belt of middle Georgia was described as a region of "red old hills stripped of their native growth and virgin soil, and washed with deep gullies, with here and there patches of Bermuda grass, and stunted pine shrubs, struggling for a scanty subsistence on what was one of the richest soils in America." Before 1860, the supposedly inexhaustible new cotton lands of the Southwest had already exhibited the "painful signs of senility and decay" familiar to residents of the seaboard states. The complaint of a Georgia editor in 1858 that from the Chesapeake to the Mississippi there was "something fundamentally wrong in Southern agriculture" was little more than a stock refrain.

Within a generation, the planters monopolized the agricultural wealth of any given area with the land and transportation facilities suitable for plantation agriculture. Five per cent of the South's farmers owned 36 per cent of the region's agricultural wealth; the poorest 50 per cent of all farmers owned only 6 per cent of the land. Indeed, even in the uplands and pine barrens—regions where the plantation never took root and that were supposedly the haven of the small farmer—a slaveholding elite controlled more land and more valuable land than the majority of the yeomanry. With their large labor force, extensive credit arrangements, and the capital resources to buy and utilize the best lands, the planters enjoyed competitive advantages over their small farmer neighbors and gradually were able to displace them.

This encroachment of the planter was not a matter of economic necessity only. As much as the planter needed fresh land to replace what he had destroyed or as a hedge for the future, he was also concerned about the security problems of having his slaves come into contact with nonslaveholders. The poorer whites were accused of interfering with slave discipline by setting an example of shiftlessness and by encouraging the slaves to steal plantation property to exchange for liquor and cheap trinkets. A Louisiana sugar planter told Frederick Law Olmsted, perhaps the most perceptive of all Northern travelers in the South, that he

wanted to buy out all the poor whites living around his plantation.

> It was better that negroes never saw anybody off their own planta-
> tion; that they had no intercourse with other white men than their
> owner or overseer; especially, it was best that they should not see
> white men who did not command their respect, and whom they
> did not always feel to be superior to themselves, and able to com-
> mand them.

Wasteful agricultural practices, monopolistic patterns of land
ownership, and displacement of the yeomanry combined to create
the South's land hunger. Down to the 1850's, there had always
been a new cotton frontier—whether in the Georgia-Carolina uplands before the War of 1812, the prairies of Alabama and Mississippi in the Jacksonian period, or the river valleys of Arkansas
and Texas just before and after the Mexican War—to satisfy this
hunger and prevent social tensions from building up. "The way
we have been able to give land to the lacklanders, to extend this
great country, and to supply the landless with land, has been by
the extension of the empire by arms and by money," boasted
Senator Robert Toombs of Georgia, as he argued in 1859 for the
acquisition of Cuba. Even the moderate Jefferson Davis claimed
an economic right of expansion: "We at the South are an agricultural people, and we require an extended territory. Slave labor
is a wasteful labor, and it therefore requires a still more extended territory than would the same pursuits if they could be
prosecuted by the more economical labor of white men."

The Failure of Expansionism

The 1850's witnessed a widening gap between the South's desire to gain more territory and her ability to do so within the
Union. The decade opened with the loss of California to the
free-soil North. California was the great prize in the lands recently wrested from Mexico. Already noted for its deep ocean
ports and its rich valley agriculture, the area became, with the
discovery of gold, a mecca for fortune-seeking Americans.

The antislavery forces, with some backing from Southern

Whigs, argued that the United States was honor-bound to respect the Mexican decrees that had prohibited slavery in the provinces of California and New Mexico. Southern Democrats reacted scornfully to this position. They stressed that the South had contributed more than her fair share of men and arms to the conquest of these territories and thus had a military, as well as a constitutional, right to carry slaves there. Racial stereotypes were employed. "Do they mean to assert," wondered Senator Albert Gallatin Brown of Mississippi, "that the victorious and proud-hearted American is to go, cap in hand, to the miserable, cringing Mexican peon, and ask his permission to settle on the soil won by the valor of our troops at Buena Vista, or before the walls of Mexico?"

To arguments that the climate and soil of these territories were unsuitable for slavery, that the institution was debarred by a "decree of Nature," Southerners responded by citing the great profitability of slavery in mining. "Slave labor is never more profitably employed than in mining," said Brown in a letter to his constituents, "and you may judge whether slaves could be advantageously introduced into that country, when I inform you . . . that an able-bodied negro is worth in California from two to six thousand dollars per annum." The slaves were so valuable in the mines, contended a Virginia senator, that, unless the black race were excluded altogether from California, slaveholders could bring them in by the thousands under contracts calling for their manumission within a few years, work them until then, and still show a large profit. Senator Jefferson Davis of Mississippi was certain that, with irrigation, southern California could support a lucrative commercial agriculture in cotton, grapes, and olives. This agriculture, however, required slave labor. The individual pioneer could not settle upon this dry land and support his family with his own exertions as he had traditionally done in the more humid East. Associated labor was needed to establish and maintain the irrigation system. Because Mexican peonage was clearly inconsistent with American law, Davis concluded that black slavery was the only solution.

The admission of California as a free state was a bitter blow to the South. A small but strategically placed proslavery wing of

resentative William Porcher Miles of South Carolina wanted Kansas as a "wall of defense" for Missouri—and for the two additional proslavery votes she would provide in the Senate. In a racist appeal, Brown of Mississippi accused the free-soilers of wanting to force a government upon the white settlers and thereby create a free Kansas that "makes the negro free by enslaving the white man; but my free Kansas makes the white man free, and leaves the negro where the Constitution left him —subject to the authority of his master." As to charges of corruption and irregularities surrounding the Lecompton Constitution, Southern Democrats replied that these were no worse than similar problems that had beset California. "Are we of the South to be made to see California hurried into the Union against all law and all precedent *because she is a free state* and Kansas subjected to the rigors of the inquisition because she *has a chance* of being a slave state?" demanded a Mississippi congressman.

In March of 1855, David Atchison, a Missouri senator and leader in the struggle to open up Kansas for slavery, offered an early version of the domino theory: "If we win we carry slavery to the Pacific Ocean; if we fail we lose Missouri, Arkansas, and Texas and all the territories; the game must be played boldly. I know that the Union as it Exists is in the other scale, but I am willing to take the holyland." In the view of Python, a pseudonymous contributor to *DeBow's Review* in the late 1850's, all the dominoes would fall if the South lost Kansas; for the entire western flank of slavery would be endangered. The emboldened abolitionists, he warned, would first attack slavery in Missouri, then move south into the Oklahoma Indian territories and Texas, and finally turn west into New Mexico and Arizona. The Upper South would be the next target, and soon slavery would end up confined to the Gulf states.

Southern Whigs, on the other hand, while conceding that the admission of new slave states was vital to Southern interests, refused to believe that Kansas represented slavery's Armageddon. For one thing, the South, they argued, was capable of standing on higher ground than the Lecompton Constitution, which one Whig denounced as the "most barefaced fraud and cheating the world ever saw." For another, few of them expected slavery to take permanent hold in Kansas. Senator John Bell of Tennessee, for example, pointed out, in the spring of 1858, that the number of slaves in Kansas had declined in the previous year from about three hundred to no more than one hundred.

In the end, the South was hoist with her own petard. If the eventual admission of Kansas as a free state was a humiliating defeat, it was largely because too many Southerners had made the issue a test of sectional strength and determination. "It will be useless to attempt explanations and excuses, we are condemned, and I think justly," wrote a Georgia judge to Alexander Stephens in June of 1857. "We have made the people believe it will be a slave state and we ought to make it good or not assume to hold the reins of power."

Cuba and Mexico offered unique advantages to Southern expansionists. The former was already a slave society, and the latter seemed ripe for the taking. Although the unyielding Republican opposition to the expansion of slavery was sufficient to block most designs on these areas, internal resistance within the South was itself a major deterrent.

The pro-Cuban forces were centered in the Democratic party, and they had some support from the Northern wing of the party, as exemplified by James Buchanan's acquiescence in the Ostend Manifesto of 1854. In this declaration, three American foreign ministers crudely served warning on Spain that the United States meant to have Cuba. Many of their arguments would sound familiar a century later. Cuba, lying just ninety miles off Florida, was deemed the key to the commerce and defenses of the Caribbean. But, of course, slavery was the overriding issue. "I want Cuba, and I know that sooner or later we must have it. . . . I want Tamaulipas, Potosi, and one or two other Mexican States; and I want them all for the same reason—for the planting or spreading of slavery," announced Albert Gallatin Brown in a speech at Hazlehurst, Mississippi. Cuba was to be the linchpin in a tropical empire founded on outright annexation or on the creation of satellite states. This empire, by giving the South a virtual monopoly over the production of tropical goods, would ensure the perpetuation of slavery.

The annexationists charged that the British were scheming to effect emancipation in Cuba. Furthermore, they warned that the unstable Spaniards might decree emancipation in order to punish the rebellious Creole planters or to make the island unattractive to Americans. A free black government in Cuba was depicted as a threat to slave security all along the Gulf Coast. "Indeed," in the vivid phrase of John Van Evrie, a proslavery propagandist, "Cuba would be a volcano of 'free negroism', constantly vomiting fire and blood on the neighboring coast. . . ." Annexation not only would eliminate this threat but would also prove a boon to the Cuban slaves. Stephen Mallory of Key West assured his Senate colleagues that, under the paternalism of a Southern master, "the plantation negro in Cuba would be what he is in Florida, the freest from disease and care, the happiest and the most enduring of his race on the face of the earth."

The Southern opposition, once again led by the Whigs, contended that, if Cuban sugar were admitted duty-free, the sugar planters of Louisiana, Texas, and Florida would be ruined. These planters depended on tariff protection for their economic survival. If hurt by Cuban competition, they might shift their resources to cotton production, thus depressing the price of that staple. The Whigs stressed that Cuba, unlike Texas in the 1840's, was a settled, heavily populated country that had no room for Southern emigrants. The living conditions of the slaves would improve under American rule, but this would result in an even higher population density, which could not absorb the South's own rapidly increasing slave population. "We want land without people on it, and not land and people together," said a Tennessee representative. The problems of assimilating the Cuban people were seen as insurmountable. Their language, religion, and extraction differed from ours, stressed Senator John Thompson of Kentucky, "and our people have regarded them as aliens and outlaws from the pale of humanity and civilization. . . . Saying nothing about color, I think I have been at more respectable weddings than it would be to bring her into the household." The Republicans agreed. Cuban whites were "ignorant, vicious, and priest-ridden," according to one Republican senator, and another wondered what the United States would do with the 200,000 free blacks on the island.

The Whigs could not see how Cuban annexation would strengthen slavery. The old fear of the future of slavery in the Upper South was revived. If, as most people expected, the African slave trade with Cuba were prohibited under the Americans, the planters would turn to the Upper South to replenish their labor supply and thereby hasten the abolitionizing of these states. One Whig congressman based his opposition on the ground that he did not want to see the area of slavery contracted. Because Spain hated and feared the United States, he reasoned, she would spitefully free the Cuban slaves if she ever became convinced that the island was about to fall into American hands. On the other hand, if Cuba, by some unexpected stroke of good fortune, were acquired with slavery intact, the Whigs foresaw an explosion of antislavery agitation. England and France, suspecting that the United States coveted, and would therefore try to seize, other West Indian islands, would be poised for war.

Despite considerable influence within the Pierce and Buchanan administrations, the Cuban annexationists got nowhere. Their most flamboyant leader, Governor John Quitman of Mississippi, was in constant difficulty with federal authorities over his open defiance of the neutrality laws through his filibustering activities. Quitman was convinced that the South would be able to expand within the Union only if she forced a drastic revision of these neutrality statutes, which barred Americans from private military enterprises against other sovereign powers. Then, Southern armies, privately financed and recruited, would be free, he hoped, to carry slavery into the Caribbean and Central America. Quitman was immensely popular in Mississippi, but most Southerners rejected his dramatic program. After all, even in the case of Cuba, the expansionists had not resolved certain paradoxes. On the one hand, they predicted that, as a result of the closing of the African slave trade and of American paternalism, the Cuban slave population would be better treated and would increase rapidly by natural causes. With a longer life expectancy, their value would rise, and this, in turn, would inflate the production costs of Cuban sugar, making it more competitive with American sugar. Yet, if the slave population grew after annexation, the island could hardly serve as the outlet the South demanded for her own increasing numbers of slaves.

For some, Mexico could serve as that outlet. In a speech before Congress, Representative O. R. Singleton of Mississippi reasoned that, because there was no settled government in Mexico, the United States had every right to intervene to promote order and set up a stable government. And, "when we have wound it up, there being no better heirs than ourselves, we will be compelled to hold that territory." Such altruism had its rewards. Much of Mexico, Singleton declared, was suitable for cotton, rice, and sugar cultivation. The South would have her outlet. "In my opinion we must, and we are compelled to, expand in that direction, and thus perpetuate it [slavery]—a hundred or a thousand years it may be."

In 1858, William Burwell of Virgina, in urging Senator R. M. T. Hunter of Virginia to exert pressure for a more aggressive Mexican policy, suggested that the acquisition of all Mexico could serve both as a popular issue for the next Presidential election and as a means for the South to re-establish her political equality within the Union.

> . . . you have within your grasp a country accessible, abounding in all the metals and staples which civilised man most values, and a territory so extensive as that you can by only promoting the existing communities of Mexico to an equality with the present members of the Union preserve the balance in the Council of States, and so guarantee the peculiar rights of those States of which you are one of the guardians and representatives.

Burwell was confident that Southern whites could easily control the racially mixed population. Movement into Mexico would be relatively easy on the railroads, and, with the telegraph, communications would be no problem. In that sense, Mexico was no farther away from Washington than Alabama or Tennessee had been twenty years earlier. If Mexico were not won for slavery, Burwell contended, it would be abolitionized by the North. "And if the worst should befall us could we not cut loose from the Union, throw an emigrant army into Mexico and make it as

safe as Texas?" There was no alternative. "The North has more
states and more territory than the South. It has the immigration
of Europe to aid it. Your subjugation is as certain as the unrelent-
ing operation of these great causes can render it." Out of self-
protection, the South must "seize upon all the territory which
produces those great staples of social necessity which the world
cannot go without. Do so and you are safe."

Southern Democrats did implement a pale replica of the Sin-
gleton-Burwell program. The Buchanan Administration tried to
purchase the northern Mexican states or at least establish a protectorate over them, to extract commercial concessions, and to
win diplomatic recognition of the right of the United States to
intervene directly in Mexican affairs. These approaches, which
met with some success, were held back by the same racial antip-
athies that had defeated the All-Mexico movement in the aftermath of the Mexican War. This racism was common to nearly
all Americans. To Senator A. H. Sevier of Arkansas, the Mexicans were "a people bigoted, superstitious, cruel and ignorant;
crossed, in the first place, in blood with the Moor and Spaniard,
and recrossed with the negro and Indian." Representative C. Delano of Ohio believed that this intermixture produced a "slothful, indolent, ignorant race of beings." In his Barnwell, South
Carolina, speech of 1858, Senator James Hammond used these
racial slurs in denouncing any effort to take slavery into Mexico.
Not only were Mexicans incapable of self-government, he asserted, but they could not even sustain slavery. Moreover, any
attempt to incorporate them into the Union would result in a loss
of racial purity.

> Sweep in Mexico at present, and it is the beginning of amalgamation.
> That is a people of mixed race and blood. So far from marking a
> line of discrimination between black and white, it is almost utterly
> obliterated, and would step over, and gradually spread itself over,
> and instead of aiding this country, debauch it.

There was no better indication of the difficulties, if not outright futility, plaguing the expansionists than the opposition
within the South to the reopening of the African slave trade.
There were many factors behind the opposition: the vested in-

terest of the Upper South in high slave prices; fear of losing racial control by importing savage, heathen Africans; the wish to avoid agitating such a divisive issue; the threat of lower-class discontent if wages were severely depressed by cheap slave competition; and the conviction that the trade was morally wrong. These factors combined to hamstring the expansionists, for Southerners of both parties agreed that, without a surplus of cheap slave labor to throw into the territorial competition with free labor, the South had little chance of adding any more slave states. "This great truth seems to take the people by surprise," wrote the Georgia Whig, Alexander Stephens. "Some shrink from it as they would from death. Still it is as true as death." Albert Gallatin Brown realized this truth, but, ever sensitive to the land hunger of his piney-woods constituency and aware that land prices in Mississippi had more than doubled during the 1850's, he demanded more land before the trade was reopened. "If . . . labor is trenching, is close upon the lands—I mean lands worth cultivating—then we ought to get more land before we get more labor, since labor without land will be a burden rather than a profit."

The positions of Stephens and Brown were irreconcilable as long as the South remained in the Union. The South needed the slave trade in order to expand, but, even if the North consented to the reopening of the trade, the South feared that she had insufficient land on which to support the additional slaves. As an independent country, however, she would no longer face the political necessity of matching the Northern expansion of free labor with her slaves and, even without reviving the African slave trade, could stake out additional slave territory to be occupied whenever economic pressures dictated.

The Lack of Alternatives

The extent to which the social and economic exigencies of plantation agriculture demanded an expansionist solution reflected the particular class and racial structure of the South. Agricultural reform and industrialization were the two main avenues by which the South could ostensibly have increased her prosperity and met the challenge of the free North without acquiring more slave territory. The South haltingly tried both approaches. Neither resulted in more than a halfway palliative, which was abandoned or allowed to wane as it impinged upon the class prerogatives of the slaveholders or the racial accommodations of Southern society. Each approach highlighted the ambivalence of the slave South and set up tensions that, far from being creative, were simply debilitating.

The agricultural reform movement was launched in the mid-1840's, during an economic depression. Soil deterioration, the overproduction and low price of cotton, and the heavy emigration from the older states had convinced the planters that reform was necessary. Despite some notable successes, particularly in Virginia and Maryland, the reform movement failed to achieve its major objectives of soil restoration, economic diversification, and application of improved agricultural techniques. An agricultural press was established, societies were founded or revivified, and geological surveys were undertaken, but the fundamental problems of Southern agriculture persisted. "Deep and horizontal ploughing and hill-side ditching are ridiculed," noted an 1860 article in the *Southern Cultivator*. "Manuring is almost wholly neglected, except a handful of cotton seed in the hill; a very light and temporary affair. Our ploughing averages from two to six inches deep." These, of course, were the same wasteful practices that had led Daniel Lee, editor of the *Cultivator*, to estimate in 1858 that 40 per cent of the Southern soil was already exhausted.

There is no evidence that the reform efforts in South Carolina even arrested the agricultural decline. In an address before the South Carolina Institute in 1850, Governor Hammond admitted that "neither our agricultural societies, nor our agricultural essays, have effected any thing worth speaking of." Five years later, the reformer A. G. Summer called for a new and vigorous state agricultural society. He cited the state's declining economy: "'She is actually and rapidly retrograding. Her old fields are enlarging, her homesteads are decreasing in numbers . . . her stock is dwindling into ghostly anatomies of vital semblance, and her sons of energy are seeking the more remunerating, hence more genial, fields of the southwest. . . .'"

The reform movement failed because the rewards of staple-crop monoculture were too great and the fears of altering the Southern political economy too intense. In the 1850's, much of the original impetus behind reform was blunted when the average price of cotton rose 30 per cent over the depressed levels of the previous decade. With cotton prices holding at about 10.5¢ per pound, its cultivation was once again profitable, especially for the large-volume producers on the better soils. Most planters were constantly in debt; whether they were about to enter a boom or a bust cycle depended on the size and price of their cotton crop, not on their commitment to better agricultural practices. Plantations were too large to permit profitable use of commercial fertilizers, and most small planters and farmers showed little interest at all in fertilizers. The relative merits of diversification versus concentration on cotton continued to be debated, but the discussion became increasingly a political one. The radicals won the debate, and apotheosized King Cotton. They argued that the South should use her cotton monopoly as an economic bludgeon to win concessions within the Union or political independence outside it. Thus, although the South was normally self-sufficient in foodstuffs, her agriculture grew less diversified in spite of the reformers.

The utter dependence of the South's political economy on slave labor precluded any far-reaching agricultural reform. Slave labor was expensive and inefficient. Thomas Cobb, in his *Inquiry into the Law of Negro Slavery*, flatly stated that the slave would never put out as much work as a free laborer. "This he never will do, and the Southern-bred master does not look for it. The security of his place, as well as the indolence of his nature, do not furnish the necessary stimulus." Planters continually complained that their slaves were excessively careless and wasteful. One frustrated slaveholder told Olmsted that his slaves worked just enough to avoid punishment, but added, "It seems on the plantation as if they took pains to break all the tools and spoil all the cattle that they possibly can, even when they know that they'll be directly punished for it." Whereas Southerners most often invoked racial explanations for the slave's poor work record, Northerners blamed it on the lack of incentives inherent in forced labor. What both overlooked was that, for most slaves, the only available means of

resisting the slave system and expressing their humanity was
through seemingly indifferent work and even the deliberate destruction of plantation property. It was a mark of the competitive
advantages conferred upon the South by her soil and climate and
the world's demand for cotton that the use of such inefficient
labor proved not only profitable but as remunerative as other
investments.

The return of cotton prosperity doubled slave prices over those
of the mid-1840's and was proof that the profitability of slavery
should not be confused with its efficiency. This sharp rise in prices
acted to confirm the maxim that slavery could be profitable only
where there was a very valuable cash crop. Mere grain or vege-
table farming did not yield a sufficiently high return, because the
master had to support not only the slave but the slave's family
as well. By the late 1850's, slave prices had climbed so high that
purchasers could show a profit only with a good cotton crop on
rich land. In the Upper South, planters were forced to continue
expanding the cultivation of tobacco, a soil-exhausting crop, in
order to meet labor costs. The limits of agricultural reform were
drawn ever tighter. Slaves "cannot be employed in planting on
poor and worn out fields, much less in making and carting manure
upon them, without a serious loss, if bought at the present time,"
noted the Southern Cultivator. The Augusta Constitutionalist concurred and sought to revive the moribund reform movement
through a reopening of the African slave trade. The paper reasoned that only much lower labor costs would enable the restoration of old lands to be profitable and offer any realistic inducement for planters to be more careful in their cultivation of new
lands. The conclusion was inescapable: "Without laborers to cultivate and improve the indefinite millions of acres of impoverished
lands, our present practice of skinning and bleeding the soil will
not be abandoned for many years."

The irony of the call for revival of the African slave trade was
not lost on its opponents. In the first place, they argued, the prime
cause of soil exhaustion was overreliance on slave labor at the expense of improved methods of cultivation and land-management
techniques. A steady supply of cheap labor would simply encourage slaveholders to waste the land, as they had done for

generations. Furthermore, with or without cheap labor, the South's worn-out lands would be reclaimed only when an inducement was offered for the grain and livestock production of diversified farming. This inducement, noted one reformer, depended on the creation of a home market, "for we have not a consuming population to afford a market for grain and meat." The lack of a home market, which necessarily thwarted any thorough agricultural reform, was a consequence of the dominance of plantation agriculture. Cassius Marcellus Clay, an antislavery crusader from Kentucky, hammered away at this point throughout his career. He lashed out at slaveholders for driving out white Kentuckians "by the unequal competition of unpaid labor." He preached that no slave state could ever be prosperous so long as so many of its inhabitants were slaves who consumed only a small fraction of what a comparable number of free laborers would, and he attacked the plantation for destroying the prospects of a vigorous town life. "All our towns dwindle, and the farmers lose, in consequence, all home markets. Every farmer bought out by the slave system sends off one of the consumers of the manufacturers of the town: when the consumers are gone, the mechanic must go also."

Finally, the opponents of the trade argued that reopening it would quickly lead to the ruin of slavery in the Upper South. Here they were touching on one of the paradoxes of the reform movement. As Eugene Genovese has pointed out, the success of the agricultural revival in the Upper South depended upon continuation of the same old wasteful agriculture in the Lower South. In the generation before the Civil War, most Southerners were convinced that, solely as an agricultural institution, slavery was no longer profitable in the Border states and some of the Atlantic states. Nevertheless, it was still economically feasible in these areas because of the sale of surplus slaves to the Southwest. Profits from the domestic slave trade were enormous and provided the capital needed for agricultural improvements in the Upper South, as well as protecting the region's economic stake in slavery. Flooding the South with cheap African slaves, cautioned a Mississippi Whig at the Vicksburg Commercial Convention in 1859, would eliminate these profits. States in which the hold of slavery was already precarious, such as Maryland, Delaware, and Virginia, *"would be compelled in less than ten or fifteen years to emancipate their slaves.* They cannot work them profitably on farms. . . . *Therefore, the permanence of the system depends on keeping the prices high."*

The slave traders reversed this argument. They maintained that slavery was doomed in the Border South unless the price of slave labor came down. George Fitzhugh of Virginia, perhaps the most famous propagandist of the antebellum South, saw no choice but to revive the trade.

Half the lands in these border States are without labor to cultivate them. At the present prices of negroes these lands must remain uncultivated, unless white labor, which is much cheaper, is introduced. . . . If introduced, it will gradually expel and drive to the South the negroes and their masters by its superior economy, or emancipate the negroes by the ballot-box or servile insurrection.

No one contributed more to agrarian reform than Edmund Ruffin of Virginia, and no one saw more clearly the contradictions of the program. In an 1859 essay in *DeBow's Review,* he explained that the very drain of slaves on which Virginia depended for her agricultural capital was itself a limiting factor in her agricultural revival, in that it made slaves too scarce and valuable for the average farmer. Like Fitzhugh, Ruffin overcame his initial opposition to the African slave trade when he realized that its reopening was essential for the survival of slavery in the border South, which was faced with the advances of free labor.

The fears of Fitzhugh and Ruffin were justified. The new agriculture could not simply be grafted onto the social structure that had supported the old methods. New markets had to be developed and a network of internal improvements built. The slave force had to be pared to a more workable and efficient number. At a serious competitive disadvantage vis-à-vis both the cotton and tobacco planters of the Southwest and the grain farmers of the Northwest, who had fresher and more productive lands, the diversified farmer of the Upper South could survive only by being integrated into the free-market economy of the Middle Atlantic and Ohio Valley states. "The new life that had come to Virginia and Maryland was more like that in the northern states than like that in the lower south" was the conclusion of Avery Craven in his classic study of soil exhaustion and agricultural readjustment. The slaveholders of the Deep South could see this for themselves. Their response was one of foreboding, tinged with scorn and bitterness, as they sensed that slavery had become an expedient, and thereby expendable, institution in the Upper South.

In a fundamental sense, the agricultural reform movement was misnamed. Its adherents had always made it clear in their resolutions and literature that their main goal was the preservation of slavery. Typical was the circular of the Southern Agricultural Society of Georgia in which W. C. Daniell urged his fellow Southerners "to combine our energies and vindicate ourselves, our institutions, and our country. . . ." There was never any doubt in the minds of most as to where their loyalties would adhere should a conflict arise between the dictates of reform and those of slavery. Faced with the choice, Ruffin "would not hesitate a moment to prefer the entire existing social, domestic, and industrial conditions of these slave-holding States, with all the now existing evils of indolence and waste and generally exhausting tillage and declining fertility, to the entire conditions of any other country on the face of the globe." Reform, then, was the handmaiden of slavery and had few defenders on its own terms when the movement was absorbed first into economic and then into political nationalism.

The hard times of the 1840's, together with mounting frustration at the South's colonial bondage to the North for many of her economic needs and with apprehension over the growing political power of the antislavery crusade, as symbolized by the Wilmot Proviso, which sought to exclude slavery from the territories won in the Mexican War, spawned the debate over industrialization. There had been previous efforts at industrialization—notably in the early 1800's and again in the 1820's, before the nullification crisis—but none were so prolonged or so intense. Industrialization was touted as a vital cog in a program of economic self-sufficiency that would ensure the South's economic independence. Home manufacturers would free the South from reliance on the North for manufactured items, just as direct trade with Europe would free her from commercial dependence on the Northeast and agricultural diversification would free her from requiring the foodstuffs and livestock of the Midwest. No longer an economic satellite of those who scorned and abused her, the South would have the power to demand respect. A Florida editor believed that, by building up Southern industry, "we will add to our own wealth, and stop to a great extent the slanderous tongue of Northern fanatics; for their pocket and conscience is one and the same thing." Prosperity would vindicate slavery by proving that the institution was not to blame for the South's soil exhaustion and lack of schools and industry. "The whole matter will turn in the end on the point of dollars and cents," lectured the Augusta *Chronicle.* "We can only prove our view by attaining prosperity."

The industrial gospel promised a regenerated South, with advantages for all. The emigration of whites and slaves from the older states would be reversed by creating jobs in manufacturing. Surplus and unproductive labor would be drawn off the land into small industrial centers, where it would furnish a market for the more efficient agriculture of those remaining in the countryside. Planters were courted by the offer of expanded employment opportunities for their slaves, the yeomanry tempted by the prospect of becoming commercial farmers for the expanded home market, and the poor informed that they could finally become useful citizens. Increased economic and status rewards were promised for the small urban middle class. The industrial promoters preached painless, almost effortless, change. J. H. Lumpkin of Georgia blended enterprise and morality in imagery that would have done a Yankee proud: "First, the factory goes up: and soon it is surrounded with a beautiful village, with its hundreds, perhaps, thousands, of clean, contented, and thrifty inhabitants. . . ." For the skeptics, the promoters could fall back on the harsh reality of sectional competition. In 1851, J. D. B. DeBow, the influential magazine editor of New Orleans, wrote to members of the Southern Railroad Convention that the South "had nothing to lose." "Every day increases the distance between ourselves and our enterprising neighbors and makes the contest between us a more hopeless one."

Yet, for all its apparent attractiveness and even the sense of urgency so evident in DeBow's 1851 statement, industrialization produced surprisingly meager results in the South. Measured in terms of its own minimal goals of self-sufficiency and substantial employment for slaves and poor whites, the movement was a failure. By 1860, only 5 per cent of the slaves worked in industry, and most of these were in small, rural enterprises. Less than a quarter of the free work force was employed in manufacturing, as opposed to 41 per cent in the North. To be sure, impressive gains were made in some areas. From 1840 to 1860, capital invested in cotton factories nearly doubled and the value of their output rose by more than 40 per cent in the 1850's. Industrial production doubled in the same period. But the entire picture reveals that the South was falling behind the rest of the country in relative amounts of all manufacturing. In 1840, the South contributed 20 per cent of all the capital invested in U.S. manufacturing; by 1860, her share was less than 16 per cent. During the 1850's, the Southern rates of increase in the average capitalization per manufacturing establishment and the number of such establishments were well below the national average. And, of course, the industrial inferiority of the South relative to the North had been one of the catalysts of the Southern industrial effort. Its failure in this crucial area was obvious. Moreover, the bulk of industry was in the Upper South, the very area that radicals in the Southern heartland feared was being converted into a free economy. In short, the price of industrialization seemed to be the end of slavery.

The problems encountered by cotton manufacturers are illustrative of those that plagued the entire industrial movement. Cotton textiles were highly touted because of the availability of cheap water power and the ready access to raw materials. The drive for cotton factories peaked between 1845 and 1850. After 1851, however, there was little growth, and profits declined. The industry was squeezed between higher prices for raw cotton and a drop in finished cotton prices; in addition, it was faced with labor problems, such as a steep rise in the cost of slaves and difficulties in training and controlling poor whites. The value of the output of cotton factories south of Maryland dropped from 8 per cent to 6½ per cent of the national total in the 1850's. A chronic lack of capital crippled the industry. Manufacturers had trouble obtaining credit for themselves, let alone competing with Northern firms in advancing long-term credit to Southern merchants or jobbers. Emblematic of the industry's limitations was its inability to drive Northern competition out of the market of providing cheap cottons for the slaves.

The direct trade movement fared even worse. Launched in the late 1830's, it sought to eliminate the Northern middleman's profits from the Southern trade with Europe. The movement flaunted economic common sense. The South had neither the funds nor the mercantile class to control the cotton trade with Europe. "Our whole commerce except a small fraction is in the hands of Northern men," wrote a Mobile businessman to Calhoun in 1847. "Our wholesale and retail business—everything in short worth mentioning—is in the hands of men who invest their profits at the North. The commercial privileges extended by the Constitution has wholly deprived us of a mercantile class—and thus deprives us (I think) of the most certain means for the accumulation of wealth." In addition, because the South lacked a home market capable of absorbing large quantities of foreign goods, cotton ships returning from Europe with manufactured goods would continue to disembark at Northern ports, where such markets did exist. State subsidies were required for the few projects that were initiated, but here also the absence of planning was often evident. For example, a state charter was obtained in South Carolina for a company to build two steamers to ply between Charleston and Liverpool. Subscription for stock was taken, and one steamer was built in a Long Island shipyard. When the steamer was brought to Charleston and loaded, however, it was discovered that it could not pass the sand bar at the entrance to the harbor. The project was abandoned.

On one level, economic considerations explain the limited achievements in industrialization. The South simply did not have the capital or markets to sustain a thorough program of industrial expansion. What progress had been made was cut short by the return of agricultural prosperity in the 1850's. The agricultural demand drove up the price and reduced the number of slaves available for industry. The "Cotton Is King" argument, which postulated an exclusively agricultural South producing cotton on isolated plantations in exchange for finished goods from outside the South, became an article of faith.

But the lack of capital and of a home market was, in turn, related to slavery. Capital was tied up in slaves, and, however quickly the slave investment could be converted into liquid funds, the fact remains that few Southerners chose to do so except out of financial necessity, and fewer yet out of a commitment to industrialization. The stunting of the home market was, as Cassius Marcellus Clay forcibly argued, a direct result of slavery and the plantation. The degree to which the plantations were self-sufficient or dependent on goods and services from outside the South, together with the monopolistic distribution of wealth, which left little purchasing power in the hands of most Southerners, meant that the bulk of the whites were not even drawn into a market economy.

In the end, the South's craving for internal stability, on the one hand, and her desperate desire somehow to match the North in material wealth and power, on the other, could not be reconciled. A key result of the tension between these conflicting aims was the restrictions placed on the industrial promoters. The promoters were given an audience, and their aims were generally applauded, but under no circumstances were they allowed to disturb the existing racial and class order. Capital accumulation that was not under the direct control of planters and a growth in mass purchasing power would have produced radical changes in this order. Southerners sensed this and reacted by erecting ideological defenses to protect themselves from the consequences of extensive industrialization. Already restricted, the industrialists had to overcome these defenses as well as the ideological contradictions generated by the debate on industrialization in order to make any progress at all.

A basic ideological roadblock confronting the industrialists was the growing penchant of the South to equate a sparse population with an orderly and moral society. The slave and free sections of the Union had been about equal in population density before the War of 1812. But by the 1850's the density in the North had increased to thirty per square mile, whereas in the South it had consistently remained at one-third that figure. In her sectional competition with free society, this disparity put the South at a grave disadvantage. Aside from contributing to and aggravating the South's colonial inferiority, this low population density meant a continual loss of relative political power within the Union. It hindered efforts directed toward internal improvements or toward upgrading what passed for a common school system, because the social and economic capital to support such programs was too widely scattered. The South accepted these limitations. As in most cases in which she was faced with her internal weaknesses, she made a virtue out of her defects.

"A dense population is one of the greatest evils a republican government has to fear," intoned Professor W. J. Sasnett of Georgia. Social order itself could not survive:

> The collision of interests, the result of this multiplication of the points of contact between men, originate and present facilities for the indulgence of criminal passions and purposes from which sparser populations are comparatively free. Dense populations always present a larger class who are seeking to live by fraud, and without legitimate employment, and among whom are to be found the worst elements of discontent and insubordination.

Equally unacceptable were the political consequences of a dense population. In 1859, Roger Pryor, a Democratic editor and congressman from Virginia, insisted that free republican government was already a failure in the North. "When you amass men together, they become agrarian [i.e., socialistic], their individuality and manhood are destroyed, and every power, physical and mental, is directed to an effort to clothe and feed himself and family."

Many Southerners felt that, by keeping her population sparse, the South was not only sparing herself such social deterioration but was also protecting the economic viability of slavery. They worried about the internal crisis that would arise when slave labor was no longer cheaper than free labor. This was not a serious threat so long as the population did not become too dense. Where workers were packed together, as in the festering cities of Europe, the price of labor was driven down to the subsistence level. Slave labor could not then be competitive, "for the amount invested," argued Thomas Cobb, "either in the purchase or rearing of the laborer, is necessarily that much more than the cost of food and raiment, which both free and bond must have, and which is all that, under such circumstances, competition and necessity leave to the free laborer."

The Southern fear of cities was a special case of the commitment to a sparse population. In part, this antiurban bias was the traditional response of agrarian cultures to the social upheavals wrought by the rise of cities. When Jefferson Davis told an audience in Augusta, Maine, "Crowded together in cities originality is lost, mind becomes as it were macadamized, and though the intercourse is favorable to the acquisition of knowledge, it is most unfriendly to that individuality, independence, and purity, without which republican governments rapidly sink into decay," he was repeating a homily familiar to his Yankee listeners. The farmers of both the North and South had been reared on the agrarian myth—the notion that the farmer, because of his close association with the land and nature, uniquely embodied the republican virtues of self-reliance, sound judgment, and sobriety. There was also a green-belt tendency in the early industrial efforts of both sections, a desire to locate the factory in the pure and wholesome countryside, away from the vices and corruption of the city. What better place for a cotton factory than Biloxi Bay, Mississippi? asked one enthusiast. "The operatives would be pretty much a community to themselves; at least, they would be free from the epidemics, vices and maladies, which cannot be prescribed against by the forms of law, and which will be consequent upon a location near New Orleans." The textile lords of Massachusetts shared much of the paternalism of William Gregg, a South Carolina manufacturer, who noted that rigid control over his work force was far easier in a planned, rural community than "in a town or city where the people live in rented houses, beyond the control of the proprietors."

Nevertheless, the cumulative effect of growing industrialization in the North soon broke down traditional attitudes to an extent not possible in the South. For the Southern prorural bias rested not just on the agrarian myth, nor even on the enshrinement of the planter as the sum of all aspirations, but also on the belief that cities weakened the institution of slavery.

Southerners never trusted their slaves in an urban environment. Insolence and insubordination were said to be rife among urban slaves. The New Orleans *Crescent* charged that the city's slaves were "demoralized to a deplorable extent, all owing to the indiscriminate license and indulgence extended them by masters, mistresses, and guardians, and to the practice of *forging passes*, which has now become a regular business in New Orleans." Similar complaints were voiced in the newspapers of other cities. Yet, Olmsted described the behavior of urban slaves toward whites as "invariably either sullen, jocose, or fawning," and other travelers agreed. It was not the insubordination that worried Southern whites so much as the commingling of whites and blacks in a setting that inevitably blurred the distinction between free and slave.

These misgivings, plus the increased rural demand for slaves in the 1850's, accounted for the decline of urban slavery in both relative and absolute terms after 1820. From then until the outbreak of the Civil War, slaves decreased from 22 per cent to 10 per cent of the urban population. Most of these slaves were service tradesmen and domestics, and ownership was more diffuse than in the countryside. Despite strict municipal codes, special housing and police measures, and a host of restraints designed to keep the slaves isolated and submissive, the problem of discipline was never solved. By the very nature of the urban environment it could not be solved. This is hardly to suggest that urban slaves were quasi-free or went around sassing whites, but only that the city offered a range of experiences, opportunities, and desires unknown to most field hands. The urban slave was not so utterly dependent upon his master as was his rural counterpart. The city's grog shops, marketplaces, churches, and brothels offered him a community life and the chance to try out various social roles. Back alleys provided a geographical, and the association of free blacks a social, distance between the slave and his master. Self-respect and self-reliance could at least be tested in this environment, if not always won, and the institution was that much weaker for every slave who gained the least bit of independence from his master. Thus, it was no coincidence that proslavery literature idealized slavery solely in a rural setting. The city was either completely ignored in this fiction or included only to be attacked.

Paradoxically, slavery was a source of both comfort and apprehension to Southerners as they contemplated industrialization. They had convinced themselves that slavery was the ultimate conservative institution, the only one capable of resolving the vicious antagonisms between capital and labor that were hampering industrial societies everywhere in the nineteenth century. In the South, not only were capital and labor combined in the person of the slave, but the slave belonged to an inferior race, which accepted its status. The opposite was true in the North. There, the menial work that must be performed in every society fell to whites, who resented their lowly status. "So far as the mere laborer has the pride, the knowledge, or the aspirations of a freeman, he is unfitted for his situation, and must doubly feel its infelicity," reasoned Chancellor William Harper of South Carolina. Exploited and ruled by capital, free labor was bitter and vengeful. As industrialization progressed, class warfare became inevitable. Juxtaposing these two contrasting images, a Virginia congressman could warn the North: "The black horse that we are riding is a docile and willing animal—the white one that you have saddled is restive and impatient. Ours will keep us above the mud, yours may drag you into it—beware!"

Comforting as this labor theory may have been to the South, the hard fact remained that industrialization meant change, and the planter elite was naturally wary of any disturbance of the existing order. A large industrial force of slaves posed a threat to racial discipline and control, whereas keeping the slaves on the land and employing poor whites as factory hands raised the very specter of class antagonisms that the South was so certain she saw in the North.

These anxieties over the composition of the industrial labor force were analogous to the Southern distrust of urbanization as a social solvent. Whether slave labor or free would entail the greater threat to class and racial stability was at the core of a debate that was never resolved. The debate turned on competing visions of Southern society—one that looked to a thoroughly rationalized slave society dominated by a planter elite, and another, more democratic, that sought to integrate the free labor force into a market economy. The planters held the economic and political power to control the industrial effort and to ensure that a majority of the industrial work force were slaves, but their own commitment to an aristocratic, seigneurial society centered on the plantation was sufficiently strong to keep the vast majority of slaves in agriculture. Concurrently, although the advocates of free industrial labor could be held in check, their mere presence as the spokesmen for the majority of white Southerners limited any efforts to put more slaves into industry.

The proslavery forces reasoned that the chief threat to slavery was the creation of a white working class. The party that would exclude slave labor from industry, mechanical pursuits, and everything but agriculture "is, in truth, the only party from which danger to our Institutions is to be apprehended among us," argued the Charleston lawyer-politician Christopher Memminger in a letter to James Hammond.

> Drive out negro mechanics and all sorts of operatives from our Cities, and who must take their place? The same men who make the cry in the Northern cities against the tyranny of capital—and there as here would drive before them all who interfere with them & would soon raise here the cry against the Negro, and be hot abolitionists—and everyone of these men would have a vote.

The abolitionism of the cities would spread to the countryside, and soon an urban-rural alliance would be forged against the planters. "For you know that even in our lower Country, there are many that could be marshalled against the Planters, upon the idea that they were fighting against the aristocracy," cautioned Memminger.

The white laborers whom Memminger accused of abolitionist sympathies could have either entered the South as immigrants from the North, or even Europe, or been recruited from among native poor whites. All these sources were suspect. Distrust of foreign immigrants had been a precipitant of the Know-Nothing movement in the mid-1850's. A Virginia member of that party explained, "I think opposition to foreign influence, indeed to immigration of foreigners into our portion of the union, is necessary to the safety of the south and her institutions. We want none such as labourers amongst us, for the negroe must give way to them." Most immigrants were poor; they therefore concentrated in cities, where they came into direct competition with slave labor. Where-ever possible, they sought to eliminate this competition by ex-cluding slaves (and free blacks) from the trades, public works, and dockyards. In most cities, free labor was gradually replac-ing slave labor, and this trend alarmed the proslavery enthusiasts. L. W. Spratt of South Carolina, who spearheaded the effort to reopen the African slave trade, ominously noted on the eve of the Civil War that, within the previous decade, ten thousand slaves had been sold out of Charleston and their places taken by immi-grant labor. Immigrants already had pushed slaves out of many jobs and, as the immigrants increased in numbers and political power,

. . . they will question the right of masters to employ their slaves in any works that they may wish for; they will invoke the aid of legislation; they will use the elective franchise to that end; they may acquire the power to determine municipal elections; they will inexorably use it; and thus the town of Charleston, at the very heart of slavery, may become a fortress of democratic power against it. As it is in Charleston, so also is it to a less extent in the interior towns.

The same strictures applied to Northern workers. They also had been born in a free society, where men "drink in abolition senti-ment from their mothers' breasts." In addition, these laborers were tainted with "infidelity, licentiousness and agrarianism"— derogatory clichés for what slaveholders interpreted as the inevi-table failings of a free society—for which they considered Northern social changes responsible. It would be foolhardy for the South to import carriers of such subversive doctrines. Northern mer-chants, gentlemen of property and intelligence, were welcome, but not common laborers. "Most of them are pests to society, dangerous among the slave population, and ever ready to form combinations against the interest of the slaveholder, against the

laws of the country, and against the peace of the Common-
wealth," lectured a South Carolina editor. A Mississippi planter
wrote to *DeBow's Review* in 1859 to express his hope that some
day Northern mechanics would find no employment at all in the
South, for "not one in one thousand would I trust among my
negroes."

In contrast to imported laborers, Southern nonslaveholders
were thought to be quiet, docile, and loyal. The rub was that
planters felt the poorer whites would retain these endearing qual-
ities only as long as they were kept ignorant and tied to the land.
The planters were quite willing to see the bulk of the whites remain in the pine barrens, mountains, and uplands. There, they
were generally segregated from plantation agriculture and slave
competition. The nonslaveholders became a threat only where
such competition did exist. White mechanics constantly decried
the use of skilled slave labor, but they were in a weak position.
Not only could slaves usually be brought in as strikebreakers, but
many of the white artisans depended on the planters for their
employment. Their most renowned victory was an 1845 Georgia
law forbidding black mechanics, free or slave, from entering into
contracts for the construction or repair of buildings. The bitterness of this class was epitomized in a letter from a carpenter that
appeared in the Rome (Georgia) *Southerner* in 1849. The carpenter violated a Southern taboo by declaring himself in favor of
immediate emancipation. He maintained that the underbidding
of slave labor depressed his wages to less than $2 a day and that
working in competition with this labor was "unjust, oppressive,
and degrading."

In many cases, the planters undoubtedly exaggerated the danger to slavery posed by white labor. On the alleged disloyalty of
immigrants, Olmsted commented, "No native even can exceed, in
idolatry to Slavery, the mass of the ignorant foreign-born laborers." Few workers, no matter what their feelings, were so boldly
opposed to slavery as the Georgia carpenter. Frequently, the
planters had such intense class fears they failed to appreciate that
Southerners of all classes preferred slavery to the social and
economic consequences of emancipation. In short, racism sub-
sumed internal class antagonisms. What Southern workers were

demanding was not an end to slavery but a curtailment of the planters' absolute power to use their slave labor in any way they saw fit. Yet, even this limited demand was excessive. "If you have the right to say, I must not teach my negro a trade and not use him thus, you can do anything with my negro," postulated M. W. Phillips of Mississippi. "If you array public opinion against me for this, you can for anything."

In the long run, Phillips was correct. If confined to agriculture, slavery would have lost the flexibility essential to its continued profitability. This point had been reinforced in the 1840's, when Southerners fretted over an agriculturally redundant slave population slowly exhausting the land in the overproduction of commercial staples. Despite the return of prosperity in the 1850's, the older states still faced the problem of a surplus of unprofitable agricultural slaves. Unable to compete on their depleted soils, they were rapidly losing slaves to the Southwest. The future profitability and extended use of slave labor in these states would depend on maintaining the option of using slaves in manufacturing.

Thus, for all their arrogance, the planters were justified in keeping whites out of industry. No one could have predicted the sequel to the creation of a large free industrial class, but at the very least the hegemony of the planters would have been undermined. The new class would have reached out for allies among the urban middle classes and the nonagrarian sector of the economy. New sources of capital accumulation and new status rankings would have altered the political economy. The planters, with everything to lose, naturally opted for limited industrialization under their control and for employing slave labor.

The free-labor ideologists insisted that their road to industrialization provided the surest defense for slavery. Basically, they argued that the planter had more to fear from the status quo than from change. Everyone realized that the safety of slavery rested upon the continued loyalty of the nonslaveholders, who constituted three fourths of all Southern families. Racism and the threat of economic competition from the freed slaves traditionally had ensured this loyalty, but the doubt persisted that slavery could ever be secure so long as it was beholden to a white majority that could not expect constant or remunerative employment. In 1860, Python warned that

> . . . the slaveholders themselves, by pursuing the unwise and selfish policy of training up their slaves, and hiring them out in competition with white mechanics, *thus degrading mechanical pursuits to the condition of menial services,* have originated in all directions, among the no-property men of the South, whether from the North, or born to the manor, *a feeling of deep-rooted jealousy and prejudice, of painful antagonism, if not hostility, to the institution of negro slavery, that threatens the most serious consequences, the moment Black-republicanism becomes triumphant in the Union.*

The restriction of slaves to house and field work was portrayed as the panacea for Southern ills. Restriction would take away from the abolitionists their greatest weapon, the alleged hostility between free and slave labor. The potential threat of internal class conflict would be eliminated. James Taylor, an associate of William Gregg in cotton textiles, reasoned that, if whites were encouraged to enter manufacturing and the skilled trades, "every man, from the deepest principle of self-interest, becomes a firm and uncompromising supporter of our institutions. But crowd from these employments the fast increasing white population of the South, and fill our factories and our workshops with our slaves, and we have in our midst those whose very existence is in hostile array to our institutions." Python and others predicted that the confinement of slaves to the soil would automatically make all other labor aristocratic by reserving it for the "superior" race. In the words of Python: "Dignify the trades to the level of the professions, in common acceptation, and idling, loafing, lounging, fox-hunting, or, in other words, general dissipation of health, energy, and time, among the young men of the South, would almost entirely cease, and in their place be substituted general and busy industry."

No longer would Southern whites perform work as if they were half-ashamed of it and allow more efficient Yankees to replace Southern teachers and mechanics. Nor, presumably, would Southerners be subjected to such platitudes as that voiced by James L. Orr, the Democratic champion of the South Carolina yeomanry, when he had asked, "Can labor be disreputable since its requirements are universal and its necessities of Divine origin?" Addressing the South Carolina Institute for the Promotion of Agriculture, the Mechanic Arts, and Manufactures, Orr had sought to refute the notion that "manual and mechanical labor was inconsistent with intelligence, gentility, and dignity of character." If Orr and the other free-labor advocates had had their way, the very work that was so degraded when performed by the "inferior" blacks would serve as a moral testing ground for Southern whites as they repented their sins of idleness and worthlessness.

Once the dignity of labor was restored and all classes were given an economic stake in slavery, significant economic reforms could be carried out. This position was brilliantly summarized in an unsigned letter entitled "Policy of the Planter," which appeared in the Charleston *Daily Courier* in December, 1856. With the competition and contact of slaves removed from nonagrarian pursuits, the "more industrious and worthy of the immigrants" could be invited into the South without fear of subversion. All white mechanics would support black slavery—"not only, as now, upon conviction of its fitness, but by ties of interest, and with improved means each would aim to become a slave owner, for the purpose of alleviating that domestic drudgery which in non-slaveholding States falls so heavily on the wives and daughters of men of limited resources." Young Southerners would no longer shun mechanical work, "the great lever of modern advancement, under the guidance of the educated mind." More of these young men would remain in their home communities and, with the increased population density, would be able to manufacture goods as cheaply as the North and provide a home market for Southern agriculture. The influence of churches and schools would be far greater as villages grew more compact. Lastly, keeping the slaves on the land "would give a definite and determinate popular policy to the South in this expression: *The greatest power to the white majority, consistent with the greatest enjoyment of the social state of which they are capable to the black minority.*" Slavery, if properly restricted, gave the South a unique opportunity to educate the Negro and "*to enable the superior white race*

*to rise above that slavery of caste which exists in all countries in
which wealth and privilege enable one class to control the other
through its physical necessities. . . ."*

A major goal of this racist populism was to make useful citizens out of the poor whites. The presence of these whites was both a burden and a challenge to the slaveholders. Travelers noticed them and were taken aback by their condition. To Frances Kemble, an Englishwoman who spent two years on her husband's Georgia rice plantation, the poor whites of Georgia were "the most degraded race of human beings claiming an Anglo-Saxon origin that can be found on the face of the earth—filthy, lazy, ignorant, brutal, proud, penniless savages . . . they will not work, for that, as they conceive, would reduce them to an equality with the abhorred negroes. . . ." Southerners were chagrined by these discoveries, but, except for propagandistic flights of fancy, they really could not deny their accuracy. A South Carolinian characterized the sand-hillers of his state as, for the most part, the "most wretchedly inert, and therefore continually stinted people to be found anywhere."

Ranging from 20 to 30 per cent of the rural population, the poor whites were those who owned neither land nor slaves. They squatted on the public lands and favored hunting, grazing, or fishing over farming. They rarely accepted farm work, except during harvest time, and would then refuse to perform certain jobs such as caring for cattle or fetching wood and water, asserting that such tasks were fit only for slaves. The women lost caste if they hired out to do servants' work, and those who did restricted themselves to sewing or quilting. Accused of stealing cattle and of plying the slaves with liquor, the poor whites constituted a nuisance to most planters. The opinions expressed by a Virginia planter to Olmsted were typical. Although the planter acknowledged a sort of equality with the poorer whites and would not assert any superiority in his relations with them, "yet he, all the time, recognized them as a distinct and a rather despicable class, and wanted to have as little to do with them as he conveniently could."

Not all Southerners, however, shared the planters' class derision of the poor whites. Richmond editor Edward Pollard, in his semi-autobiographical *Black Diamonds Gathered in the Darkey Homes of the South* (1859), sympathized with these folk, whom he significantly defined not just as landless rural whites but as nonslaveholders, the "working classes and yeomanry of the South." Their cause, he wrote, "cries to Heaven for justice." They would defend the South with their lives; yet they were "a people treated with the most ungrateful and insulting consideration by their country, debarred from its social system, deprived of all share in the benefits of the institution of slavery, condemned to poverty, and even forced to bear the airs of superiority in black and beastly slaves!" It was this last point that especially infuriated Pollard; for, if some blacks could act superior to any whites, the entire value structure of his racism was reversed. Indeed, a prime source of his sympathy for the nonslaveholders was the shame and embarrassment he felt for his race when he saw poor whites allegedly treated with disrespect by black men.

> Of all things I cannot bear to see negro slaves affect superiority over the poor, needy, and unsophisticated whites, who form a terribly large proportion of the population of the South. My blood boils when I recall how often I have seen some poor "cracker," dressed in striped cotton, and going through the streets of some of our Southern towns, gazing at the shop windows with scared curiosity, made sport of by the sleek, dandified negroes who lounge on the streets, never unmindful, however, to touch their hats to the "gem'men" who are "stiff in their heels" (i.e., have money). . . .

Whereas Pollard would have raised the status of the poor whites by importing enough African slaves to enable everyone to become a slaveholder, the more popular course was that offered by the free-labor industrialists—factory employment under strict, paternalistic controls.

These industrialists labeled as absurd the slave traders' position that the South was suffering from a labor shortage. The true picture was, in the words of William Gregg, "that one half of our white people, who are willing to work, cannot procure employment—that able-bodied men are roaming about the country, glad to get work at seventy-five cents per day . . . when similar labor commands a dollar or more at the North and

West. . . ." To employ and train these whites, Gregg received a
state charter and founded the textile town of Graniteville in the
South Carolina upcountry. Here, the South's "poor, degraded,
half-fed, half-clothed, and ignorant population, without Sabbath-
schools, or any other kind of instruction—mental or moral—or
without any just appreciation of the value of character," were to
be educated and "Christianized." As much a missionary venture
as a manufacturing establishment, this company town provided
an ordered, regimented, almost antiseptic environment, which,
it was claimed, molded productive citizens. Every member of
the family found employment—the husband on a rented plot of
land, the wife attending to the rented house, and the children in
the mills. "But the great advantage of this system," pointed out
James Taylor, "is its safety to the morals of the people." The
youth were under constant supervision; liquor was strictly prohibited; schools and churches, even a public library, were established.

Taylor's boosterism had some factual basis. The factory workers in Barnwell District, South Carolina, had come down from
the hills "bare-footed, dirty, and in rags," observed William
Cullen Bryant in 1849. They were "scoured, put in shoes and
stockings, set to work, and sent regularly to Sunday-school, where
they are taught what none of them have been taught before—to
read and write." At the same time, Taylor and others usually
overlooked the brutalizing working conditions. A correspondent
of the Augusta *Constitutionalist* even predicted that slaves would
replace free labor in the cotton factories because the former,
aside from being more manageable, were better able to "endure
the heated atmosphere of a confined room—to which hundreds of
the whites are daily falling victims."

The moral uplift of these whites would be paralleled by a dramatic increase in their purchasing power. Far from threatening
planter rule, argued Gregg and his followers, the newly productive citizens would be thankful for their jobs, the first steady
employment and source of income most of them had ever known.
Dreading free black competition, they would enforce the color
line and fight against emancipation. The cotton-textile workers
would have an economic stake in slavery, the only feasible sys-

tem of supplying the cheap raw cotton essential to their jobs. The more prosperous workers would save their earnings and become slaveholders themselves. Labor unions to regulate wages were prohibited, but the workers would be encouraged to form voluntary benevolent associations. Capital and labor were in conflict in other societies, admitted Gregg, but in the South "this cannot be the case; capital will be able to control labor, even in manufactures with whites, for blacks can always be resorted to in case of need."

Southern fears that skilled or industrial slaves constituted a threat to slave discipline were effectively exploited by the free-labor forces. James Hammond seriously doubted whether the extensive and permanent use of slaves in manufacturing and the skilled crafts was "consistent with safe and sound policy. Whenever a slave is made a mechanic, he is more than half freed, and soon becomes . . . the most corrupt and turbulent of his class." Hammond's doubts were traditional ones. Typical of editorial opinion was the 1822 statement of the South Carolina *State Gazette* that black mechanics "are placed, by the nature of their employments, much more from under the eye and inspection of the masters, and they acquire vicious habits injurious to themselves as well as their owners, and of evil example to other slaves."

The plantation was used as a foil to highlight the dangers of training slaves. There, the slaves could be awakened in the morning, counted, put to work in the fields under the direction of the master or an overseer, and then recounted and herded into the cabins for the night. White patrols roamed the countryside disciplining any slaves who left the plantation without permission. In short, the slaves lived in a controlled environment where most of their moves and time could be accounted for. They stood far less chance of being "corrupted" by lower-class whites, free blacks, or other slaves than if they lived in town or were hired out. Some manufacturers tried to re-create these conditions by providing slave living quarters within the same compound that housed the factory and by requiring workers to wear badges or carry passes as a security measure. But the average industrial slave belonged to a small, rural concern where such steps were rare, and this, indeed, was the most common complaint against industrial slavery. A Virginia planter who rented some slaves to an iron manufacturer, for example, commented: "They worked hard, and had too much liberty, and were acquiring bad habits. They earned money, by overwork, and spent it for whiskey, and got a habit of roaming about and *taking care of themselves;* because, when they were not at work in the furnace, nobody looked out for them."

Another advantage of keeping slaves in agriculture was that the performance of their work normally did not necessitate any special incentives. But trained slaves required these enticements because their work involved more care and discretion. As Olmsted put it, most nonagricultural slaves "are, nearly always, 'gratified' with some sort of wages, or perquisites, or stimulants, to skill and industry, in some form; and are more intelligent, more privileged, and more insubordinate than the general mass." The result was what Southerners called the "ebony aristocracy." At the top were those slaves permitted to hire their own time. Most urban slaves, except domestics, fell into this category. The evil was clear enough. In return for a stipulated amount from his wages, the slave bought his own time and was free to a great extent from the discipline and surveillance of his master.

All the states had legislation prohibiting or restricting this practice. Vigilance committees sporadically sprang up to enforce these laws, and grand-jury indictments were handed down to the same end; yet, the practice persisted. "We are accustomed to black labor, and it would create a revolution to drive it away" was the pragmatic conclusion of a committee of the South Carolina legislature, formed in the 1850's in response to petitions demanding a stop to the hiring-out abuses and the use of slave artisans. The committee pointed out that most of the domestic servants and common and semiskilled laborers of the state were slaves. Strict enforcement of the laws—which would involve such details as a separate contract with the owner for each specific job performed by his slave—was utterly impracticable.

Once again, the slaveholders probably magnified the dangers facing them. Much of the industrial work was just as routinized and spiritually deadening as the most monotonous farm labor and hardly encouraged a sense of self-reliance and independence. Slaves could be controlled—as was proved at the Tredegar Iron Works in Richmond: Cash payments and bonuses were cleverly used as control devices and, by extracting more work, increased the profitability of slavery and thereby strengthened it. Nevertheless, Hammond's prediction proved more than half-right. The leaders of all the major slave revolts of the nineteenth century had been artisans or industrial slaves. This class comprised nearly all of the rebels who threw the South into a panic in the fall of 1856. The incentives program tended to create an economic hierarchy among the slaves, just as social rankings existed that were related to the types of jobs. Membership in each of these strata carried its own level of aspirations and expectations. Industrialization was breaking down the undifferentiated mass of untrained slaves that had always been considered the safest social structure for the control of slaves. Moreover, disciplinary problems would have increased as more slaves were shifted into manufacturing and as industrialization grew more sophisticated.

The debate over free labor or slave for Southern industry ended in a compromise. The poor whites were left in possession of the upcountry cotton mills, white artisans were given a limited veto over slave competition in some areas, and slaves made up the bulk of the remaining work force. Neither side had won so much as both had lost. The free-labor forces had educated or employed very few whites, and the proslavery enthusiasts had failed to take many slaves off the land. The fears of both sides had not materialized, but neither had their hopes.

In appealing for the essential support of the planters, the industrial promoters had no choice but to play on their vanities and extol the agrarian virtues. Governor Hammond of South Carolina, for example, was engaging in more than a rhetorical flourish when he concluded an 1850 speech in favor of increased manufacturing with the assurance that under no circumstances was he "desirous to see the mechanical and manufacturing spirit and influence prevail over the agricultural, in this state, or in the South." The planters simply had to be convinced that industrialization would be stopped short of creating competing centers of power and status. They were promised increased profits. If

enough slaves were put into factories, the agricultural remnant
would produce a smaller cotton crop that would fetch higher
prices. At the same time, finished goods would be cheaper because they could be purchased within the South. Still, most
planters hung back and favored little more than self-sufficiency
in basic manufactured items produced in small, rural units. The
lack of entrepreneurship and the persistence of aristocratic
standards of consumption hindered capital formation. "Our planters and farmers are even too timid when invited to make outlays
of capital in anything new; and yet they carry their liberality
even to prodigality in satisfying their own or the wants of
friends," complained James Orr. "This timidity is a barrier to enterprise, and some useful lessons might be learned by them from
our northern rivals."

Ultimately, the industrial effort foundered on its own self-
contradictions. The agrarian South was being asked to defend
herself against the industrial North by herself becoming indus-
trialized. George Fitzhugh, though an advocate of limited manufacturing, fairly spat out the words when, in 1857, he asked the
South whether she wished "to imitate the little 'truck patches,'
the filthy, crowded, licentious factories, the mercenary shopkeep-
ing, and the slavish commerce of the North." The conundrum was
obvious, and the Republicans seized it. Congressman James Mc-
Kean of New York dared the South to develop her manufacturing.

> Sir, let her proceed with her manufactures and her home industry.
> She can do nothing that will so strangle slavery. . . . Let her turn
> her attention to all departments of manual industry and intellectual
> inquiry, and she will thereby create demands which ignorant, in-
> dolent slave labor cannot meet, and which intelligent, industrious
> free labor can alone supply.

2. Benevolent Diffusion

Racism left Southerners in a black-and-white dilemma of their own making. They simply could not conceive of a free biracial society; yet, they were literally surrounded by blacks. The solution was obviously to keep the blacks enslaved; yet, racial stereotypes decreed that the pressure of a rising slave population confined to a fixed geographical area would ultimately break down racial control. Since the free states had made it clear that they would not accept a large influx of freed blacks, the South could relieve herself of her increasing slave population only by exporting them to new areas. Eventually, the logic of diffusion predicted that slavery extension would create safe conditions under which the South could emancipate her few remaining slaves and, if she waited long enough, be blessed with an all-white society. The South's racial dilemma would not be solved so much as its root cause—the presence of the black man—would be removed.

Racial Blinders

The black man was unwanted in nineteenth-century America. Whites of all classes and from all sections feared and despised him. In large measure, this racism was attributable to the white egalitarian ethos and the intense social competition of democratic capitalism. For, if America was a truly egalitarian society that dispensed to all comers wealth and status commensurate with their talent—if, in other words, economic success was a measure of moral worth—then the lower classes were somehow deficient, either morally or in natural ability. The wealthy could easily accept this conclusion, but the poor and the middling groups, en-

gaged in daily competition for the rewards that were supposedly
theirs if only they worked hard enough, could hardly consent to
denigrate themselves. Consequently, they either blamed imperfections in the society, such as monopolies based on privileged
orders, or vented their frustrations on allegedly inferior races—
especially in the early nineteenth century, when, as the last rem-
nants of aristocratic legal prerogatives were eliminated, a full-
blown racist ideology developed. The result was a rather vicious
"democratic" racism that served as an outlet for the competitive
tensions and aggressiveness of American society. The upper
classes shared in this racism, but, to the extent that they were
sheltered from economic combat and assured of their status, their
racism was glossed over with a paternalistic sheen.

The generation that later fought the Civil War had begun to
interpret American history in racial terms. Southerners had always appealed to Northern racism in their ideological defense of
slavery, but, with the institution under increasing attack, these
appeals, particularly after the Mexican War, became more specifically linked to the vision of national greatness and progress
with which Americans compulsively identified. Speaking before
a Democratic convention at Portland, Maine, in 1858, Jefferson
Davis rhetorically asked why the United States had far surpassed
her neighbors to the south. A stern moral creed was his answer.
Not yielding to the temptations of miscegenation with the Indians, the colonial forefathers "preferred to encounter toil, priva-
tion and carnage, rather than debase their lineage and race." On
the other hand, in Central and South America "we see the Caucasian mingled with the Indian and the African. They have the
forms of free government, because they have copied them. To its
benefits they have not attained, because that standard of civilization is above their race."

Racial purity maintained a white stock fit to appreciate and
benefit from democratic institutions but could not by itself explain America's unique success. For many Americans, the line
between egalitarianism and anarchy was a fine one and had been
crossed repeatedly in France and elsewhere. Political equality
would inevitably lead to social instability, argued the proslavery
ideologists, unless a counterweight was provided by the enslave-

ment of an inferior race that would perform the menial physical work and permit an aristocracy of race to replace the traditional aristocracy of wealth. It was the "presence of the black race in the United States," wrote A. J. Donelson, a nephew of Andrew Jackson and a key figure in the annexation of Texas, that had "enabled the white man to treat as his equal all his own race. A basis was thus formed for liberty as broad as the population; and hence popular sovereignty was a reality, not a fiction. The absence of such a basis in Europe is the secret of the failure of all its attempts to found popular institutions." The poor in Europe were at the bottom of society, resentful of their status and anxious for change. The comparable class in America comprised the black slaves, and the whites, no matter how poor, were co-equals in a racial brotherhood where membership automatically imparted its own superiority.

Ironically, then, the unwanted black man by his own inequality had become indispensable for the equality of white Americans. His presence, however, entailed problems of racial control. In the North, where blacks made up less than 2 per cent of the population in most states, control was handled through Jim Crow statutes and, particularly in the newer states, exclusion acts. In the South, slavery was the solution, and, pointing to the sheer number of slaves (one-third of the population), Southerners were positive that it was the only solution. Emancipation, stated the Charleston *Mercury*, would mean "the loss of liberty, property, home, country—everything that makes life worth living."

In their general view of race relations, Americans assumed that, if large numbers of two races were forced to inhabit the same territory, the inferior race would become naturally subject to the superior, or amalgamated with it, or exterminated. The case of the American Indians constitutes a classic example of genocide. Although they were never enslaved to the same extent as the Indians of Latin America, they were usually treated contemptuously by white Americans. The eastern tribes, who, according to Jefferson Davis, were as "deceptive, as bloodthirsty, as treacherous, as cowardly a race of men as are to be found on the globe," had been all but destroyed; those that remained were pushed west of the Mississippi. Their fate was similar to that of other nonwhite and non-Anglo Saxon groups with whom Americans had come into contact. "Our people believe it is no harm to take away from a Spaniard or a Mexican or an Indian anything he has got, and they want," declared Senator Thompson of Kentucky. When he added that "they do not believe it is homicide or murder to kill him either," his fellow senators laughed.

The size and irreplaceable economic contribution of the slave labor force ruled out the ruthless policy of extermination, but even more unacceptable was the option of amalgamation, or racial fusion. The concept of amalgamation had explicit sexual overtones and was used interchangeably with miscegenation. Because most white Americans believed that whiteness was the universal standard of truth, beauty, and grace, they interpreted racial interbreeding as an unconscionable defilement of this standard. With supreme ethnocentrism, Chancellor William Harper wrote, "If man be the most perfect work of the Creator, and the civilized European man the most perfect variety of the human race, is he not criminal who would desecrate and deface God's fairest work, estranging it further from the image of himself, and conforming it more nearly to that of the brute?"

Since these white Americans wanted so desperately to believe that interracial offspring were biologically inferior, they eagerly accepted the half-truths and myths of the racist anthropology prevalent in the mid-nineteenth century. Senator James Bayard of Delaware announced, "It is an undeniable truth, though the offspring of the white and the negro is not strictly hybrid [sterile], that in the mixed race produced by their union, the capacity of reproduction is lessened, and the duration of life shortened." This mixed progeny was also deemed socially dangerous. An article on amalgamation in *DeBow's Review* warned that "to encourage amalgamation is to encourage the commission of crime and cruelty, the increase of ignorance and misery, and to insure the destruction of two races in attempting to elevate one." The alleged evils of amalgamation were cited by Dr. J. C. Nott of Mobile as the most obvious obstacle to the suggestion of antislavery critics that the South should gradually educate and emancipate her slaves and allow them to be absorbed into the white population. "There is no doubt that the intellectual grade of the negro races may be greatly improved by crossing them with the whites," conceded Nott, "but it must not be forgotten, on the other hand, that the white races would be *dragged down* by the adulteration, and their civilization destroyed."

Trapped by their racial attitudes, white Southerners told themselves and the rest of the world that they must keep the blacks enslaved. There was really no choice, they insisted; for, "so long as the white and African races constitute the same community, and the latter in point of numbers approximate anywhere near the former, the safest and happiest, and indeed the only, safe and happy relation for both races, is that of master and servant." Emancipation was unthinkable. Frances Kemble astutely noted that, "besides the natural fact that the slaveholders wish to retain their property, emancipation is, in their view of it, not only a risk of enormous pecuniary loss, and of their entire social status, but involves elements of personal danger, and, above all, disgust to inveterate prejudices, which they will assuredly never encounter."

The economic cost of reimbursing the slaveowners for their property was staggering. By 1860, the slaves were estimated to be worth nearly $2 billion—at a time when the entire national income stood at barely twice that sum. Yet, property rights, according to the American credo, were sacred, and so Northerners, with the exception of hard-core abolitionists, agreed that it was only fair to require proper compensation for emancipation. Various funding programs were therefore introduced periodically in Congress. Although tentative and even somewhat utopian in their expectations, these programs nevertheless made compensation an integral part of the national commitment to rid the country of slavery (and of freed blacks as well, in some cases). But, one by one, all the various proposals—which ranged from the setting up of a fund, with proceeds from public-land sales, for the purchase and expatriation of slaves to Lincoln's wartime effort to issue federal bonds as grants-in-aid to the loyal Border states—were summarily rejected by the slaveholders. It was not the heavy cost that acted as a major deterrent to emancipation but the fears of what the racial consequences would be.

What could be done with all those freed blacks? Colonization was one solution, but it had been tried and found wanting. Citing the Southern fear of insurrection, the ineradicable prejudice of most Americans, and the wretched condition of the freed blacks, the American Colonization Society tried to implement the Jeffersonian program of gradual emancipation coupled with colonization of the freed slaves outside the United States. By providing for the removal of the blacks, the Society hoped to encourage voluntary manumissions and to create socially acceptable conditions for eventual large-scale emancipation. Part of the reform impulse of the post-1812 generation, colonization was another effort at social control by a declining elite centered in the Federalist party. Desiring an ordered, homogeneous society, this elite sought to regain its slipping social leadership by assuming control of a host of reform movements that would guide the fallen and the disorderly. The sinner was to be saved, the heathen converted, and the alcoholic reformed, but, significantly, the black man, a social outcast whether free or enslaved, was to be removed.

Henry Clay and several prominent Virginians were leaders in the movement, but the Society was never popular in the Deep South. In his 1828 pamphlet *The Crisis: or Essays on the Usurpation of the Federal Government*, Robert Turnbull of South Carolina sounded the usual alarm. "Discussion [of colonization] will cause *death* and *destruction* to our negro property. Discussion will be equivalent to an act of emancipation, for it will universally inspire amongst the slaves, that hope." Although temporarily revived by white fears in the aftermath of Nat Turner's rebellion in the early 1830's, the movement failed to receive the federal subsidies essential for the success of its program. Its elitism and broad, nationalistic outlook put it increasingly out of touch with the politically triumphant egalitarian individualism and states'-rights philosophy of the Jacksonian era. At the same time, the abolitionists, who placed their faith in an end to racism through the ultimate moral perfectability of man, denounced African colonization for capitulating to racism and serving as a bulwark of slavery by expelling potentially troublesome free blacks.

Suspected in the North of strengthening slavery and in the South of weakening the institution, and ambivalent about whether its goal was to make America all white by removing the blacks or all free by helping to end slavery, the colonization movement was a failure. Nevertheless, the African nation of Liberia remained as an enduring legacy of America's philanthropic racism. And the concept of colonization, because it represented such an apparently clear-cut and direct solution to the racial dilemma, never lost its appeal.

Republicans, especially those from the Midwest and the Border states, proclaimed black expatriation the key to the solution of the inseparable problems of race and slavery. Land in Central and South America was to be acquired by the federal government. Blacks "who are now free, or who may hereafter become free" were to be encouraged to migrate there, take up homesteads, and live among a racially mixed population, where the color of their skin would not be a mark of degradation. These regions were closer to the United States than Africa, and transportation costs would be greatly reduced. In addition, because the climatic determinism of the day postulated that dark-skinned peoples were biologically better equipped to survive and prosper in warm, tropical climates, the Republicans could argue that they were merely fostering the migratory instincts of American blacks. The black colonists, grateful for all the assistance they received, would presumably maintain trading ties with the United States and thus provide Northern manufacturers with an entree into the potentially rich markets of tropical America. The argument, as summarized by Republican Representative Francis P. Blair of Missouri, one of its chief advocates, was that colonization would block the expansion of slavery, build up stable and friendly republics in Central America, and rid the nation of "a class of men who are worse than useless to us. . . . For, whether as a slave or free man, the presence of multitudes of the black race is found to be fatal to the interests of our race; their antagonism is as strong as that of oil and water. . . ."

The cotton South found colonization no more appealing in the 1850's than it had a generation earlier. As Robert Turnbull had warned in 1828, the mere talk of colonization was dangerous to slave discipline. Ever sensitive to the slightest sign of federal interference with slavery, Southerners worried that colonization was the entering wedge of federally imposed emancipation. They announced that they, too, had designs on the territory to the south of them, and that, if their blacks went there, they would do so as slaves. To the Southern mind, blacks were by nature lazy savages who would not work without compulsion, and therefore the very idea that free blacks could ever accomplish anything worthwhile seemed utterly preposterous. "As a general rule, free negroes will not follow any steady employment," pronounced Congressman T. H. Bayly of Virginia. "With them, idleness and liberty are synonymous. He only values freedom that he may not be forced to work." Dr. Nott charged that what limited success had been achieved in Liberia was due solely to the white agents of the Colonization Society and to the white blood of the mulattoes. The former slave colonies of Haiti and Jamaica were frequently cited as illustrations of the blacks' inferiority. "Slavery was abolished, and what followed?" asked DeBow. "Wealth decreasing to poverty, commerce rapidly disappearing, population steadily diminishing, and the unfortunate negroes, who, in the language of philanthropy, had been elevated to the rank of freemen, are fast sinking into that state of barbarism from which slavery alone seems to have elevated them."

These strictures against colonization applied with even greater force to the prospect of allowing the emancipated slaves to remain in the South. The area would be "Africanized." "To leave these negroes free to follow their own inclinations," wrote Hammond in an 1860 article for the New York *Journal of Commerce,* "would be a virtual annexation of the Southern States to Haiti or to [the] Congo; for it would establish the same state of things that there exists in [the] Congo—free polygamy, free laziness, free stealing from the nearest sheep fold or hen-roost, and free seizures of the most docile by the most savage, to be held as slaves." The South, debased to anarchy and barbarism and abounding in sexual license, would become the antithesis of the moralistic and hard-working community so idealized by white Protestants. White sensibilities could never endure such a spectacle. Rather than have their ex-slaves live among them, "to be our equals, to disgust us by their vices, insult us by their insolence, to

degrade our name and posterity by a vile commingling of races,"
Southerners, according to Representative John Savage of Tennessee, would "pray to God that the ocean's wave might blot us
from the world—yea, gladly accept the glories of the past, and hope
for us, no future might be written."

Emancipation, then, would benefit no one, least of all the
blacks. For, released from the constraints of slavery and turned
loose upon white society, this poor and ignorant population, predicted John Townsend, a South Carolina planter, would "ramble
in idleness over the country until their wants should drive most
of them first to petty thefts and afterwards to the bolder crime
of robbery and murder; or until their excesses, their impudence,
their filth and starvation shall bring pestilence among them and
sweep them off by thousands." No longer under the protection
of their masters and incapable of caring for themselves, they
would be reduced to misery, want, and eventual extermination.
Asking his fellow Southerners to assume the white man's burden,
Dr. Nott explained that, "as experience proves that the negro is
better off in slavery at the South, than in freedom elsewhere, it is
the part of philanthropy to keep him here, as we keep our children in subjection for their own good."

The inherent duality in white attitudes toward the blacks was
brought out by the emancipation issue. Whites were genuinely
attached to the docile slave. Identifying the black's true nature
with that of a child, Edward Pollard wrote, "I love the simple
and unadulterated slave, with his geniality, his mirth, his swagger,
and his nonsense. . . . I love to mark that peculiarity in him,
which beneath all his buffoonery exhibits him as a creature of
the tenderest sensibilities, mingling his joys and his sorrows with
those of his master's home. . . ." But let the black step outside
the role of Sambo, let him exhibit signs of independence, intelligence, and self-reliance, and he becomes, in Pollard's words, "altogether another creature, and my especial abomination." In
short, when blacks' behavior fed the white ego, it was approved,
even rewarded, but, when their behavior challenged the white
ego in any way, it was denounced and punished. This dichotomy
between good (submissive) and bad (impudent) slaves was un-

avoidable because it reflected for Southern whites an inbred tension in the black between his "savage" behavior in freedom and
his "civilized" state under slavery.

According to the racist mythology, slavery was a school that
tutored and civilized the savage African. "The first lesson in
civilization and Christianity to be taught to the barbarous tribes,
wherever to be found," lectured Alexander Stephens in the Senate, "is the first great curse against the human family—that in the
sweat of their face they shall eat their bread. Under our system,
our tuition, our guardianship and fostering care, these people,
exciting so much misplaced philanthropy, have attained a higher
degree of civilization than their race has attained anywhere else
upon the face of the earth." As proof both of their missionary
zeal and of their assertion that blacks were receptive to religion
only when slaves, Southerners quoted statistics showing that the
majority of all African Christians lived in the slave South. All
in all, slavery had wrought a wondrous transformation. Challeng-
ing the abolitionists to name another institution that had so
helped the black race, Senator Solomon Downs of Louisiana invited a comparison:

> Go among the Africans on their continent, and you see them starv-
> ing, killing one another, robbing one another, and plunged into all
> the degradation of the most abject state of barbarism, sinking lower
> and lower, from one grade to another, until it is almost impossible
> to distinguish them from the savage brutes that roam their forests.
> Here you will find them attaining a civilization highly creditable to
> them, and living in the comfort and enjoyment attendant on a happy
> and prosperous people.

Yet, if slavery was a school, it was a most peculiar one, for the
students forgot their lessons as soon as they left the classroom.
Once released from slavery, the happy, civilized, and docile
black man reverted to the sullen, brutish, and dangerous savage.
All the racial traits slavery had kept in check, if not eliminated
—the coarse, animal feelings, lack of mental abilities, idolatry,
disregard of family ties, laziness, and a tendency toward thievery
—would re-emerge, making the blacks totally unfit for white society. Nothing could prevent this atavistic behavior, for it had

all been biologically predetermined. Referring to the alleged failure of emancipation in Jamaica and Haiti, Senator Stephen Mallory of Florida declared that

. . . just as there are certain grains and fruits which the industry of man has redeemed by careful culture from their original and savage nature—from some wild grass or bitter nut, which, if withdrawn from his care, will relapse back to their original type—just so does the African in these colonies, when left to himself, relapse back, stage by stage, to the original barbarism of his fathers.

Sambo, then, was just a guise artificially created by slavery under white masters. Once free, the black beast would emerge again.

Most Southerners believed that there was no halfway station to which they could safely assign their ex-slaves. There was no legally defined, subordinate class position the blacks could occupy, for American society, North and South, was committed to a nonhierarchical and fluid class structure. A racist egalitarianism could decree that the blacks were not free and equal, most Southerners could hold that the blacks should be enslaved, and most Northerners, that they should be ejected. But, as long as enough Americans believed that the blacks were entitled at least to the minimum rights set out in the Declaration of Independence—life, liberty, and the fruits of one's own labor—slavery would remain under attack and a rigorous apartheid would not be possible.

Southerners were not certain, however, just what kinds of barriers they could erect, or be permitted to erect, to protect themselves from their liberated slaves. Ultimately, it was the logic of egalitarianism that explained the Southern contention that the blacks, if emancipated, would dominate Southern life. Not only politics but society itself would be overrun by the freedmen—for didn't the majority rule? In 1850, Congressman John Savage of Tennessee asked what would prevent liberated slaves in such states as Mississippi, Louisiana, and South Carolina from electing congressmen. Significantly, as a good egalitarian, he equated this expected political power with a collapse of all the walls slavery had erected between the races. "Instead of the pure white blood which now sits here," he told his fellow representatives, "we would have over on that side of the House some twenty or

thirty shining darkies, sending forth their odoriferous fragrance
to gladden the olfactories of God's 'peculiar saints' from Massachusetts and Ohio, while their southern white brethren would
be ground down into hopeless infamy and ruin; their wives and
daughters the victims of negro brutality."

The nation's free black population was a social and ideological
anomaly. In the South, free blacks were obviously incompatible
with slavery; by the racial definition of slavery, they should have
been slaves themselves. Hedged in by a web of humiliating restrictions and discriminations, which went so far as to define
the degree of public submissiveness demanded by the whites, the
free blacks were barely tolerated. An 1822 memorial from the
citizens of Charleston—which noted that "they have sufficient of
liberty to appreciate the blessings of freedom; and are sufficiently
shackled to be sensible they enjoy comparatively few of those
blessings"—recommended that all free blacks be expelled from
the state as a threat to public safety. Demands for expulsion
increased during the antebellum era until, in the wake of John
Brown's raid, some states began offering their free blacks the
choice of leaving or being enslaved.

Confined and insecure as the Southern free blacks were in
their quasi-freedom, their brothers in the North fared little better.
They faced many of the same disabilities. Many states required
them to post bond and security for good behavior; they were
rarely allowed to vote, hold office, serve on juries, or send their
children to the public schools. Several states totally excluded
them. They lived in grinding poverty with but a faint hope of
advancement, subject to the whims of the white majority. Despite his smugness, a Southern congressman could justifiably
taunt Northerners with their own racism. The Southerner "is
told that by nature the negro is equal to the white man, and entitled to all his rights and privileges, while, at the same time, the
laws made by these very men deny him all the means by which
these rights are to be enjoyed. . . . Life is permitted to him, but
it is poisoned at every turn by marks of degradation, legal and
social." Another Southerner wondered whether, if Northerners
abolished slavery, they would grant full citizenship to the black

man. "Why, you do not do that in the non-slaveholding States. What privilege prized by the freeman do you extend to him?"

Inevitably, invidious comparisons were drawn between the contented slaves and the degraded Northern blacks. The slaves, alleged Jefferson Davis, were "comfortable and happy . . . advancing in intelligence . . . provided for in age and sickness, in infancy and disability . . . in useful employment, restrained from the vicious indulgences to which their inferior nature inclines them." But, alas, the Northern free blacks, far from being cared for or treated with kindness, "are, with few exceptions, miserable, degraded, filling the penitentiaries and poor-houses, objects of scorn. . . ." This analogy was hopelessly self-serving, but it was more than mere myth-making. Although only a racist could believe that the slaves were happy, only a moral charlatan could maintain that free blacks in the North were permitted to live in anything approaching human dignity.

Foreign visitors saw that the color line was a national phenomenon and puzzled over the motives of the antislavery movement. William Chambers, a Scottish author-publisher, noted "that the people of the Northern States, though repudiating slavery, did not think more favorably of the negro character than those further South." An alliance with a black, he felt, would cause any white person, in any part of the country, to lose caste. Accusing the abolitionists of hypocrisy, he challenged them to live up to their beliefs: "If they think that negroes are MEN, let them give the world an evidence of their sincerity, by moving the reversal of all those social and political arrangements which now, in the free States, exclude persons of color, not only from the common courtesies of life, but from the privileges and honors of citizens." Chambers was too harsh on the abolitionists; for, despite their undeniable prejudice, many of them were aware of the limits and contradictions of their racial attitudes. In attempting to overcome their ambivalence, they at least recognized that racism was a matter of moral concern and not a permanent and justifiable pattern of human relations. Many joined with the Republicans in a struggle to win some recognition of black equality.

The Republican party, drawing heavily from native white

Protestant stock, represented those Americans who, though challenged by newer religious and ethnic groups, were still the accepted leaders of their communities, especially in rural areas.
They were removed from the bitter economic competition experienced by the Negrophobic immigrant Irish who flocked to the
urban Democratic machines and from the ingrained prejudices of
the transplanted Democratic Southerners who had moved into
the lower Midwest. This social distance, plus their tradition of
moral stewardship, frequently enabled them to combine their
antislavery position with a commitment to black civil rights.
Republicans and abolitionists fought to gain for blacks suffrage,
access to public schools and public facilities, and equality before
the law. Above all, they struggled to have blacks recognized as
American citizens free to compete economically and to live in
peace. Their idealism was real enough and should not be minimized, especially because their stand on black rights was normally a decided political liability.

There were distinct limits, however, to the Republicans' conception of a biracial society. Congressman Owen Lovejoy of
Illinois, whose crusading brother had been killed by an anti-
abolitionist mob, constantly deflated the pompous proslavery arguments of Southern congressmen, and in turn was roundly hated.
Affirming his faith in the Jeffersonian dictum that all men are
created equal, he declared repeatedly that he would free the
blacks and assure them protection of life, liberty, and property.
Yet, he was just as adamant on what his concept of racial equality did not include. The races were *not* equal "in gracefulness of
motion, or loveliness of feature; [nor] in mental endowment,
moral susceptibility, and emotional power; not socially equal;
not of necessity politically equal. . . ." Obviously, even in Lovejoy's America the black man would be a second-class citizen
posing no challenge to white supremacy.

Why, then, did the South so exaggerate the Republican commitment to black equality, and why did she refuse to accept
the Northern brand of racism as a feasible alternative to slavery? Emancipation would, of course, destroy the class structure of
the South. In particular, the planters would lose that direct and
absolute control over fellow human beings that was the source

of their special hubris and power. An unsigned article in *De-Bow's Review* exalting the plantation as a way of life explained the planter's conception of himself: "The cultivator of the soil is a ruler. The slave owner is more—he is, to a certain extent, necessarily a despot. He makes the regulations which govern his plantation and he executes them." The planter was ultimately subject to public opinion, but most plantation activities were beyond the reach of the law. How necessary, then, for the planter to be endowed with the higher virtues! "He is daily called upon to exercise the virtues of forbearance, mercy, generosity, and, above all, of justice."

Quite aside from the class factor was the numbing fear of a black inundation. Southerners readily admitted that, where there were relatively few blacks, as in the North, they could be confined to allegedly menial and degrading jobs, such as barbering, boot-blacking, and other service trades that reputable whites shunned. But, in the South, the sheer size of the slave population meant that the blacks could never be so confined. If they were freed, they would leave the land and would need more than these restricted job opportunities in order to survive. As Dr. Van Evrie, a proslavery Northerner, warned, "The physical necessities, the absolute overwhelming pressure of hunger, would impel them to crime, robbery, insurrections, to violence and blood, and [would be] certain to end in complete and total destruction." The fear of such an eventuality aroused Southern anxieties in a way incomprehensible to the North and accounted, declared L. Q. C. Lamar of Mississippi in Congress, for the different ways legislators from both sections regarded the black issue; for "the negroes are not sufficient in numbers at the North to make it necessary to reduce them to the condition of domestic servitude, while with us that condition is indispensable to the good order and welfare of the whole society."

James Hammond reasoned that, where one black was outnumbered by one hundred whites, society could safely absorb the otherwise deleterious consequences of harboring such an inferior race. Legal masters or guardians would not be required. Some member of the overwhelming white majority might teach the black how to work, either out of charity or out of a desire to profit from his labor. "And even should the negro grow up a mere vagrant and parasite, there are so many industrious white men around, for him to prey upon, that his pickings and stealings will not fall ruinously hard upon any one." In the South, on the other hand, the situation was radically different. The only choice was between slavery and barbarism. "The industrial education of a *negro multitude* cannot be managed without fixed and responsible masters, endowed with all necessary authority by law, and stimulated by some surer reward than the chance wages to be derived from negro conscientiousness and negro gratitude." Because blacks could not care for themselves and would not work unless physically compelled to do so, emancipation would force the planters to feed and clothe their ex-slaves out of charity or witness their starvation. Hammond's arguments were part of racial folklore. A poor dirt farmer told Olmsted, "It would n't do no good to free 'em, and let'em hang round, because they is so monstrous lazy; if they had n't got nobody to take keer on'em, you see they would n't do nothin' but juss nat'rally laze around, and steal, and pilfer, and no man could n't live, you see, war they was."

Their racism left Southerners with no choice but to endorse slavery. "We could not live in the midst of a large black population without the law of slavery," said Congressman Robert McLane of Maryland. Northerners subjected their blacks to a degree of bondage through discriminatory regulation, he added. This bondage "was necessary to them—he was not reproaching them for it. They could not live without it. It was thus limited in degree with them on account of their free sparse black population, and their overwhelming proportion of whites." Unfortunately, far too few Americans were prepared to take issue with McLane. If, as the failure of Radical Reconstruction was to reveal, Southern whites had overreacted to the Republican stand on black rights and had placed too much faith in the leveling tendencies of egalitarianism and too little in the power of racism to segregate and control even large numbers of blacks, this was a lesson that only hindsight could teach. Ironically, it was the very racial fears of Southerners that had blinded them to the alternative between slavery and racial chaos.

An Outlet for Blacks

The slaves in the United States experienced a rapid rate of reproduction unique to the slave societies of the Western Hemisphere. In the Caribbean as well as the rest of Latin America, the slave populations could be maintained only by continual massive imports from Africa. In the United States, both before and after the closing of the African slave trade in 1808, the slaves increased only slightly less rapidly than the free population. This rate of increase, which averaged 27 per cent per decade from 1810 to 1860, became a Malthusian time bomb for the South. Painfully aware, after the Mexican War, that the North was determined to exclude both slaves from the territories and ex-slaves from the free states, white Southerners began to feel a kind of racial claustrophobia.

Denying the South an outlet for her black population, warned Jefferson Davis, would "crowd upon our soil an overgrown black population, until there will not be room in the country for the whites and blacks to subsist in; and in this way destroy the institution and reduce the whites to the degraded position of the African race." This warning was common; Southerners of both parties repeated it whenever they were challenged to defend the right of the South to expand. Congressman A. W. Venable of North Carolina predicted that restriction would "compress the white and black race within such a narrow compass that the white race must abandon their country to blacks, or come under their political control by the mere force of numbers." He charged that such a policy was designed "to overwhelm and ruin the South"; it was "degradation aggravated by the most refined cruelty."

An outlet for blacks was the South's racial safety valve. Just as land functioned as the economic elixir for a wasteful agriculture, so would it also provide social space in which the slaves could be controlled and their density prevented from reaching unmanageable proportions. Lieutenant Matthew F. Maury of Virginia merged the racial and class pressures behind expansionism when he noted in 1852, "There will soon be no more Mississippi lands to clear, no more cotton fields to subdue, and unless some means be devised of getting rid of the negro-increase, the time must come,—and sooner or later it will come,—when there will be an excess in these states of black people."

Two factors would account for this excess—the natural increase of the blacks and the emigration of whites. If slavery expansion was blocked, the percentage of slaves in the total population would inevitably rise. No matter how much this black population increased, it would have to remain within the fixed geographical limits of slavery that had been established by the 1850's. Southerners ruled out colonization of freed slaves as both financially impractical and a threat to slave discipline. The North had made it clear that she would not accept any appreciable numbers of liberated slaves. Lewis Henry Morgan, a Northern intellectual and noted anthropologist, wrote to Calhoun in 1848, "We [of the North] are afraid of the indefinite propagation of the colored race, upon which the South seems determined." There was no respect for the black race or any wish for its improvement, he added, "but on the contrary a strong desire to prevent the multiplication of the race so far as it is possible to do so, by such legislation as shall be constitutional and just."

Between 1850 and 1857, Indiana, Illinois, Iowa, and Oregon prohibited, by constitutional stipulation, the further entry of free blacks across their boundaries. Afro-Americans were, in effect, barred from many other states by restrictionist legislation that required legal proof of freedom and the posting of bonds guaranteeing good behavior. Often, indeed, Northern mobs prevented the settlement of blacks altogether, as in southern Ohio, where the 518 manumitted slaves of John Randolph were forced to leave the state. An Ohio congressman boasted that his state would never accept freed blacks. "Three hundred thousand freemen of Ohio would . . . receive them on the points of their bayonets, and drive them from [the] State." Predictably, the South reacted to these exclusionist policies with righteous indignation. "You, gentlemen of the North, denounce slavery, and tell us it ought to be abolished. You wish to exterminate it. But you will not suffer our emancipated slaves to go among you. . . . Your people will steal, but will not accept them as a gift," scornfully noted Congressman E. Carrington Cable of Florida. Representative Richard Meade of Virginia drew a disturbing moral from the Randolph incident: "If Ohio was unwilling to receive in her territory a few hundred [emancipated] slaves from Virginia . . . is it not an unequivocal declaration on her part, that Virginia is right in keeping her slaves in bondage? And if she is unwilling to add a few hundred to her free black population, can she consistently blame Virginia for objecting to half a million?"

While the blacks would be penned up, the whites would be free to leave. This emigration, it was predicted, would accelerate as slavery began to sink of its own weight. When planters ran out of fresh lands on which to employ their slaves profitably, they would sell the slaves or leave them behind and emigrate. Those whites who were too poor or too proud to leave would be at the mercy of a growing black majority. Initially, the South would be brutally exploited by the cunning Yankee. The living conditions and comforts of the slaves would decrease in proportion to their increase in numbers and to their masters' inability to care for them. As the racial imbalance culminated in unrest and insurrection, the plight of the South would parallel that of Santo Domingo in the 1790's, when the slaves plunged that island into bloodshed in their fight for freedom.

For most Southerners, the exact timing and outcome of this racial catastrophe were the only issues in doubt. "These consequences may be remote, but they are, nevertheless, equally certain," said Senator James Green of Missouri. In 1850, Clingman of North Carolina felt that his generation would escape the consequences of restriction, but they "would be certain to overtake our children or grandchildren." The turn of the century was most often cited as the period when restriction would have precipitated a racial crisis. By then, the slave population, doubling approximately every twenty-five years, would have reached at least 10 million. The South would be surrounded by a cordon of free states. In the vivid imagery of Richard Meade, the "Abolitionists in and out of Congress will wave to and fro the incendiary's torch, until the countenance of every negro will glare with demoniac hate of the white man. From the scarcity of fertile soil, his services as a slave are no longer wanted; he is permitted to roam at large, and the triumph of the Abolitionists is complete."

The whites would own the land and all property, and, even if
the indigent freedmen were willing to work, there would be
nothing for them to do. The South would be on the threshold
of a race war.

Most Southerners predicted that confining slavery would result
in the ultimate extinction of the black race. Once it became economically impossible for its masters to feed it, this inferior race
would suffer a slow death by starvation, according to Jefferson
Davis. Van Evrie exclaimed that "the cry of no more slave States
. . . is tantamount to no more room for the blacks, and *death
to the negro.*" Van Evrie and others foresaw the extermination of
the blacks through a violent race war. It would be, prophesied
Representative Richard Bowie of Maryland, "a war in which
there would be no quarter, no prisoners—victory or death—in
which the South, like ancient Sparta, must strangle the children
born[e] in her own bosom." Invoking the racial stereotype of
the black savage, a South Carolina congressman spoke of a general massacre "in which the black race are to light the midnight
torch of assassination, and bathe themselves in the blood of the
men, the women, and babes of the whites."

Other Southerners understandably recoiled from the nightmare of exposing their loved ones to such remorseless warfare.
Instead, they felt that the whites, faced with the uncontrollable
numbers of blacks that would follow in the wake of restriction,
would prudently abandon the South to their ex-slaves. Representative William Brockenbrough of Florida argued that such a result
should be unthinkable to all white Americans. The North would
have abolished slavery, he admitted, but only at a staggering
cost. Whites would have been exiled from half of their country.
Driven from their homeland, Southern whites would stream into
the territories and compete for them with Northerners more
greedily than if they had remained with their slaves in the South.
The glorious South would become a wasteland incapable of producing crops or revenue. Above all, charged Brockenbrough, the
North would have created a monster, an "empire of negrodom."

Good order—religion—the spirit of improvement—the schools established—all the institutions of humanity and civilization are gone, and

gone forever, from the whole South. . . . One-half the republic is dead, not paralyzed, but dead and corrupting; and yet adhering a lifeless mass to you the living half, and there must adhere a loathesome burden for ages yet to come, as the price of your unnatural lusts for exclusive dominion.

As in most areas of Southern life in which blacks were involved, white fears of a potential slave surplus were tinged with paranoia. Common sense seemed to support those who minimized the threat of a black excess. In 1850, the population density of the slave states was about ten per square mile. Primarily because of the higher infant and child mortality rates of the blacks, the whites were increasing faster. If both races maintained their average antebellum decennial gains for another century, the South of 1950 would still have a population density only one-third that of the England of 1850 and two-thirds the figure for Massachusetts in 1850. In the meantime, pressure on the land might have been relieved by reclamation projects, economic diversification, and greater productivity. The number of slaves would rise dramatically, but there was no necessary reason to dread this development. "Slaves can be as dense as freemen," assured L. W. Spratt. Discipline, order, and economy of resources would increase as the slaves were brought under centralized management. Spratt cited as proof the effective racial controls on plantations. In the rice districts of South Carolina, the slaves often outnumbered the whites by more than one hundred to one. The boldest assertion of those who welcomed more slaves was made by James Hammond in a letter to the antislavery leader Lewis Tappan: The South, he wrote, with no extension of territory, could support profitably 100, or even 150, million slaves. Nevertheless, like so many who professed to have no qualms over the confinement of slavery, Hammond weakened his case by adding that, in any event, tropical America was destined to be the future home of the black race and would serve as an outlet for any surplus slaves.

In 1847, Senator Andrew Butler of South Carolina conceded that most Southerners did not agree with his opinion that the South needed no more room for her population; thirteen years later, a Virginia congressman could label as the "universal sentiment of the South" the belief that slavery restriction was a doctrine "leading ultimately to her certain destruction." Clearly, those who confidently predicted that the South of the 1850's could absorb many more slaves had won no more converts than had the African slave traders. Ideologically, the position of the two groups coincided, and their memberships often overlapped. Both embraced the concept of a thoroughly hierarchical slave society and welcomed the spread of slavery into every sphere of Southern life. This vision, however, clashed with the dominant egalitarian racism. Except in so far as it promised all whites eventual slave ownership, this social model precluded any meaningful participation by the white majority in the black South of the future. Restriction would render agricultural slave labor unprofitable, reasoned T. H. Bayly of Virginia, and would necessitate a massive shift of slaves into industry. White laborers, displaced first from the skilled trades and then from the factories, would be forced to leave the South. "It will be the indigent white men who will be injured more than the large slaveholder," he concluded.

For the white egalitarians, slavery was more crucial as a technique for race control than as a labor system. They wanted no part of a South in which black slaves gradually monopolized the labor force, under the aegis of a reactionary planter class. The extremist spokesmen of this class were already arguing that slavery was a natural and necessary ordering of society and that, therefore, all labor, regardless of race, should be enslaved. A writer in the Richmond *Enquirer* admitted that "it is far more obvious that negroes be slaves than whites—for they are only fit to labor, not to direct." But he added, "Yet the principle of slavery is in itself right, and does not depend on difference in complection." An 1856 editorial in the Charleston *Mercury* argued, "The great evil of northern free society is, that it is burdened with a servile class of mechanics and laborers, unfit for self-government, and yet clothed with the attributes and powers of citizens." Consequently, it continued, only the introduction of the master-slave relationship, as normal and beneficial to society as the relationship of parent and child, could save the North from anarchy. This ultraconservatism, however, was shared by only a small minority. What, rather, conditioned the Southern response to the threat of encirclement and the prospect of a more intensive use of slave labor was the anxiety of the white egalitarian majority. Acutely aware that slavery was not just another economic system, and convinced that trying to prevent its expansion would force a fundamental restructuring of the South's racial and class balance at the expense of the nonslaveholders, this white majority demanded that an outlet be kept open for the hated black man.

The preservation of racial purity and white values was the ultimate Southern justification for the right of slavery to expand. This theme of self-defense was itself part of a comprehensive racial world view. By the 1850's, the South had combined two central racial tenets—the black man's inherent inferiority and his greater adaptability to tropical climates—into a deterministic vindication of expansion.

Slavery in the United States had been pushed steadily southward since colonial days. Racial theorists explained this trend by postulating that, in a cold or temperate climate, white labor was always the most productive. Its superior efficiency, plus the constant growth of the population through natural increase and European immigration, enabled white labor to displace slavery in the Northern economy. The key variable was race, not the labor system. The free states were more prosperous, noted Van Evrie, only because they contained far fewer blacks and enjoyed the "immense superiority of the white race." White labor "pays better [than], not as erroneously supposed slave labor, but better than negro labor," he insisted; "therefore the latter falls back, is pressed southward, and demands new outlets and fresh fields of industry suited to the constitution and wants of this race."

The irreversible movement of slave labor was toward the tropics—the black's "natural home." "The negro is as much a product of the tropics as the orange or the banana," wrote Van Evrie, "and the instinct of his nature prompts, as well as urges, him onward to his original and final home." If disciplined and supervised by white masters, black labor would be immensely profitable in a tropical climate that would kill off any whites who attempted to do physical work. Even in the American South, the climate allegedly took a terrible toll of white lives; during the summer, planters and their families left low-lying rice and sugar districts for health reasons. Dr. Samuel A. Cartwright of Louisiana, another pioneering racist ethnologist, pitied the poor whites who were the common laborers of New Orleans. "The sickness and mortality among that class of persons who make negroes of themselves in this hot climate, are frightfully great. . . ." He contended, for instance, that, during the hot season, a railroad company building below the city required fifty fresh white hands a day to replace the sick and the dead. In the same area, on the other hand, black slaves performing equally grueling work were said to be as healthy as any Northerners. Cartwright cautioned, however, that the black man was so incapable of caring for himself that freeing him or permitting him to hire out his own time would result in an excessive black mortality rate. To Cartwright the moral was clear: "In the cotton and sugar region, Nature has ordained that the negro shall serve the white man, and the white man shall take care of the negro."

Thus, slavery, under the higher law of Nature, would regulate itself. Eventually, it would survive only in those tropical regions where the climate rendered white labor inefficient and unprofitable. Its transformation in the Upper South was well under way before the Civil War; nothing could stem the gradual abolitionizing of the northern tier of slave states. Slavery was virtually abolished in Maryland and Delaware, emphasized Dr. Josiah Nott of Mobile in 1851, "and it requires no prophet's eye to see that emancipation is inevitable in all the farming states, where white labor can be advantageously used." This seemingly inexorable tide of emancipation did not itself frighten Southerners so long as there was an outlet for the blacks. The process was a natural one—indeed, providentially inspired—and would ultimately solve the racial problem by siphoning off all the blacks to the tropics. If allowed to run its natural course, the expansion of slavery would benefit both races and would, furthermore, even regenerate the inferior Indian and mixed races of tropical America.

Missionary Racism

The average Southerner was profoundly moralistic, compelled by his Protestant heritage to define his life as well as his society in moral terms. Combined with his racism, this resulted in an oddly skewed humanism. The Biblical defense of slavery was one by-product. But, in a broader context, the greatest and most incredible ideological flowering of this moral rationalization of slavery was a missionary racism, which interpreted slavery as part of God's plan to develop the American tropics for the enrichment of the world and, at the same time, to civilize both the black race and the mixed races of the tropics.

Southerners were appalled by the societies of Central and South America. For, in a vast region blessed with a fertile soil and a limitless growing season, and thought to contain mineral riches, all Southerners could see was unrest, miscegenation, and instability. Part of this dreary spectacle they attributed to a climate and terrain so lush that it made a mockery of the Protestant work ethic. When food could be had simply by scattering a few seeds over the ground, what value was there to energy and ambition? Moreover, they thought the climate was so enervating that only dark-skinned peoples could survive and propagate. Yet, to be sure, the area had once supported a great civilization—the Latin America of the Spanish Empire. If that civilization declined, reasoned the Southerners—and many Northerners as well—it was only because of the abolition of slavery. They assumed from the climate that only a forced labor system could produce a valuable economic surplus, and racism dictated that that labor be non-white. To clinch their case, Southerners pointed to Cuba and Brazil, two societies that, according to the critique, were stable and productive. What they shared, of course, was slavery, an institution so beneficial that it enabled these two countries to prosper in spite of despotic monarchs. They also cited the rest of Latin America, where slavery had been abolished; even with the advantages of republican government, it languished in wasteful drift. Echoing this dogmatic view, Chancellor Harper declared, in his *Slavery in the Light of Social Ethics*, that nowhere was there a tropical society "where slavery does not exist, that is in a state of high civilization, or exhibits the energies which mark the progress toward it."

Both as a Christian and as a slaveholder, the white Southerner was convinced that God had not intended tropical America to lie dormant, inhabited by a slothful race. The instrument of His redemption was to be black slavery. "Africa was designed to supply that great field of labor—which is to clothe, and, in a great extent, to feed the world; to develop the mighty wealth that lies buried in the vast and rich soil of the tropics, where the white man fleeth from toil for his life," intoned Edward Delony, a Louisiana State Senator, in a report calling for the reopening of the African slave trade. This racial fantasy assured Southerners that expansion was divinely sanctioned. The very idea of a struggle "between a whining abolitionist and the Great God, to change the order of his creation," was, said Delony, ludicrous.

Once slave-produced tropical goods began to flood world markets, the entire white race would benefit. Sugar, coffee, rice, and tropical fruits would be cheap and plentiful and become part of even a poor man's diet. Already the manufacture of slave cotton had generated countless jobs in America and Europe. Cotton goods raised the dignity of the poor everywhere by allowing them to purchase clothing at reasonable prices. Modern civilization had become so dependent on cotton that this single commodity, Van Evrie asserted, was now "revolutionizing the world, and doing more to advance democratic ideas and true civilization than all the 'universities' of Europe." There could be no doubt about what would be best for mankind. As A. J. Donelson wrote to Calhoun, "The only inquiry is whether it is better for humanity that that portion of the world should relapse into a savage negro and Indian state, or be gradually improved by permitting the white man to continue the civilization which he is capable of enforcing as the legitimate superior of the negro or Indian."

The racially mixed populations of tropical America would gain tremendously by the reintroduction of slavery. According to the racial indictment, the major problems of the region—ignorance, poverty, and instability—were directly traceable to the inferior racial stock. Once the Spanish possessions had won their independence, these countries were ruled by a mélange of red and black races. The predictable result was analogous to what had occurred in the West Indies. "In both instances," explained a writer in *DeBow's Review*, "the support of the strong will and high intelligence of the white man has been withdrawn, and, forthwith the red man and the black man, liberated but incapable and helpless, have sunk down from the position in which they had been held up and sustained, and lapsed rapidly towards their original and natural barbarism." When William Walker, an American filibusterer who gained temporary control of Nicaragua in the mid-1850's, revoked the decree abolishing slavery, he justified his action by arguing that slavery would not only furnish a plantation labor force but would also "tend to segregate the races and destroy the mixed breeds who cause the disorder which has prevailed in the countries since independence." Moreover, slavery would restore stability, end the constant struggles between the mongrel races for supremacy, and provide a secure foundation for a system of rational liberty. Both the land and the peoples would be regenerated.

For some, the southerly thrust of slavery would be peaceful and irrepressible. "Expansion is our mission, and we must advance. Civilization and religion impel us on," announced Congressman Reuben Davis of Mississippi. "We intend only to revivify these fallen Republics and restore them to respectability and position amidst the nations of the earth. With swelling hearts and suppressed impatience they await our coming, and with joyous shouts of 'Welcome! welcome!' will they receive us." A year after this euphoric imagery, William Walker was shot by a Honduran firing squad. Edward Pollard, caught between the fact of native resistance to Walker and his own preconception of a weak race waiting to be redeemed, interpreted Walker's defeat as only a temporary setback. Eventually, Southern whites "would win a peaceful and natural triumph over native imbecility, and change the destiny of the country." Even Walker would have triumphed, Pollard felt, if it had not been for the "fickleness, the jealousy, the treachery, and the revolutionary spirit of the Central American people."

Albert Gallatin Brown and most other Southerners avoided

Davis's wishful thinking and Pollard's ambivalence by making the Southern experience of seizing territory from the Indians a paradigm for expansion into the tropics. In an 1858 speech, Brown pointed out that Central America belonged to someone else, just as Mississippi had once belonged to the Choctaws. "When we wanted this country we came and took it. If we want Central America, or any part of it, I would go and take that. If the inhabitants were willing to live under a good government, such as we would give them, I would have them protected; and if they were not, they might go somewhere else." This sounded cruel, he admitted, but it was no worse than what had already been done to the Indians. Besides, these Central Americans were "semi-barbarous, conglomerate of Indian, negro, and Celt." And, as God clearly supported the South, "I would spread the blessings of slavery, like the religion of our Divine Master, to the uttermost ends of the earth. . . ."

As crucial as the expansion of slavery was for the regeneration of tropical America, it was deemed equally indispensable for the continued happiness of the slaves. Southerners rationalized that, by diffusing slavery over a larger area, they were reducing the need for harsh discipline in regions where slaves outnumbered whites and were, thereby, humanizing the institution. This belief in the benevolence of diffusion was an old one; its first extensive political use had been in the debates over the Missouri Compromise. Jefferson outlined the argument in his famous "firebell in the night" letter on the compromise: "As the passage of slaves from one State to another would not make a slave of a single human being who would not be so without it, so their diffusion over a greater surface would make them individually happier, and proportionately facilitate the accomplishment of their emancipation, by dividing the burden on a greater number of coadjutors." And Jefferson Davis expressed the theory aphoristically: "It is in proportion to its sparseness that [slavery] becomes less objectionable." Discipline would become more rigorous and the condition of the slaves would deteriorate whenever the institution was confined to a fixed area, because of rising white fears related to insecurity and the decline of the slave economy.

As a given number of slaves became more dispersed, it was assumed, more whites would have an opportunity to own them. A multiplication of small holdings would maximize the immediate personal contacts between master and slave on which the legend of paternalism rested. "It is only when the slaves are assembled in large numbers, on plantations, and are removed from the interested, the kind, the affectionate care of the master, that [slavery] ever can partake of that cruelty which is made the great charge against it by those who know nothing of it," assured Jefferson Davis. It was also assumed that slavery generally would expand only into areas where it would be quite profitable. If this was true, the comforts of the slave would increase in proportion to his greater productivity. On the other hand, if slaves were taken into areas where their labor proved too expensive or unprofitable, they would be emancipated, for their numbers would probably be so small that society could safely afford to liberate them. According to this logic, the Northwest Ordinance of 1787, which prohibited slavery in the old Midwest, actually retarded the cause of emancipation. The few slaves who would have been transported there, reasoned Senator Solomon Downs of Louisiana in 1850, would in all likelihood have been freed. Left in the South, they would certainly still be slaves.

However, the diffusion theory was but one more myth promulgated by whites to buttress their contention that the South was really a Christian society with the best interests of the slaves at heart. No evidence was ever adduced to show that, as slavery spread westward, the slaves carried into new regions were treated better than those left behind. Indeed, the opposite seems to have been the case. What paternalism slavery possessed was a product of old and mature plantation societies where the original economic impulse had slackened and slavery had mellowed and provided the prop for an aristocratic way of life. On the frontiers of plantation agriculture, the profits were greater, but so were the economic pace and the harsh demands made on slave labor. Blacks may have been treated better when they were part of small or single holdings, but diffusion did not democratize the pattern of slaveownership. Holdings were more concentrated and absenteeism was higher in the wealthier plantation regions, whether the old rice districts of South Carolina or the newer cotton and sugar areas of Mississippi and Louisiana. By creating fresh markets for slave labor, expansion did make it possible for planters in the old Atlantic states to rid themselves of surplus slaves at high prices, but the institution as a whole was no more diluted. From 1790 until 1860, a period of nearly constant accretions of slave territory, the slave population remained at 33 to 34 per cent of the total Southern population. Because both races were increasing in numbers at about the same rate, the proportion of blacks could be lowered only if large numbers of whites came into the South or large numbers of blacks left.

Jefferson's argument that a wider range of owners would facilitate emancipation by spreading the burden overlooked the fact that emancipation was more a social than an individual decision. By the nineteenth century, most states forbade voluntary manumissions unless the freedmen were removed. Moreover, even if all Southerners had owned slaves, emancipation conceivably could have been more difficult. The dictum that expansion into unprofitable areas offered some slaves a chance for freedom was just as inconsistent. Assuming that the owners would not even have been permitted to retain their slaves as status symbols, nothing would have prevented them from selling their slaves or taking them back South.

An End to Slavery?

The popularity of the diffusion theory did not rest on its inherent logic. It did assure Southerners of their good intentions toward their slaves, and it did idealize in humanitarian terms the economic thrust of slavery's expansion. Most important, it offered the illusion of a socially safe solution to the racial dilemma. Racially, whites feared and despised the black man, but economically they were absolutely dependent upon his labor. Although the inherent instability of these conflicting relationships was accommodated in the institution of slavery, tensions and frustrations remained. So did consternation about the future: What if slavery became, as most Americans predicted, unprofitable when confined? What could be done with the blacks when their numbers stitution, in most areas, was not vital to the economy. Society as a whole, therefore, could accept abolition because freedmen would be too few in number to present any real threat to white dominance or security. Nevertheless, the North proceeded with extreme caution. Emancipation was gradual and applied generally only to those born after a certain date. The Pennsylvania Act of 1780, for example, provided that those subsequently born of slave mothers were to be freed only when they reached the age of twenty-eight. Consequently, slaves were still legally held in the state as late as the 1840's. This conservative approach was justified as the only means, short of compensation, of respecting the property rights of the slaveowner.

Since the slaves constituted less than 5 per cent of the Northern population when the emancipation plans were adopted in the 1780's and 1790's, the later Southern insistence that the North needed an outlet for the liberated slaves was overstated. Yet, the axiom that whites could face emancipation only when they far outnumbered their slaves was borne out with amazing precision. In the two states with the smallest proportion of blacks, New Hampshire and Massachusetts, slavery was ended suddenly by judicial decree; in Pennsylvania, Connecticut, and Rhode Island, however, where slavery played a slightly larger role, gradual emancipation laws were passed; and, in New York and New Jersey, where slaves approached 10 per cent of the population, the slaveholders held out the longest. Although documentation is spotty, the extremely low rate of increase in the black population of these last two states during the early federal period supports the contention of contemporary abolitionists and later Southerners that slaves were illegally transported from there to the American South or the British West Indies.

The diffusion theory of emancipation, by removing the blacks, rendering a fair compensation to the slaveowners, and ensuring Southern control, met the major obstacles to abolition. The theory also provided a psychological release for the South. It promised that, as the black race gradually dispersed over equatorial America, the racial and class tensions generated by slavery would eventually be resolved. The theory conformed to the prevalent racial attitudes and left the class order undisturbed. A "Lady of

outgrew the capacity of the South to control them? In short, v
did the South eventually plan to do with her black slaves? S
a biracial society without slavery was unthinkable, and s
Southern whites had no intention of abandoning their cou
to the Afro-Americans and Northerners would not accept en
cipated slaves, the only solution was to remove the slaves f
the United States. This removal, unlike Northern, federally
posed colonization plans, was to be under Southern contro
would be both a very gradual process and profitable because
blacks were to be sold or taken as slaves into fertile regions sc
of the United States. In the missionary rhetoric so favored by
expansionists, the blessings of diffusion would flow back u
Southern whites until they were wholly free of the black m
presence.

Southerners felt that the value of diffusion had been an
proved by the Northern abolition of slavery. This emancipa
was possible, the South argued, only because there had beer
outlet for the freed slaves. Indeed, the North, strictly speak
had not liberated her slaves but only sold them farther south.
"so-called emancipation at the North," insisted Lieutenant N
thew Maury, "was simply a transfer to the South of the slave
the North—an act of banishment; nothing more." If the Nc
wanted to proclaim to the world that this banishment represen
a humanitarian act of emancipation, that was her business,
she had no right to deny the South a similar outlet. "We h
now three and a half millions of slaves," said Albert Galla
Brown in 1853, "and in thirty years we shall have seven or ei
millions. When they have become profitless or troublesome,
too, want a South to which we can send them. We want it,
cannot do without it, and we mean to have it."

This argument had more substance than most Northern
were willing to acknowledge. To be sure, slavery was virtua
abolished in the North during the period following the Revc
tionary War, to a large extent because of the idealism and na
ral-rights philosophy that then held sway. But considerations
class and race played at least an equally important role in brii
ing about emancipation. For one thing, there was no extens
class of slaveholders to block emancipation; for another, the

Georgia" explained in *DeBow's Review* how painless the end of slavery could be. Although careful to spare white sensibilities by stipulating that emancipation was neither a goal in itself nor even to be regarded as inevitable, she did feel that the southward tendency of the black race might very well result in a "most natural termination" of slavery. The blacks would first become concentrated along the shores of the Gulf of Mexico. Then, "as population increases, and the slaves become not only useless, but a burden to us, we will get rid of this surplus population by transporting them across the Gulf to South America, and over the line to Mexico, where, in a population which seems to amalgamate readily with them, they may be free."

For the white egalitarian, the outlet theory was the one ideological device that enabled him to be loyal both to his concept of an eventual all-white South and to the needs and values of the slave society in which he lived. William Brockenbrough of Florida balanced this dual commitment by equating diffusion with the triumph of white labor. He reasoned that, as a fixed number of slaves became spread over a wider area, a labor shortage would develop. "It is very clear that slave labor which will be sufficient for 100,000 square miles, will not be sufficient for 200,000, and so in proportion; and that free labor must and will flow in to supply the demand, and every day more and more, with every expansion, diminish the relative proportion of slaves and freemen, by increasing the latter. . . ." As long as the outlet was kept open, free labor would continue its encroachments until all that remained of slavery would be a few harmless house servants. This projected free society would have no race problem at all. Initially, a few freed blacks, enough to be a nuisance, would be left; but they would be widely scattered and "diminishing every day by increasing sloth, idleness and degradation. They will diminish, without the care of a master, and disappear from the face of the earth by degrees." All this was inevitable, according to Brockenbrough. It had already occurred in the North and was under way in the Upper South. The entire process, moreover, would be peaceful and orderly. "Whatever may be the feelings or happiness of the people, slavery will, at least, go out in peace and quiet, without a convulsion or confusion, and by [a] transition so easy that all parties can adapt themselves to the gradual change of social relations."

The mechanical simplicity of Brockenbrough's model could also be infused with religious fervor. In 1844, Representative John Tibbatts of Kentucky emphasized that the hand of God could be clearly discerned in the Texas question. Annexation "will be favorable to the gradual, peaceable, and constitutional abolition of slavery on this continent, in a manner pointed out by the Almighty Creator of the universe. . . ." God, humanitarian racist that He was, had sent the Africans on a pilgrimage "from their own dark and benighted land." Passing through Europe and America, and exposed to "their superiors by nature," they would learn the rudiments of democracy and civilization. "The African race will be carried along in this pilgrimage by the interests of mankind, and by the laws of trade, gradually improved, cultivated, christianized, regenerated, and converted into beings of a different nature." This conversion, however, would be a limited one; the Africans would still be inferior. Unsuited by nature to a temperate climate and pressed upon by the tide of white emigration from Europe, they would be pushed farther south, then through Texas, "until they end their pilgrimage on the shores of the Gulf, and in a climate congenial to their nature, and become blended with the mixed population of Mexico."

In the racial fantasies of the diffusionists, everyone would benefit. The North would be rid of a wretched black population that clogged her jails and poorhouses. The South would have improved her population and increased her wealth. Hardy, industrious whites would replace the lazy blacks, and capital would flow in to pay for the slaves who were taken out. The African finally would have found a permanent home. Since the mixed races of tropical America were not themselves superior to the African, they could not reject him because of his color. The black would blend in, biologically and culturally, and would enjoy the limited social rights of which he was capable. "Who is there that will object, if all of this unfortunate race shall thus gradually and peaceably finally be withdrawn from our republic?" asked Tibbatts. "Who will set himself up to oppose the decrees of the Almighty?"

The North rejected this road to emancipation, especially after the annexation of Texas proved not to be the panacea that Southerners, and many Northern Democrats, too, had claimed it would be. Slavery *"will certainly disappear, if Texas is reannexed to the Union,"* asserted Senator Robert Walker of Mississippi. And James Buchanan asked hopefully, "May not, then, the acquisition of Texas be the means of gradually drawing the slaves far to the South . . . and may they not finally pass off into Mexico, and there mingle with a race where no prejudice exists against their color?" As time passed, the answer increasingly became no. In addition to providing, through slave sales, an economic motive for retaining slavery in areas where it was no longer profitable, expansion would never free a slave. It would simply transfer them from one place to another. The area of freedom would expand in the American South as it contracted in Central America. The timing of the eventual emancipation was so distant and vague that the antislavery forces justifiably denounced diffusion as a cruel delusion that completely ignored the problem of the Afro-Americans where they already stood enslaved. They pointed out that the South normally spoke of emancipation through diffusion only as a defensive measure when faced with Republican efforts to keep slavery out of the territories. The belief that confinement, and not expansion, would destroy slavery continued to motivate Republican policy. As Senator Jacob Collamer of Vermont put it, "The more limited the extent of territory to which slavery was confined, the sooner it would come to an end."

In fairness to the South, diffusion was always far more a visionary hope than a practical policy. The openendedness and uncertainty of diffusion accounted for much of its appeal. The South did not have to commit herself to any particular course and was not called upon to sacrifice any of her interests; all that was asked of her was that she be patient and allow for time. How much time can be gauged by Brockenbrough's "general law of population." Slavery, he argued, had attained its maximum growth by 1830; from then until 1840, the percentage of slaves in the South had dropped from 34.29 per cent to 33.67 per cent. When the slave states were new, the proportion of slaves to whites rose steadily until all the rough, pioneering work had been done. Then the tide turned, and the slaves moved on to another wilderness.

Since the first federal census of 1790, slavery had receded from
Delaware and Maryland. He estimated in 1847 that Arkansas and
Texas would be the only states in which slavery would not have
peaked by 1850. What all this meant, Brockenbrough continued,
was that, "by the natural laws of population, the days of slavery
are already numbered, though distant, and may be calculated
with mathematical precision. . . ."

Brockenbrough spared his fellow congressmen the calculations, for they would have been interminable. In the first place,
he had greatly underestimated the expansive capacity of slavery
within the South. During the 1850's, and in addition to Arkansas
and Texas, the number of slaves was still increasing faster than
that of whites in five states. What Brockenbrough had based his
hopes on was the small proportional drop of slaves in the 1830's,
but at that rate centuries would have to pass before the South became significantly "whitened."

The expansion of slavery was at the core of the political debate
that came to dominate the public life of the 1850's. Whether free
labor or slaves were to settle the future states was, of course,
translatable into sectional power at Washington. But to visualize
the issue only in political terms is to overlook the incalculable psychological value that diffusion had for white Southerners. As de-
lusive and contradictory as the diffusion theory was, Southerners
clung to it because it offered an effortless way out of the racial
morass. The option of evolving into a white egalitarian society,
no matter how tenuous, had to be kept open. Like any myth,
diffusion reminded Southern whites of what they could be. Ultimately, diffusion was not even a hope but, rather, the self-
deception of a society trapped between its inability to accept the
black man as an equal and its fear of the consequences of keeping
him enslaved.

3. The Radical Effort

Of the many ironies associated with the efforts of prewar radicals to achieve Southern independence, few are so striking as the relative lack of attention the radicals received. The constitutional issues raised by them have been studied, as have their racial arguments, but there is no over-all perspective that integrates their ideology, their social origins, and their relationship to the power structure of the slave South into a cohesive interpretative framework. In short, how did the radicals, those who desired secession as a goal in itself, fit into the mainstream of antebellum Southern history?

The Radical as Outsider

A distinct image of radical leadership, in large part propagated by their more conservative opponents in the 1850's, has persisted in the historical literature. A political confidant of John Calhoun's once described Robert Barnwell Rhett, one of the most prominent radicals, as "a rash and ultra man in his politics, frequently bent upon extreme and desperate courses, very excitable and unstable and intolerant and contemptuous of all about him, with neither tact [n]or discretion and without sympathy or popularity with the great mass of men." This vivid if unflattering portrait was typical. Bold, impetuous, uncompromising, greedily ambitious— these were the adjectives consistently applied to radical leaders. The collective image was that of the fire-eater, the swaggering hothead plotting to break up the Union. Even allowing for the partisan bias of many of the contemporary accounts, it is still clear that a distinct type existed. An examination of the public careers

of the most influential fire-eaters will show why such a type of
leader emerged and why individuals with such doctrinaire and
extremist views were able to wield significant influence.

The three men usually singled out as classic examples of
radicals are Edmund Ruffin of Virginia, Robert Barnwell Rhett of
South Carolina, and William Lowndes Yancey of Alabama. Just
below them in prominence would rank John Quitman of Mississippi and J. D. B. DeBow of New Orleans. The careers of these
men followed a common pattern: All were self-made men whose
relationship to the recognized channels of power and prestige in
the South was that of social and political outsiders.

Both Quitman, born and reared in the North, and Yancey, a
Southerner by birth but reared in Troy, New York, and educated
in New England, moved to the Deep South as young lawyers
intent on making their fortunes. They readily identified with their
adopted society.

Shortly after his arrival in Natchez in the early 1820's, Quitman
wrote to his former law patron Platt Bush that "these 'niggers,' as
you call them, are the happiest people I have ever seen . . . they
are oily, sleek, bountifully fed, well clothed, well taken care of,
and one hears them at all times whistling and singing cheerily at
their work." The planter aristocracy impressed Quitman with its
wealth and sense of propriety. He reported back approvingly to
his father that here there was to be found a "genteel and well-
regulated society." The planters were wealthy but not ostenta-
tious. They "affect great simplicity of costume themselves—straw
hats and no neck-cloths in summer, and in winter coarse shoes
and blanket overcoats." This sense of balance was important to
Quitman, for he had been taught by his minister father that ambition must be tempered with integrity and purpose. He admitted
having been attracted to Mississippi by the opportunity to grow
wealthy, but he was aware of the pitfalls. "Many young men who
go South grow careless on account of the facility of making
money, and plunge into every kind of excess. Young men born
there to hereditary wealth, who have never felt what it is to want,
set them the example."

When Yancey moved to South Carolina in the 1830's, he was
returning to a society he had known briefly as a child, before his

stepfather, the Reverend Nathan Beman, had taken his family
north to Troy. A unionist during the nullification crisis, Yancey became increasingly radicalized as marital difficulties intensified between his abolitionist stepfather and his mother. Deeply angered
by what he construed to be Beman's cruel and hypocritical self-
righteousness, Yancey seems to have projected his resentment into
an indictment of the entire abolitionist movement. His need to reject an antislavery stepfather he had come to hate was paralleled
by a deeper commitment to slave society. Whereas Quitman embraced slavery as a means of enforcing the order and stability so
revered by his father, Yancey posed as the defender of slavery in
order to flout more strongly the values of his stepfather.

Both men quickly acquired land and slaves through favorable
marriages. But any dreams of planter status that Yancey might
have entertained were shattered in 1839 when his slave labor
force was accidentally poisoned. Forced to liquidate his agricultural holdings, he turned to the law to support his family. Quitman came closer to achieving the ideal of planter status. Only his
poor business judgment prevented him from acquiring a large
fortune. Heavily in debt at the beginning of the 1840's, he required most of the decade to pay off his creditors but did manage to retain his land and slaves.

Of the two, Quitman was always the more comfortable in a
political role. From his election to the Mississippi legislature in
1825 until his death in 1858 while a member of Congress, he was
politically active. In the 1850's, he was the recognized leader of
the states'-rights faction of the Mississippi Democracy, and he
was mentioned twice as a potential vice-presidential nominee on
the national ticket. But, with these exceptions, Quitman's influence rarely extended beyond the confines of Mississippi. Although
growing sectional tensions after the Mexican War probably made
it impossible for a radical of Quitman's stripe ever to exercise
power on the national level, he clinched matters by first advocat-
ing secession in 1850 and then identifying himself with filibustering
groups intent upon the military conquest of Spanish Cuba for the
slave South. He delighted in his maverick's role, but control of
the Mississippi Democracy increasingly passed into the hands of
the more moderate Jefferson Davis and Albert Gallatin Brown.

To Quitman, the expansion of slavery seemed necessary to prevent the British from building up hostile concentrations of black power to the south of the United States. "The European policy is to establish near us negro or mongrel states. Such a result would be fatal to us," he warned. Cuba was the only slave state left in the Caribbean and Central America, and Quitman was certain that the British were plotting to force emancipation there. Once they did so, they would establish a protectorate over this free black empire and use it to halt American progress and harass the slave South. The only course open to the United States, therefore, was to destroy this empire in its infancy, because, in Quitman's words, America "could have no relations, political or diplomatic, with a black empire. Such intercourse would taint with incurable leprosy our political system, already affected to an alarming extent by negrophilism. The end would be internal convulsion, disunion, and death." Cuba had to be saved for slavery. But, since the federal government was too much distracted by the sectional dispute, Quitman insisted that only private Southern armies, working with Cuban planters, could accomplish the task. Quitman never won Cuba for the South, and his own party denounced his filibustering, but, in his emphasis on the threat of a free black empire, he revealed how radical politics could function as a vent for racial phobias.

Yancey had neither the temperament nor the self-discipline necessary for a successful political career. In the 1840's, he served briefly in both houses of the Alabama legislature and in Congress. A distaste for the mundane tasks of the officeholder, the financial enticement of legal fees back in Alabama, and, perhaps above all, an inability to cope with the give and take of political debate without resorting to an invective so bitter and sarcastic that it resulted in his fighting one duel and nearly a second—all induced Yancey to resign his congressional seat in 1846 and retire from politics. He made futile attempts to obtain a post in Buchanan's cabinet and a Senate seat in the late 1850's but held no other political office until the war. His fame, as well as his influence, rested upon his oratory. In mid-nineteenth-century America, especially in the rural South, where illiteracy was high, life was hard, and amusements were few, a gifted orator, whether at a revival meeting or at a political barbecue, was a source of both information and pleasure. Yancey could hold an audience for hours with a rhetoric that would strike a modern listener as hopelessly pompous and long-winded. Yet, his speeches were also marvelously effective because of their rich imagery, Biblical allusions, and reiteration of simple themes that appealed to the prejudices and aggrieved sensibilities of his white audiences.

The violence and other excesses of the slave rebellion on Santo Domingo during the 1790's were stock themes of Southerners whenever the mere suggestion of emancipation arose. Yancey, however, made the scene grotesquely vivid by describing it as one "where wives were violated upon the bodies of their slaughtered husbands, and the banner of the inhuman fiends was the dead body of an infant, impaled upon a spear, its golden locks dabbled in gore, and its little limbs stiffened by the last agony of suffering nature." Yancey's comments on the repeal of a Massachusetts law prohibiting interracial marriage revealed his skill at employing sexual imagery to convey the depths of white racism. He dehumanized the free Negro into "the black son of Africa, with flat nose, thick lips, protruding [c]hin, and skin redolent of rare odors." Although purportedly free to compete on equal terms with the white man, "to ally himself with, ay, and even [be] invited to the arms of, the fair-skinned[,] cherry-lipped, and graceful daughter of that famed [Puritan] race, [he] still retains his nature—rejects with scorn the tendered connection, and prefers to revel in the brothel, until imprisoned in a jail or penitentiary." As for the problems rocking the country in 1860, Yancey had a simple answer: The absolute equality of the states must be recognized. "The only issue of this campaign is the integrity and safety of the Constitution." Such were some of the themes and imagery upon which Yancey built his fame. Never brilliant, rarely subtle, he simplified issues, gilded Southern racial fears with an ornate rhetoric, and talked his way to leadership.

Politics was one of the many vocations in which James DeBow dabbled before he finally settled on journalism in 1845, at the age of twenty-five. The son of a Yankee businessman who had done moderately well in Charleston, South Carolina, DeBow was a quiet, bookish youth. The failure of his father's business forced

DeBow to take on a succession of odd jobs. Clerking for a wholesale grocery concern, schoolteaching, and law were some of the
professions he tried. He was bored with all of them, for his real
interests lay in speaking and writing, two talents he cultivated
at the College of Charleston in the early 1840's. Known in
Charleston circles as a minor worker for the Democrats and as a
contributor of staunchly pro-Southern articles to newspapers and
magazines, DeBow was appointed a delegate to the Southern
Commercial Convention in Memphis in the fall of 1845. His
attendance there convinced him of the need for, and the feasibility
of, a monthly journal devoted to promoting the economic resources of the South. In January, 1846, he published, in New
Orleans, the first issue of *DeBow's Review*, soon to be acclaimed
as the most influential and widely circulated of all Southern
magazines.

When DeBow launched his magazine, he was a young man in a
strange city, lacking money, friends, influence, and experience.
Sheer hard work and perseverance, plus timely contributions
from wealthy benefactors, enabled him to survive the lean early
years. By the mid-1850's, enough advertising revenue was coming
in (ironically, most of it from the North) to make the magazine
profitable and provide DeBow with a considerable surplus to invest in real estate.

From the start, *DeBow's Review* preached a New South brand
of boosterism. Article after article explored and computed the
South's material wealth, tapped and untapped. The goal was a
strong, unified South, in league with the agricultural West if
necessary but ultimately able to stand alone and defend herself
against the aggressive North. Any program of economic better-
ment was extolled—whether it was industrial diversification, agricultural reform, direct trade with Europe, or internal improvements—as long as it respected the inviolability of slavery. Always
a Southern nationalist, DeBow became an outright radical only in
the late 1850's. At a time when he was plagued by personal trag-
edy—the death of his infant son in the fall of 1857, followed a few
months later by that of his young wife—his boosterism shaded
into radicalism. He endorsed with increasing shrillness the reopening of the African slave trade and the expansion of slavery into

tropical America—programs that were clearly unattainable within the Union. In concluding his presidential address at the Knoxville Commercial Convention in 1857, he outlined the imperialistic glories awaiting a free South:

> Free thus in her industry and her enterprise, the growth of the South would be commensurate with the extent of the regions and the inclinations of the peoples who surround her. Mexico, Central America, Cuba, the West Indies, generally, would probably, in the remote future, become parts of a system which assimilated so much in its necessities with their own. Slavery, in its natural increase, or by the reopening of the slave trade . . . will supply to us the labor that will be the indispensable agent in this great development.

In his zealous defense of slavery and his support for secession, DeBow was strengthening the same class interests and feeding the same racial fears that kept the antebellum South riveted to the old values based on land and slaves. The leading propagandist of the New South never freed himself from the demands of the present or the traditions of the past.

At first glance, Edmund Ruffin and Robert Barnwell Rhett appear to have been prepared by birth and family tradition for secure positions of public leadership. Both men were born into the Tidewater gentry and could boast an aristocratic genealogy stretching back to the colonial era. The only rub was that they were born about a generation too late, at a time when the economic base of their families' fortunes had eroded, leaving them with elitist aspirations without the wealth to support them. The result was a gap between expectations and social position.

Ruffin inherited a worn-out plantation on the northern neck of Virginia. His genius for agricultural reform soon restored the land, but young Ruffin was dissatisfied. As was a gentleman's due, he wanted to lead and to command respect from others. The natural channel for these ambitions was politics, and, in 1823, he entered the Virginia Senate. Much to his chagrin, however, Ruffin soon discovered that he lacked certain essential political talents, especially the ability to speak effectively. This weakness, plus his disdain for electioneering or serving the private interests of constituents, led to his resignation. In later years, he explained to a friend:

. . . in the first place, I felt sour that I had no talent for oratory, or to influence popular assemblies, and I was too proud to be willing to be deemed below any station in which I might be placed. Next and mainly, if I could have obtained popular favor (which I never procured, or sought to gain) and political eminence as its reward, I never knew the time that I would have been willing to purchase the honor at the cost of paying the necessary price for popularity.

The bitterness and disillusionment of thwarted ambition never left Ruffin. At first, he turned to agricultural reform as a means of vindicating himself and gaining the public approval he craved so desperately. Although he succeeded in the 1830's in compiling a record as a soil chemist that was no less than brilliant, he remained alienated and frustrated. Convinced that his efforts had gone unappreciated—indeed, had often been ridiculed—he resigned from the State Board of Agriculture in 1841 and resolved to abstain from all public service.

Although he would later return to his agricultural work, Ruffin committed himself to another crusade in the 1840's, a crusade that eventually consumed all his energies. Agitating for secession fulfilled a real need for Ruffin. It mattered little if his position was unpopular, for it was the aristocrat's duty to lead the masses. In the Yankee he had found the perfect scapegoat for all his frustrations. Not only was the Yankee, with his factories and cities, threatening to destroy the agrarian way of life, which Ruffin loved, but, with his fanatical attacks on slavery, he was undermining the racial order, gentility, and system of labor that had combined in the slave South to create a patriarchal civilization far superior to the crass materialism north of the Potomac. For Ruffin, such an idealized Southern society may well have been a projection back into the past of a golden age, when his ancestors, as gentlemen, naturally ruled, and where birth, talent, and recognition naturally meshed. But in the reality of Virginia politics, where he found himself incurring the "odium of opinions so unpopular with the many," Ruffin used this idealization to persuade himself that a South had existed that was worthy of his sacrifices.

Nearly crushed by a series of sudden family deaths in the late 1850's, Ruffin found solace in his role as an agitator. Fellow radicals could always be counted on to flatter him and appreciate his work. With John Brown's raid and the gathering momentum of secessionism in 1860–61, he began to glory in the role of a prophet whose time had come. In South Carolina for the secession of that state, he wrote back to his sons: "The time since I have been here has been the happiest of my life, in which personal feelings and interests were not concerned. The public events are as gratifying to me as they are glorious and momentous, and there has been much to gratify my individual and selfish feelings." For once, if only briefly, Ruffin had vindicated himself and won public approval.

In contrast to Ruffin, Rhett was a skilled politician. In spite of his fine family name, Rhett approached politics not with the complacency of an aristocrat accepting his just due but with the hunger of a parvenu on the way up. Financial failure forced his father to abandon a couple of rice plantations, and young Rhett, reared by a grandmother and largely self-educated, had to make his own fortune and carve out his own career. If the path he chose was the traditional one of law and politics, his leadership in the South Carolina nullification controversy of the early 1830's, while he was still just a young state legislator, immediately stamped him as a firebrand eager to challenge established authority.

Rhett would occasionally moderate his demands and tone down his rhetoric, but the notoriety he gained early in his career never left him. He would attempt, as Calhoun's lieutenant in Congress during the Van Buren and Tyler administrations, to work through the national Democratic organization, to control it in the interests of the South. But, with the collapse of the Calhoun candidacy in 1844, the emergence of the annexation of Texas as a sectional issue, and the revival of old battles over the tariff and abolitionism, Rhett reverted to the intransigence that had first won him a reputation. His return to a radical posture in 1844 may also have been influenced by the death of his younger brother Albert in the fall of 1843. He had doted on Albert, providing for his education and grooming him for politics. "In him is gone the chief personal reward I looked to in my public labors," Rhett wrote to Calhoun. With Albert gone, Rhett apparently renounced all hope of national leadership, either for himself or for a political protégé. The Bluffton movement that Rhett led in 1844 in an effort to force the Democrats to take a stronger stand for Texas and against abolitionism was short-lived; but never again would he place his trust in the Democratic Party. The Wilmot Proviso simply confirmed his worst fears. In 1848, he honestly could lay claim to a record of political consistency:

> In 1828 I declared . . . that the General Government must be driven back to its legitimate limitations in the Constitution. That if we yielded on the Taxing power, the next stride would be against our slave institutions. . . . I said the same thing in 1844. . . . Now you have this great question of Slavery upon you; and my counsel is, as of yore—meet the question at once, and forever.

The repeated disappointments and rancor of his career were the price Rhett paid for his dogmatic adherence to principle and his abrasive public personality. The merchant and planter elite of Charleston viewed him as a dangerous braggart who would carry logic to absurd extremes. After coveting the position for a decade, he was finally elected, in 1851, to a seat in the U.S. Senate by the South Carolina legislature. In office barely a year, he resigned when his party and the voters repudiated his stand on separate state secession in the uproar over the Compromise of 1850. Rhett came out of retirement five years later to promote secession once again, but so unpopular had his name and ideas become that he was frequently advised to remain in the background for the good of the cause. A fellow South Carolinian could write in 1860, with scant exaggeration, "I knew Rhett had no popularity out[side] of So[uth] Ca[rolina], but I had no idea he was so utterly *odious*."

Of all the leading fire-eaters, Rhett was perhaps the most provincial. He made his home and reared his large family on the Sea Islands of South Carolina, where he himself had been born and reared. It was there that he based his politics and distilled his social vision. Despite sharp reverses in the financial panic of 1837 and a heavy debt that he carried for years, he grew prosperous from his slaves and his rice plantation and even opened another plantation in Georgia. In return, Rhett gave this slave society his unquestioning devotion. It was a society that, for all its immense wealth and stately mansions, was haunted by a brooding insecurity. The islands, tidal flats, marshes, and inlets that made up the coastal region were the blackest and the most isolated area of the South. The prospect of slave revolts was a recurring nightmare, not because any significant uprisings actually occurred but because of the potentiality for unspeakable horrors inherent in the sheer numbers of the black slaves. With the rise of the abolitionists and their efforts to sway federal policy, white Southerners' concern over their security became a fetish. The limits of federal authority had to be strictly delineated and never broached. Rhett's admonition to the South Carolina legislature in 1833 rang just as true a generation later: "A people, owning slaves, are mad, or worse than mad, who do not hold their destinies in their own hands. . . . Every stride of this Government, over your rights, brings it nearer and nearer to your peculiar policy."

Ultimately, even this demand for home rule failed to satisfy Rhett. By 1860, complete security required not only secession but the remaking of the South into a homogeneous slave society approximating what Rhett knew at home. The repeal of the prohibition of the African slave trade, a constitutional provision forbidding the admission of any free state into the Confederacy, and full political representation for all slaves—these were the programs Rhett sought for the new Southern republic. His proposals were rejected. His dream of secession had come true, but he was already a disappointed and spurned leader before the society he so loved was destroyed by the war. In the end, few had contributed more to its destruction than Rhett himself.

In their political rhetoric, all of these radicals shared a passion for purity and principle. Scorning the compromises and half-truths of the politicians, they demanded a religious zeal from their followers. They preached a politics of the desirable, not of the possible. In 1850, Quitman pointed out the moral absurdity of compromise: "Can we compromise a question of conscience? Can we halve a moral duty?" Yancey constantly exhorted his fellow Southerners to follow him in renouncing party attachments and security. In resigning from Congress in 1846, he sounded the keynote of his career. "We [the South] shall never be able to act with that precision and energy to insure permanent success, until we make, as a *sine qua non* of political fellowship, a strict adherence to principle."

This religiosity was a function of the radicals' role as political and social outsiders shut off from the decision-making process at the state and, especially, national levels, as well as of their independence from the discipline and dictates of a political organization. Quitman and Rhett came closest to operating within a party framework. After the Mexican War, Quitman, always inclined to place his states'-rights principles before party regularity, was a Democrat in name only. He returned from the war a military hero and was elected governor by a huge majority. Increasingly, he would use his immense popularity to place himself above his party. In 1850–51, he fought hard for separate state secession. In 1852, the year he bolted his party to run for Vice-President on the Southern Rights ticket, he asked, "Of what consequence is it who is elected President beyond the securing [of] a principle? Without this the contest would be a mere struggle for office, interesting only to those who expected a share of the spoils." He urged the South to assume toward the national parties a posture of "armed neutrality."

In the loosely structured and localistic orientation of South Carolina politics, which placed a premium on a devoted personal following, Rhett had a secure power base in his congressional district. The low-country gentry regularly backed him, and, with the usual support of the powerful Charleston *Mercury*, he rarely had to trim his politics to suit party needs. As late as the 1850's, the question of whether the South Carolina Democracy should even cooperate with the national organization was a major issue in state politics. Yancey, with his oratory; Ruffin, with his work as an agricultural reformer; and DeBow, with his magazine, had never been beholden to a party for their fame or influence. Obstructed throughout most of their careers by the more moderate position of Southern parties and, perhaps, in compensation for their own inadequacies as politicians, all three viewed Southern politicians with contempt. To Yancey, most of them were "mere puppets in the show, made to wheel and dance as the party organists choose to grind the music; while others of ample ability and individuality are absorbed in their own personal advancement, which invariably requires a compromise of Southern issues."

Sharing a sense of rejection, the fire-eaters welcomed the role of agitators. Unable to function within a party structure, they felt free both to criticize and to stand above it. Reasoning that they had no greedy constituency to serve and no partisan ambitions to placate, they projected themselves as the only selfless defenders of the South. Of all the fire-eaters, Yancey understood this role best, and he reveled in it. "Error and ignorance occupy a more primitive relation to our lives than enlightenment and truth. Agitation, incentives to exertion, inducements which impel inquiry are sources of knowledge and wisdom. The prophets of old were agitators." If the South was, in fact, being denied her constitutional liberties, Yancey insisted he was duty-bound to proclaim this fact. If he was wrong, his very agitation would reveal the truth. "No good cause has ever been delayed by agitation, and every error has trembled before it." The agitator would be the conscience of the South, prodding an indifferent and submissive people to awareness of their rights. The wrongs, injuries, and insults perpetrated by the antislavery North would be exposed and publicized. Yancey realized that the South could not be united on a single issue, but "One thing will catch our eye here and determine our hearts; another thing elsewhere; all united may yet produce spirit enough to lead us forward, to call forth a Lexington, to fight a Bunker's [sic] Hill, to drive the foe from the city of our rights."

As the agitator literally forced the South to do what was right, he would purge slave society of all moral ambiguities. He interpreted as a moral stigma upon the South the 1819 statute of Congress defining the African slave trade as piracy. In demanding its repeal, Yancey acted not so much from a conviction that the trade should be reopened as in an attempt to remove the stigma, "to strip the Southern ship of state for battle—to furl and cut away every sail that would impede her movements—to cut loose every rope that would be a drag upon her progress." L. W. Spratt, a lesser-known radical, was even more adamant on the trade's tremendous symbolic importance: *"I regard the slave trade as the test of its integrity. If that be right, then slavery is right, but not without."*

The dichotomy between the fire-eaters' conception of their role and motivations and the negative image of them conveyed by the party press reinforced their belief that they were the ablest and purest Southerners. Just as a martyr ultimately finds confirmation of his faith through suffering, so also did the fire-eaters. Again Yancey expressed it best. In a Breckinridge campaign speech he told his audience: "The whole time refusing office, I have given my mind, heart, character and fortune to raise the Southern mind to the full view of Southern rights, that we may be *men* in the hour that tries men's souls. How hard that for *this* a man should be denounced as a demagogue, an office seeker and a traitor." Yet, by identifying his detractors with the same wicked men who defiled the Lord's temple, Yancey was able to take comfort. "There is a lesson in Holy Writ that, when the temple which had been devoted to the worship of the ever living God . . . was taken possession of by a people forgetful of the truth pronounced at Sinai . . . a Saviour came and with a whip of scorpions drove them out." Even defeat need not mean failure. "Revolution must be accomplished by strong hearted, powerful individualities found in a community, who choose to lose life and fortune for their country, and leave her to do justice to their memories if they fall."

Like radicals everywhere, the fire-eaters soon discovered that agitation alone would not effect change. Some organizational discipline was necessary, but the major parties had to be bypassed because they invariably put partisan needs above those of the South. Although there were suggestions for a new third party, the antiparty bias of the radicals pointed to the creation of non-partisan committees or associations. In his 1850 message to the Mississippi legislature, Governor Quitman recommended that such committees be appointed by state conventions. Functioning as "some centre of opinion and action," they would meet periodically and be invested with all necessary powers to act for their respective states in matters relating to their rights and safety. Since the states were naturally unwilling to surrender their sovereignty in so flagrant a manner, the recommendation was ignored. In 1858, Ruffin proposed that associations, known collectively as the League of United Southerners, be formed throughout the South. These clubs were to be consciously modeled after the Committees of Safety of the American Revolution. Their paramount objectives would be to propagandize for the Southern cause and to preserve sound principles. Members would retain their party ties but would pledge to work within their parties for the election of staunch Southern-rights men.

These attempts to operate outside the limits of political institutions were usually stillborn. Because the fire-eaters distrusted parties as organizations that put temporizing above principles and as breeders of jealousy and exclusiveness, they did not want to create new structures that would be equally flawed. As Yancey explained in an 1858 letter to James Slaughter of Georgia, "I hardly agree with you that a general movement can be made that will clean out the Augean stable. If the Democracy were overthrown, it would result in giving place to a greater and hungrier swarm of flies." The solution was to be an association of loyal and zealous individuals who would "fire the Southern heart—instruct the Southern mind—give courage to each other. . . ." In short, what was desired was not a political party but a cult of the faithful. Few Southerners could measure up to the high standards set by the fire-eaters. Most of them remained unconverted and, rather than rallying to the cause, waited for more convincing evidence that their rights and safety were being challenged by the North.

Ironically, the rhetoric of Southern conservatives matched that of the radicals in its moral fervor. But, whereas the former, reacting to a changing society and to their displacement as the South's leaders and natural spokesmen, clung to principle as one remaining symbol of stability and gentility, as a yardstick to distinguish the statesman from the politician, the latter invoked principle as a counterweight to a power structure they had never fully entered and as a condemnation of those sobered by the exercise of power. In their own way, both groups had been rejected and both expressed their frustration in the same metaphor.

It is clear that each of the five fire-eaters discussed here was driven by his own private demon. Yet, the common pattern of

their careers is equally unmistakable, especially their search for
a public role that would win them prestige and approval from a
society that never quite accepted their claims to leadership. This
leadership rested with the Democracy, the majority party
throughout most of the Deep South by the 1850's. Only when the
demands and the intransigence of the fire-eaters had become
institutionalized in this party would secession become a viable
alternative. The process of committing the party to radicalism
would begin in earnest during the controversy over the compromise measures of 1850, and the catalyst would be Southern anxieties over expansion.

Dividing the Spoils

In 1850, one-fifth of the United States consisted of lands recently won in the Mexican War. These huge acquisitions posed
a fundamental question concerning the destiny of the young republic: Was the division of the nation into free and slave societies
to be perpetuated indefinitely as slavery expanded into the new
territories; or was the institution to be set on the road to eventual
extinction by being confined within its present limits with the
territories the exclusive domain of free and white labor? This
was the crucial issue, and no amount of compromising or negoti-
ating could blur its stark simplicity. When a hitherto obscure
Pennsylvania congressman, David Wilmot, proposed, in August
of 1846, that slavery be forever prohibited from all the territory
acquired from Mexico, and the South responded by damning the
plan as "abhorrent . . . to every principle of religion, of honesty,
of morality, of honor, and even to that principle which binds the
basest men in society together, called honor among thieves," the
issue was joined.

The vagueness of the Constitution on the question of slavery in
the territories was a fatal defect in an otherwise masterful example of the art of compromise. Congress was given the "Power
to dispose of and make all needful Rules and Regulations respecting the Territory or other Property belonging to the United
States" (Article IV, Section 3), but whether this included the
power to exclude slavery was not clear. In the early years of the

Republic, the issue did not seem of paramount importance. There were Northern proposals to ban slavery from the territories by congressional legislation. George Thacher of Massachusetts and James Hillhouse of Connecticut, for example, introduced such resolutions in 1798 and 1804, respectively, for the territories of Mississippi and Louisiana, but their efforts received little backing and have been largely forgotten. By tacit agreement, the Mason-Dixon line was extended to the Mississippi. Where soil, climate, and the flow of migration permitted slavery to flourish, the institution was recognized, and new slave states were admitted into the Union without friction.

In 1819–20 this agreement began to break down. The North realized that slavery was about to cross the Mississippi, and its eventual extension into much of the Louisiana Purchase seemed to be only a matter of time. The panic of 1819 had resulted in a sharp depression, and both sections were measuring the Union in economic terms. Sectional tensions boiled over in acrimonious debate once Representative James Tallmadge of New York introduced a resolution to prohibit the further introduction of slavery in the proposed state of Missouri. The issue was settled by the Missouri Compromise, which, with the exception of the state of Missouri, restricted slavery in the Louisiana Purchase to the region south of the 36°30′ line. The South never interpreted the compromise as recognition of a constitutional right to exclude slavery from the territories, but she did acknowledge the utility and predictability of a measure that permitted slave and free labor to share in the territories.

The looseness and pragmatism of the old approach no longer sufficed in the expansionist 1840's. The seaboard republic of the 1790's was rapidly becoming a continental empire, and both sections wanted to define the nature of that empire. The rise of abolitionism in the 1830's had placed the South on the defensive and prompted her to look to expansion as a means of relieving external pressures against slavery. The antislavery forces, their suspicions fed by Southern opposition to the presentation of abolitionist petitions on the floor of Congress, began to project the image of the Slave Power, an all-powerful conspiracy of slaveholders intent on spreading slavery and trampling upon the civil liberties of those who opposed their aggressive designs. The mutual fears of the two sections were aggravated by the annexation of Texas and the ensuing war with Mexico. In 1850, a free-soil Whig, Congressman G. Ashmun of Massachusetts, could still refer to annexation as "that stupendous scheme for the extension of slavery—conceived in iniquity and brought forth in sin—which fully aroused the slumbering antislavery feelings of the northern people."

Southerners insisted that they wanted Texas primarily for self-defense, arguing that abolitionism, by threatening the internal security of the South, made the annexation of Texas crucial for the safety of slavery. The South, said Rhett, was motivated by a "sense of insecurity." She "has been wantonly wronged, insulted, and betrayed. And now, when her alarms have been awakened, will you refuse to quiet them?" Without additional slave territory, the South would be doomed to a chronic minority position within the Union. She would lack the economic and political power with which to compel respect for her institutions. "On it [annexation] hinges the very existence of our Southern Institutions," wrote James Gadsden, a South Carolina planter-entrepreneur, to Calhoun, "and if one of the south now prove recreant, we will or must [be] content to be Hewers of wood and Drawers of Water for our northern Brethren." Others felt that the peaceful acquisition of Texas would do more for the permanence and general welfare of the Union than any measure since the Louisiana Purchase. Senator William Merrick of Maryland summed up the safety-through-expansion ideology. "The best security for the South," he said, "is to be able to protect herself. The balance of power once restored, abolitionists would then let us alone, and this blighting agitation would die its natural death. For these reasons, . . . for the purpose of *preserving domestic tranquility*, we should admit Texas."

An independent Texas, the annexationists warned, would turn to Britain for protection. After assuming the Mexican debts of the Texans, the British would entice them into an economic alliance based on the duty-free exchange of sugar and cotton for manufactured goods. So advantageous would the terms of this free trade be that planters from the older slave states would flock to

Texas in order to avoid the 17 per cent British duty on their cotton and the 40 per cent American duty on British items. With the stimulus of free trade, Texas cotton would flood the market and put the Southern output at a ruinous disadvantage. One of the chief economic defenses of slavery, the South's near monopolization of the world's supply of cotton, would be destroyed. Yet, if the South needed Texas to preserve this monopoly, she needed Texas even more to forestall the threat of having a free country hard on the southwestern border of slavery.

Aware that the British were on public record as favoring the end of slavery throughout the world, the South accused them of encouraging the Texans to emancipate their slaves in return for recognition of their independence by Mexico. It was feared that, if this tactic failed, the British would use their predicted economic domination of Texas as a lever to force emancipation. So strong was this fear that Calhoun, as Secretary of State, cited it to the British in 1844 as ample justification for annexation. The possibility of a free Texas had to be eliminated forever. "With the South, the issue of *immediate annexation* is one of self-preservation," announced Representative James Belser of Alabama. "No non-slaveholding government will be permitted to rear its head in Texas, until those who now have slaves are exterminated." He contended that, unless the British were checked, they would establish in Texas a "mongrel population" of emancipated slaves and European paupers. Senator Robert Walker of Mississippi doubted that the mixed races of Mexico could ever subdue and govern the Americans in Texas. But, if they could do so, "ought we to consent to establish this ignorant and fanatical colored population upon the borders of Louisiana and Arkansas, in contact with the slave population, and within the very heart of the valley of the Mississippi?" The answer, of course, was no; annexation was infinitely preferable to the risk of permitting Texas "to fall into the hands of the semi-barbarous hordes of Mexico, now openly engaged in the crusade of abolition, prepared, in peace, to stimulate the servile population to revolt and massacre, and in case of another war with England, sure to be her friends and allies."

The South had too much at stake in the Texas issue to retreat.

In expressing his opinions to Calhoun on the tactics to be followed in the Presidential campaign of 1844, Hammond stressed that the South must push for annexation at all costs. "If the Union is to break there could not be a better pretext. With Texas the slave states would form a territory large enough for a *first rate power* and one that under a free trade system would flourish beyond any on the Globe—immediately and forever." At the same time, antislavery Northerners, such as John Quincy Adams, had warned that adding Texas was tantamount to dissolving the Union. This potentially explosive situation was partially defused by the Polk Administration. In a classic example of the Madisonian theory that domestic tensions could best be alleviated by expanding the political sphere so as to balance off a multiplicity of interest groups, Polk offered the Oregon Territory to the agrarian Midwest, the seaports of California to the commercial Northeast, and Texas to the slave South. The last two of these objectives could be gained only by war, but even that could be used to advantage. By prodding the Mexicans into war over their controversial Texas boundary, Polk hoped to deflect the sectional hostilities onto an external enemy. Although the war was bitterly opposed in New England, it received strong backing in the Midwest and was very popular in the South. For Southerners, the war was an opportunity not only to strengthen the bridgehead of slavery in the Southwest but also to prove their military prowess and show their critics that slavery was a source of power, not weakness.

Polk's strategy worked too well. The sheer quantity of the seized land magnified the slavery issue and contributed to the already complex problems of sectional power and morality. Mexican law had prohibited slavery. The abolitionists, who had already challenged as immoral the proposal to add a slave state to the Union, naturally felt that it would be an even greater evil to allow slavery into a formerly free society. On the other hand, Southerners argued that slavery had a constitutional right to expand into the territories and that it could not be legally prohibited until a given territory actually became a state. The Constitution was too imprecise to serve as arbiter. Soon, as both sides outlined their positions, it became apparent that the most enduring legacy of the Mexican War for American politics would be the replacement of the old economic issues of the tariff, banks, and internal improvements, which had formed the basis of party and sectional divisions for a generation, with the overriding issue of slavery in the territories. These economic issues, wrote an Alabamian to Calhoun in 1848, were "but matters of government practice—the regulation of its machinery," but the latter "affects the Soul of the Constitution."

The popularity of the Wilmot Proviso in the North, and the fact that it had passed in the House twice, added to the South's growing sense of inferiority. Southern anxieties were eloquently described by Representative Andrew Ewing of Tennessee:

> Under this disastrous state of feeling in the nonslaveholding States, with a consciousness that we are the weaker party, and becoming rapidly more so at each recurring census; with a further knowledge that there is no earthly means for a safe removal of slavery; that on its continuance and the forbearance of foreign interference depend not only our wealth, but the lives and fortunes of ourselves and families,—can it be wondered at, under these circumstances, that we are alarmed by the smallest interference with slavery by the Federal Government?

The Proviso, far from being a slight interference, called for a fundamental shift in the power balance between the sections. The sectional equilibrium had been upset in the late 1840's by the admission of Iowa and Wisconsin, which gave the North a preponderance of two states. This in itself was not alarming to the South, except as a portent of the permanent minority position that the passage of the Wilmot Proviso would force upon her. Restricted to her present limits and watching helplessly as more and more free states were admitted, the South predicted that she eventually would be at the mercy of a North with the necessary three-fourths majority to change the Constitution and abolish slavery. It was this concern that led Hammond to insist in 1850 that "We must act *now*, and *decisively*." He foresaw the addition of ten free states west of the Mississippi within thirty years and, assuming the cession of Canada to the United States, an equal number north of the Great Lakes and the St. Lawrence. "Long before the North gets this vast accession of strength she will ride

over us rough shod, proclaim freedom or something equivalent
to it to our Slaves and reduce us to the condition of Hayti. . `. .
If we do not act now, we deliberately consign our children, not
our posterity, but *our children* to the flames." What Hammond
wanted was a division of the territories to ensure permanent
Southern equality, at least in the Senate. "Our only safety is in
equality of POWER."

However much Hammond may have exaggerated the pace at
which the North would expand, the restoration of sectional equality became crucial for the South. For Calhoun, it was the obsession of his last years. Asserting that the Constitution was
formulated to create and maintain a parity between free and slave
societies, he argued that Southern rights had been endangered and
disregarded in proportion to Northern usurpations of the public
domain, first through the Northwest Ordinance, then through the
Missouri Compromise, and most recently in the prohibition of
slavery in the Oregon Territory. The South had to be granted
equality in the territories. If denied that by the stronger North,
she was justified in resorting to disunion. Calhoun's constitutional
syllogisms also led him to the conclusion that there should be a
dual executive, one each from the North and South and each with
a veto over the actions of the other. This was a logical position, but
it would be absurd in practice and had no chance of acceptance.
Calhoun's main contribution to Southern radicalism would remain his efforts to use the Constitution as a guarantee to the
South of a measure of equality that she herself had failed to
maintain when pitted against the industrializing North.

The extension of the 36°30′ line to the Pacific seemed to most
Southerners the fairest and most direct means of restoring the
lost equilibrium. Neither section would have to surrender its
principles. All that was asked was a sharing of the spoils. To
prove their magnanimity, Southerners pointed out that most federal territory lay north of 36°30′. According to this argument, if
the line was extended and if the future states were comparable
to Ohio in size, there would be room for forty more free states
but only six slave states.

The South was clearly attracted by the prospect of economic
gain, particularly from the California gold mines. In addition,

there were hopes that slave labor could be profitably employed in the old Spanish mines of New Mexico and in large-scale irrigated agriculture in the valleys of the Rio Grande, Colorado, and Gila rivers. Far greater emphasis, however, was placed on the absolute necessity of acknowledging the South's right to equity. This appeal to constitutional justice was bipartisan and reflected the belief that, if one outpost of Southern rights was surrendered, the entire structure of slavery would be endangered. In 1847 (and before gold was discovered in California), Rhett announced that the South cared but little for most of the former Mexican territory, "since it is not probable that a single planter would ever desire to set his foot within its limits. But the right is important, because it applies to future acquisitions of territory; and by refusing to acknowledge the obligations of the Missouri compromise, you force open the whole question of power." Three years later, Representative Humphrey Marshall, a Kentucky Whig, admitted that he had no idea whether slavery could be profitable in the arid Southwest. Besides, it was immaterial, he continued, for "It is not on this account I desire the settlement, but because it will afford evidence that gentlemen from the North are willing to meet on terms of equality—to give and take. . . ."

The South relied on the same themes of self-defense and *Lebensraum* that had been the crux of her justification for annexing Texas. Expansion was advocated as a means of securing territory against abolitionism, providing an outlet for surplus slaves, and furnishing a base for a possible Southern republic. The new element, by 1850, was the sense of urgency. The threat of encirclement was on the verge of becoming a reality, and the right of slavery to expand at all was being denied.

"My race and my country are threatened," proclaimed Richard Meade of Virginia; "we are even now engaged in the death-struggle. We must come to terms with the enemy, or we must either fall or triumph in the conflict." The terms demanded by Meade included sufficient space for an empire. The South needed room both to retain the power of self-protection and to instill fear and respect in her enemies if she was ever driven to independence. "To effect this you have only to demand half your rights—half justice. To the Pacific, then, I say—to the Pacific. Your future security depends entirely upon your own strength; secure to yourselves while you can, an empire."

If the South delayed until the Pacific coast and New Mexico had a large antislavery population, abolitionist pressure would be too strong to resist. To Meade, it was obvious "that this western continent is now owned by [two] distinct classes of men, who are rapidly arranging themselves in hostile attitude." The South must prepare for the storm. "We must have the southern portion of this continent for our uses; you may have the north for yours." Congressman Marshall Wellborn of Georgia, warning that the survival instinct would force slavery outward, said, "Spasmodic and involuntary irruptions of the institution on contiguous territories must under stress of threatened confinement be the natural expressions of the laws of its self-preservation—the only means, indeed, of escape from evils it is not in the power of human courage to deliberately confront." Even the loss of so rich a prize as California could be absorbed if Southern security were ensured in other areas. Thomas Clingman would let the North have all of California, provided that the South received all the land east of the Sierras up to about the fortieth parallel. This arrangement would leave the South with a safe frontier on her western flank. With its territory protected from intruders by the mountains and deserts of the Southwest, slavery would be free to expand southward at any time. "We might then acquire, at some future day, whether united or divided, possession of the country along the Gulf of Mexico, well suited to be occupied by our slave population."

Northern congressmen repeatedly voted down all efforts to extend the 36°30′ line. Some reasoned that the South could never be satisfied, since expansionism was a natural and inevitable result of white fears of a slave surplus. No matter how much land was acquired, the same fears would eventually surface. Others, angered by the loss of Texas to slavery, interpreted the Mexican War as an unconscionable Southern scheme for territorial aggrandizement. Turning the diffusion rhetoric against the slaveholders, they wondered how Texas could serve as an outlet to drain off slaves into Mexico if much of the Mexican territory was to be converted to slavery. "But if we take the very country that was to be [the slaves'] refuge, and subvert it for slavery, what becomes of the reasoning and argument of [Senator] Walker?" asked Wilmot. C. Delano of Ohio threatened that, unless the South discontinued her bloody war of conquest, "we will light up the fires of liberty on every side, until they melt your present chains, and render all your people *free*." The South felt openly menaced. As Congress tried to hammer out a new territorial dispensation during the winter of 1850, Calhoun summed up the apprehensions of the slaveholders: "Never before has the South been placed in so trying a situation, nor can it ever be placed in one more so. Her all is at stake."

Thanks mainly to the floor leadership of Senator Stephen Douglas of Illinois and the willingness of Northern Democrats to seek a middle ground, the compromise measures of 1850 were passed, and the sectional crisis precipitated by the success of the Mexican War was resolved. In its territorial provisions, the Compromise admitted California as a free state, adjusted the boundary dispute between Texas and New Mexico, and organized the territories of Utah and New Mexico with no mention of slavery aside from the provision that when they applied for statehood they were to be "received into the Union, with or without slavery, as their constitution may prescribe at the time of their admission." In two unrelated matters, the slave trade in the District of Columbia was interdicted and enforcement of the Fugitive Slave Act was tightened by giving federal courts and officials wider jurisdiction and discretionary powers.

For a minority of Southerners, the Compromise was a fraud. "Will honorable Senators point out to me a *single* concession from the North to the South which these bills contain?" beseeched Senator Pierre Soulé of Louisiana. "Sir, there is *none;* no, not ONE." According to the radicals, the South had been swindled out of the public domain. In return for no Wilmot Proviso in New Mexico and Utah, she had been compelled to surrender to free soil all of California down to the thirty-second parallel. What the supporters of the Wilmot Proviso had not been able to accomplish openly and fairly, it was charged, had been done covertly and deceitfully. They were accused of refusing to organize a territorial government in California until they could offer the settlers statehood in return for excluding slavery. In addition, over 100,000 square miles of slave territory in Texas had been ceded to New Mexico and in all probability would be lost permanently. Quitman fumed, "Every outlet to the extension of our institutions has been firmly closed. . . . We are now hemmed in on the west as well as the north. The line once fixed, to save the Union, has been contemptuously disregarded." It was true that the South had received all she demanded in the new Fugitive Slave Act, but public opinion in the North would block its enforcement. "Like the laws against duelling in all the States, they are apparently strong enough to prevent the practice, but practically they are a dead letter upon the statute book," noted Representative Jacob Thompson of Mississippi. The banning of the slave trade in the District of Columbia was depicted as a precursor of emancipation.

Most Southern congressmen backed the Compromise. To be sure, they had voted two to one against the admission of California and nearly unanimously rejected elimination of the Washington slave pens, but they felt they had saved Southern honor by forcing both abandonment of congressional restriction of slavery in the territories and recognition of the principle of constitutional right and equality. "Principles, sir, are not only outposts, but the bulwarks of all constitutional liberty; and if these be yielded, or taken by superior force, the citadel will soon follow," stressed Alexander Stephens in 1857, as he reminded a Congress caught up in the Kansas imbroglio of the value of the Compromise of 1850. The moderates also insisted that the Southwest was too parched and barren to sustain slavery and that the South had, therefore, risked little by not gaining positive assurances that slavery would be protected there.

The fact remained, however, that, if the South had won a victory, it was a purely negative one, a holding action at best. The adjustment appeared attractive primarily because it was measured against the backdrop of the Wilmot Proviso and the fears openly expressed throughout 1849 and 1850 that hostilities might erupt between the sections. Texas, which claimed the eastern half of the present state of New Mexico, had been in a surly mood. Reports filtered out that she was prepared to take the Santa Fe country by force if necessary. William Duval, a minor politician active in Texas affairs, wrote to Senator Hunter of Virginia, in August, 1850, that "She has arms for herself and two Southern States, and if the union is broken, we will save the North all further trouble with California and New Mexico, for we will take them to our exclusive use." Texas and her bondholders were placated by the federal assumption of $10 million of her state debt. As a bonus, she had to relinquish claim to less land than originally anticipated.

On a broader scale, disunion had loomed as a distinct possibility. In January, 1850, Calhoun reported back to South Carolina that Southern congressmen were "more determined and bold than I ever saw them. Many avow themselves to be disunionists, and a still greater number admit, that there is little hope of any remedy short of it." A month later he spoke of disunion as the "only alternative, that is left us." In the spring of 1850, C. S. Morehead expressed his forebodings to his fellow Kentucky Whig, Senator John Crittenden: "You may think that I am inclined to be gloomy, but I do most solemnly believe that disunion will ensue . . . if there should be a failure of an amicable settlement." Morehead admitted, "I never have in my life had so deep and abiding a conviction upon any subject as at this moment of the absolute necessity of a settlement of the whole question." Other Southerners, especially Whigs and those from the Border states, shared this concern and were relieved when they were offered a way out of the sectional impasse with Southern honor intact. As relieved as they were, however, events would soon reveal that nothing had been settled. The all-important question of congressional jurisdiction over slavery in the territories had been ignored. Even before the Compromise had been agreed upon, Thompson of Mississippi had foreseen that any step short of extending 36°30′ "will be but laying the foundation of greater trouble in the future." Southern radicals realized this better than anyone and were determined to convert the uncertainties and indecision regarding the territories into an issue that would unite Southerners in defense of their rights.

Rehearsal for Revolution

In their opposition to the compromise measures, the radicals forged the first serious threat to the Union. They launched their movement in the winter of 1848–49. Earlier in the year, the Treaty of Guadalupe Hidalgo had been signed and the scope of the Mexican cessions became known. A new and untested President had just been elected. Although Zachary Taylor was a slave-holder and war hero, Southerners distrusted him and suspected that he would be manipulated by such Whig leaders as Clay and Webster. It was thought that Taylor might sacrifice Southern interests by agreeing to the Wilmot Proviso. The slave states had announced their repudiation of the Proviso, and the Virginia legislature, soon followed by others, had provided for the calling of a state convention to consider the proper means of redress should Congress pass the Proviso or other anti-Southern legislation. Calhoun's Southern Address of December, 1848, outlined the grievances. He accused the North of systematic aggressions that could culminate only in emancipation or war.

Throughout 1849, Southerners debated the tactics of resistance. Senator David Yulee of Florida suggested to Calhoun that all the states should follow the example of South Carolina and form committees of safety and correspondence that might come together in a grand convention. Perhaps a States'-Rights party might be organized, he added, as a counterbalance to the Free-soilers. "We must have some distinctive organization by which we may *be separated* from the enemies of the Rights of the States, whether those enemies claim to be democrats, whigs, or abolitionists." Others argued that Southern rights could be won only by equipping volunteer regiments and sending them into the territories as military protection for Southern settlers and their slave property. Armed intervention entailed too many risks, and the debate turned on cooperative action through a Southern convention or separate action by individual states. Largely because Calhoun favored it, the former course was adopted, and the call was issued from Mississippi in the fall for a convention to meet in Nashville, Tennessee, in June, 1850.

Just as the specter of the permanent confinement of slavery had energized the radical movement, so, too, did the defeat of the Wilmot Proviso sound its demise. When the Nashville Convention assembled, a conservative reaction had already set in. The death of Calhoun in March had deprived the radicals of their most effective leader. Only nine states sent delegates, and most of these were from the Lower South. There was a call for the extension of the Missouri line, some fiery speeches, and an agreement to convene again within six weeks of the adjournment of Congress, but the long-desired Southern convention was plainly anticlimactic. Its reassembling caused hardly a stir, and a proposed convention for Montgomery in early 1852 never met. What had happened?

As the radicals sought allies within the South, they found enemies everywhere. Wilson Lumpkin, a retired Georgia political leader, told Calhoun, "Our own beloved South has many, very many, antislavery people in her bosom. People whose sympathies are with our vilest enemies." The cities were made uncertain and unsound by the influx of Northerners and foreign immigrants. These groups hated blacks because they were all rivals in the same labor pool. Immigrants had replaced black labor in New Orleans, and "they will not let a negroe drive a dray," reported a Charleston merchant-banker, H. W. Conner. "He would be mobbed or killed." More and more, steamboat captains were Yankees with white employees, he added. His ominous conclusion was that "the issue of the Free labour against Slave labour will soon be made at the South."

Since it was commonly accepted that slavery was dying in the Upper South, the loyalty of that region was automatically suspect. Regarding Virginia, Calhoun's close friend and biographer, R. K. Crallé, fretted that "She is already deeply infected with the spirit of abolitionism, much more deeply than most persons think. . . ." In a time of crisis, the nonslaveholders appeared to constitute a likely fifth column. "As to the boys up the hollows and in the brush who form a considerable part of our country they are not to [be] relied on in any contest against the Union," cautioned Representative John McHenry of Kentucky in early 1850. Radicals cited class jealousies against slave owners as the chief obstacle to the extensionist movement. The governor of

Florida informed his South Carolina counterpart, Whitemarsh Seabrook, that many Southerners believed the Wilmot Proviso "tended to promote the prospective welfare of the poor or non-slaveholding whites."

Cutting across economic and regional lines was what radicals denounced as the divisive party spirit, the lust for place and power. "The corrupt press and office seekers of the South are daily becoming more and more reckless and bold in their prosecution of their selfish plans and objects," grumbled Wilson Lumpkin. These men were prepared "to sacrifice the last hope of the perpetuation of our good system of Government, upon the altar of combinations of office seekers." He sneered, "Look at our little *pigmy* [Alexander Stephens] from Georgia, and his Southern associates on the Compromise Bill . . . they can only hope for the distinction of infamy, but they prefer that to obscurity."

Events confirmed the pessimism of the radicals. Fewer than half of the Southern congressmen endorsed Calhoun's Southern Address, and only two of these were Whigs. Once concrete compromise plans had been offered, radicalism became moribund, except in South Carolina and Mississippi—the only states where slaves outnumbered whites. Racial fears fed extremism in both states. Although the decade of the 1840's was one of agricultural depression, the radical effort was not spearheaded by those who had suffered the heaviest economic losses. In South Carolina, the leadership came from the coastal planters, who had continued to do quite well with their crops of rice and sea-island cotton. In Mississippi, resistance was centered in the newly opened cotton areas. Nevertheless, economic discontent did provide an undercurrent of resentment that was effectively exploited. Cotton prices hit their antebellum low in 1845, and the small planters in the South Carolina uplands and the interior of Mississippi were hurt badly. Ironically, when the sectional crisis was approaching its peak, good times had begun to return. After traveling across central Georgia in the summer of 1850, James Hamilton, the former "Nullification governor" of South Carolina, noted that "thirteen cents a pound for cotton was a powerful contributor to make civil war and revolution exceedingly distasteful to her people." Rather disgustedly, Governor Seabrook told Quitman that "prosperity makes the masses indifferent to the crisis."

Racial and class pressures had always been most intense in South Carolina because of her singularly high slave concentrations and the problems of economic readjustment in an old cotton state stung by Western competition. Her planters thoroughly enjoyed the aristocratic amenities of the slave-based culture of Charleston and the low country and had clung to a reactionary and elitist political structure in an attempt to protect their prerogatives by confining the masses. The chief threats to this established order were democratic stirrings from the back country and slave uprisings. South Carolinians also feared that their state was the prime target for the abolitionist crusade, the one that would be, in the words of Representative John McQueen, "the first on the East at which a [test] is to be made, or the general massacre to commence in this unhallowed work. . . ." Wealthy but insecure, exulting in yet despairing of slavery, the planters were susceptible to radical agitation.

South Carolina had earned a reputation for rash and unpredictable belligerency since her lone defiance of the federal government during the nullification episode. Precisely because no one doubted her radicalism, she had to refrain from boldly assuming control of the resistance movement in 1850, lest she frighten away more cautious states. In addition, Carolina firebrands had impugned the loyalty of their fellow Southerners for so long that resentment had set in. Feelings were especially bitter between South Carolina and Georgia. An informed Carolinian, James Hamilton, noted that "Georgia came to dislike us . . . more than the people of Massachusetts."

Economic rivalries had contributed to the coolness. In 1847, Charleston merchants, seeking to tap the export trade of the central Georgia cotton belt, had the effrontery to petition the Georgia legislature for the incorporation of a trunk line that would have diverted the traffic of the Atlanta and Macon Railroad from Savannah to Charleston. Naturally, the Georgians were angered, and, in 1850, the Carolinians worried with good reason that their neighbors would gladly favor the Union so as to leave Charleston

economically isolated and choking on its own bluster. Since
Georgia was the economic and strategic heart of the Deep South,
Carolina radicals swallowed their pride and avoided any rash action that might ruin any chance of converting the Georgians to
their cause.

Above all, they tried to cajole the Empire State of the South
into leading the resistance movement. Governors Seabrook of
South Carolina and Quitman of Mississippi repeatedly told Governor George Towns of Georgia that they would wait for his
state to act. When Towns informed them, in late September of
1850, that the cause looked "cheerless and discouraging" and that
a coalition of Georgia Whigs and Union Democrats appeared to
be unbeatable, the game was about up. The November election
results sealed the radicals' fate. The Union ticket outpolled the
Southern Rights nominees in all but ten of Georgia's ninety-three
counties. At the state convention the following month, the moderates repudiated disunionism and laid the foundations for a state
Union party. All that the radicals could salvage was the stipulation that Georgia's acceptance of the Compromise of 1850 was
contingent on a faithful adherence to the adjustment by the
North, especially in regard to enforcement of the Fugitive Slave
Act and the implied promise to give slavery an equal chance in
the territories. The radicals hung on for another year in South
Carolina and Mississippi, but it was largely a face-saving gesture.
The action of Georgia had proved decisive.

The gap between the radicals' rhetoric and their performance
was so striking that it is tempting to dismiss their efforts as mere
gasconading. Yet, of deeper significance than their failures was
their ability to analyze what had happened, pinpoint their mis-
takes, and fashion a revolutionary ideology that would blend tactics and goals into an effective strategy for future action. The
goal of the radicals was clear from the start—to convince their
fellow Southerners that slavery and the Union could not safely
coexist. Because the masses were apathetic, they would have to
be persuaded of the dangers. "The great difficulty is to make the
Masses see beyond their noses," explained a Calhoun follower,
Hilliard Judge of Alabama, in 1849; "they do not see and feel that
the necessary consequences of allowing all the outposts of Slav-

ery to be carried, involves a certain destruction of the Citadel itself. The public mind is rapidly being prepared for what must
come at last—the dissolution of the Union, *but we must have
time.*" Educating the common folk was essential, and clubs and
associations would be used for proselytizing, as would the editorial page and the orator's platform. Legislatures would be committed to the principle of secession. But class, sectional, and partisan differences persisted and were ineradicable. Thus, when
Hershel Johnson, a Georgia radical, complained to Calhoun, "I
seriously fear that the people of the South are not properly awake
to the danger—not thoroughly nerved to united resistance," his
disappointment, in fact, stemmed from false hopes. A united
South was a delusion. Once the radicals learned this, they had
found the tactical key to secession.

As they surveyed their failure, the radicals were not surprised
by the unionism of the Whig party, the Upper South, the cities,
and the upland regions of the yeomanry. More bitter to accept
had been their inability to dispel the aura of social and political
respectability that surrounded the unionist cause. The best and
most prominent families spurned extremism. Even in South Carolina, Seabrook had to confess that the radicals were "comparatively unknown to the public. It can not be said, therefore, that
they have the confidence of the people. Without this support it
is impossible for men, however distinguished for talent and patriotism, successfully to pull down one government and establish
another." In Georgia, hardly any of the radical leaders held political office in 1850.

Despite these obstacles, the more perceptive radicals realized
that the tactical decision to await unity before action had practically foredoomed their efforts. Rhett had foreseen this during
the abortive Bluffton Movement of 1844. "It may be next to impossible, as I fear it is, to obtain any cooperation amongst the
Southern States, to make the proper issue with the General Government, while it will be very easy to obtain their aid and cooperation (in case it should be needed by the action of the General
Government), *after the proper issue is made by the conduct of a
single State.*" He pointed out that the American colonies united
only after a single colony had created an issue by dumping the

tea overboard and forcing the British into coercive acts. "One
State made the issue in our Revolution, and one, I think, will
have to make it again with the General Government. A Southern
cooperation will then be as natural and easy a consequence as
the first Congress in 1774." Rhett's revolutionary analogy was
sound, but, without the prestige and authority of a Calhoun, he
was unable to translate it into a general policy for the radicals in
1850. Not a single state—not even South Carolina—supported his
position. The dream of unity still held sway, and the pursuit of it
had not yet been discredited.

By 1851, an increasing number of radicals had come to see that
Rhett was correct. "So long as the several aggrieved states wait
for one another, their action will be over-cautious and timid,"
wrote Quitman. "Great political movements, to be successful,
must be bold, and must present practical and simple issues."
Angered that the opportunity for action had slipped away while
they waited in vain for Georgia to take the lead, the radicals began to reassess the assumptions behind the cooperative approach
to resistance. Even if a representative Southern convention did
assemble, they reasoned, tensions would be so high that the delegates might be too easily satisfied. The greatest menace would
come from the Upper South, whose loyalty to slavery had constantly been questioned by the radicals because of the region's
heavy slave sales. Some had suggested that the cotton states
should prohibit the internal slave trade and thus, as a Mississippi radical, C. R. Clifton, told Calhoun, "force Virginia, Maryland, Kentucky, Missouri, to stand their ground, and make common cause with us." Acting as a Trojan horse, these states would
grasp at any compromise, even if it meant irreparable damage to
Southern rights. The radicals also saw that cooperation was a
time-consuming process and that delay aided the conservatives
by allowing passions to cool. In the meantime, they felt, promises of federal money and patronage would buy off the uncom-
mitted. Quitman warned that, the longer effective resistance was
put off, the greater became the risk that "the public sense of the
insult, injury, and oppression inflicted upon the slaveholding
states, will become blunted by time and acquiescence, until it
will be very difficult to arouse the people. . . ."

For the hard-core radicals, the very notion of cooperation had become a dangerous anachronism. Much of the appeal of cooperation rested on the belief that a united South might have the power to wrest justice from the North through constitutional amendments or guarantees. But, for those who believed that slavery could never be secure within the Union, talk of reform through united action was a snare that delayed the South from facing the inevitable and preparing herself for separation. "We now live under an anti-slavery government, whose will, openly hostile to the institutions of the South, is expressed at all times by a majority," said Seabrook in 1851. "What security can such a government give to the endangered party? None whatever." Nor could the South defend herself against antislavery aggressions. By the simple, yet insidious, expedient of admitting free states to the Union and excluding slave states, Congress could constitutionally build up the strength of the North to crushing proportions. For this reason, Rhett was sorry to see the Wilmot Proviso defeated. It was obviously unconstitutional, he felt, and, more important, it was an issue around which the South might have rallied. The same was true of the abolition of slavery in the District of Columbia. "Would to God, they would do both, and let us have the contest, and end it once and forever. It would thus accomplish our emancipation, instead of that of our slaves."

The South herself, the radicals concluded, must create the revolutionary issues and spirit. Secession by separate state action would meet the radicals' criterion of presenting daring and easily grasped issues. Southerners would be confronted with the most direct issue of all—submission or resistance. By a single stroke, the South's internal enemies would be neutralized and placed on the defensive. They would have to declare their loyalties. Gone would be the drift and futility that had plagued the Southern struggle. The politicians and temporizers would be bypassed and the people asked to decide. The moral example set by just one state would fire the South's imagination and force mass discontent out into the open. Other states would quickly join the movement. Once the initiative had been seized, the free states would have to give in to Southern demands for security and let the seceders go in peace—or, more probably, try to force them back into the Union. Coercion would, in effect, drive the Upper South out of the Union because even these states, the radicals conceded, would come to the defense of their sister slave states once blood had been shed. By such a course, Quitman reasoned, "an active and cordial union of the whole South would be instantly effected, and a complete Southern confederacy organized."

Out of the failure of 1850–51 came not only wider acceptance of the possibility of separate state secession for the radicals' objectives but more realistic expectations and a determination that the South would not be impotent during the next sectional crisis. Still, many were discouraged and felt that slavery was doomed. "In my own judgment, submission now will seal the fate of our institutions," worried Seabrook in June of 1851. "The operations of the 'Compromise' measures, and the influence and patronage of the central authorities, will prove sufficient not only to maintain the division that unhappily exists in the South, but in time to effect the very end at which our enemies aim." After his repudiation in South Carolina, Rhett retired from politics; Yancey, too, in time would tone down his rhetoric and stump for the election of Buchanan in 1856. The radicals were quieted, but Seabrook's pessimism proved unwarranted. The hope of the conservatives for a national Union party evaporated by 1852. Partisan differences remained; the subsiding of the sectional agitation that had originally alienated Southern Whigs from their Northern counterparts would alienate them from Southern Union Democrats who no longer saw the need for a bipartisan coalition to save the Union. Moreover, if the radicals' contention was valid that the conflicts between a free and a slave society coexisting and competing within the same nation were irreconcilable, then sectional controversy was bound to erupt again. For this reason, Quitman exhorted others to work with him in order that "we may preserve and extend sound principles, until the day shall come when it may be necessary to strike a blow for their defense."

The radicals did not have long to wait. In 1854, the Kansas-Nebraska Act reopened the entire question of slavery in the territories. By expressly repealing the Missouri Compromise line and thereby theoretically leaving slavery free to spread into areas previously barred to it, the Act set off an explosion of anger and indignation in the North. The Whigs, already gravely weakened by the 1850 crisis, were now destroyed as an organization. The anti-slavery forces demanded, and got, a new party dedicated to pre-serving all the territories for freedom. The parties were becoming purely sectional.

Writing in 1858, on the eve of the congressional vote on the Lecompton Constitution, Quitman foresaw that the Kansas ques-tion, and by extension the whole problem of the expansion of slavery, placed the one remaining national political organization, the Democrats, in an untenable position. For if, on the one hand, Northern Democrats honored their party's pledge to uphold Southern rights, they would be committing political suicide, and the Republicans would accuse them of being proslavery and sweep them out of office. Thus stripped of her Northern allies, the South would have no recourse but secession. If, on the other hand, Northern Democrats acted against Southern interests, then "the South must regard the plighted faith of the Northern De-mocracy violated. It will assure us that no more reliance can be placed on them to aid in protecting our rights; that National De-mocracy is worthless." Again, disunion was the only alternative. No sooner had the uproar over "Bleeding Kansas" subsided than John Brown's raid threw the South into panic. Not even the fieri-est radical could ever have made the threat of an internal holo-caust appear so real and imminent to Southerners as had the grim, dedicated Brown.

Within a decade, events revealed that the radicals had not been proved wrong in 1850, only premature. Perceptive conserv-atives had seen as much. "The present crisis may pass; the pres-ent adjustment may be made," wrote Alexander Stephens in early 1850 to his brother Linton, "but the great question of the per-manence of slavery in the Southern States will be far from being settled thereby. And, in my opinion, the crisis of that question is not far ahead." Throughout the 1850's, the radicals would con-tinue to dramatize the issues, exploit fears, and popularize and ideologically justify the concept of secession. They told the South that she must rule herself and expand, or perish.

To a great extent political unknowns in 1850, the radicals were outsiders. Their energy and drive were those of men struggling to gain power and approval by charting a course in defense of Southern rights well beyond what established authorities and institutions would sanction. They were impatient and ambitious. Henry Benning, a young Georgia radical who was to play an important role in the secession of Georgia twelve years later, explained in 1848, "I am no Calhoun man. He in fact is off the stage, the coming battle is for other leadership than his, a leadership that is of this generation, not of the past." By 1860, the radicals had won the battle. Paradoxically, although the more outspoken extremists, such as Yancey and Rhett, were never entrusted with positions of leadership, the ideas of Southern nationalism and expansionism that they had first preached and disseminated on a broad scale had helped to convince a generation of Southerners that only an independent South could fulfill white ambitions for land and slaves and forestall a loss of racial control.

4. Prelude to Secession

Rarely has an election mirrored the social conflicts of a nation so vividly as did the Presidential contest of 1860. The Republicans put forward Abraham Lincoln, the Whigs ran John Bell, one wing of the Democrats sided with Stephen Douglas, and the other, centered in the South, backed John Breckinridge. Befitting a young, growing nation, the central issue was expansion and the future of the American empire. What made this issue so divisive was its inseparability from the problem of slavery. Each candidate represented a different social coalition that sought to resolve the dual issue of expansion and slavery in its own best interests.

Ideologically, all four groups shared the prevalent American world view, which held the individual to be the basic social unit and master of his own destiny. With the exception of the Whigs— conservatives who desperately wished to maintain the status quo —these groups also shared a desire for economic expansion, which they equated with the preservation and strengthening of social and political liberties. In Madisonian language, enlarging the economic sphere would prevent any one faction from dominating the others. Because most formal and legalized class privileges and advantages had been removed during the Jacksonian era, an individual's status and worth came to be measured increasingly in economic terms. The individual thus had a personal stake in a growing economy, for such expansion, by widening access to wealth, democratized and heightened aspirations. The result, whether measured in terms of the multiplication of small entrepreneurs or the huge agricultural and commercial surpluses, was a tremendous release of individual energy, which, in turn, fed the vision of an America uniquely destined to rule over the Western Hemisphere. The untapped riches and promise of the territories inevitably became a metaphor for the expectations of both sections. Whose political economy would be secured, whose social system would prevail, and whose set of values would be honored in the territories were unavoidable questions.

The four candidates in 1860 were differentiated by their responses to these questions and the manner in which they proposed to settle them. Although Bell and Douglas tried to find a middle ground, consensus was impossible because each section believed that its prosperity, security, and values depended on the future of the territories. Too much was at stake to compromise. Not the abolition of slavery but its extension and the repercussions of this extension for white Americans defined the issue that would ultimately precipitate a civil war.

FREE LABOR OR SLAVE?

As had been predicted, Lincoln and Breckinridge, the two most sectionalized candidates, ran the strongest campaigns. Lincoln virtually swept the North; Breckinridge, the Deep South. Capitalizing on previous voting patterns and strong organizational support, each had the additional advantage of representing a clear and aggressive solution to the territorial issue which was functionally related to the visions of their respective constituencies as to how American society should be ordered and what goals and priorities should be pursued. Although they were similar in their stress on the individual and on economic growth, these visions were diametrically opposed on the use of free or slave labor.

The fundamental doctrine of the Republicans' free-labor ideology was that the South had no constitutional right to carry slaves into the territories and that Congress consequently had full power to prohibit slavery wherever it was not already protected within existing states. This doctrine, which was purely negative from the Southern perspective, had positive and crucial ramifications for Northern society: The bounty of American expansion was to be reserved solely for free white labor. "The policy of the Republican party," declared Senator James Harlan of Iowa, "invites the Anglo-Saxon . . . and others of Caucasian blood, by its proposed preëmption and homestead laws, to enter and occupy [the territories], and by the exclusion of slavery it will practically exclude the negro and kindred races." There was no need to ban free blacks expressly, he added, because "very few have the inclination or pecuniary ability to emigrate." As proof, he pointed out that in the newer Western states, where Congress had prohibited slavery during the territorial stage, the proportion of blacks in the total population ranged from an innocuous 0.1 per cent in Iowa to but 1.5 per cent in Oregon. In contrast, the black percentage in the old Southwest was as high as 51 per cent in Mississippi and was still socially "dangerous" at its low of 13 per cent in Missouri. Here was supposedly solid evidence that the Republican policy would fill unoccupied territories with the white race and the Democratic "with negroes, wherever negro labor can be made profitable."

Nearly all Republicans shared the Southern conviction that blacks were an inferior race, incapable of assimilation or meaningful participation in American society on a level of equality. Granting this assumption, Harlan asked, "Why stimulate their multiplication and coerced emigration to the most desirable part of this continent, to the exclusion of millions of our own blood?" Surely, he reasoned, Southerners ought to see the justice of peopling the continent only "with the most vigorous, the most energetic, the most enterprising, the most intellectual and powerful people to be found on the earth. . . ." Because the blacks were "out of place on the earth when in contact with the white man," said C. C. Washburn of Wisconsin, the Republicans proposed "to prevent their increase as much as possible, by refusing to open new territories to be despoiled by them, and by colonizing, in Central and South America, such free blacks as are willing to go there. . . ." Republicans contended, with pride, that their plan would benefit both races by promoting peaceful separation at the same time that it provided each with a homestead.

Racism alone did not account for the Republicans' aversion to the presence of blacks in the territories. A major premise of their commitment to free soil was the belief that slave competition necessarily degraded and drove out free labor. "It *is* impossible for any manual labor to be considered honorable, while it is almost exclusively performed by slaves, and is thereby made a badge of slavery," asserted Senator Dixon of Connecticut. For the New Englanders and their Yankee descendants transplanted throughout the North, this corruption of free labor by slavery was blasphemy. It made a mockery of God's commandment that work should be honorable—an expression of man's calling to subdue and cultivate the earth for the glorification of his Maker. In the Protestant ethic, to work was to worship, and anything that defiled labor was therefore sinful. Out of this sense of moral outrage, Dixon could denounce slavery as an institution that "does, in truth, not only enslave the African race, but, in every community where it exists, it also includes, in the chains of its bondage, the labor of the white man."

This bondage was also economic and political. Elaborating on the same themes that Cassius Marcellus Clay and Hinton Rowan Helper had dared to hurl at their fellow Southerners, the Republicans charged that slavery enabled a small elite to monopolize the best lands in any given area, prevented nonslaveholders from becoming mechanics or manufacturers by substituting nonconsuming slaves for their potential home market, and reduced most whites to poverty and ignorance through the ruinous competition of unpaid, compulsory labor. The condition of free laborers in the South, the Republicans insisted, was tantamount to political slavery. Basic civil liberties, such as freedom of speech and of the press, were denied to them. Anyone who tried to speak out against the oligarchy would be suppressed and expelled by a slaveholder-dominated power structure.

As the spokesmen and defenders of free labor, the Republicans pledged never to permit this iniquitous system to expand. They owed no less, they felt, to the Northern farmers who would be excluded from the territories by slave competition and to the Southern yeomanry who had already fled from slavery. To support their contention that nonslaveholders preferred free soil, they cited figures from the 1850 census, which revealed that the South, despite its warmer climate, cheaper lands, and sparser population, had lost three times as many of her native-born residents to the North than had immigrated from the North.

As pawns in the sectional balance, the territories were invaluable. Whoever controlled them could direct the political economy of the nation and shape policy on tariffs, other fiscal matters, and internal improvements. The Republicans frankly admitted that the North wanted the territories for her own interests. The free states looked to the territories as an outlet for their surplus population, a supply of homesteads for their farmers, and a safety valve for labor discontent. Manufacturers saw in them an expanding market for their goods and a source of raw materials, including cheap foodstuffs for the industrial work force. This territorial utilization, the Republicans reasoned, contributed to the prosperity of the entire nation and was a sign of a healthy, vigorous economy.

Quite the contrary was the case with Southern expansion. "Slavery starves out the towns and cities, wears out the soil, and leaves nothing to improve or recuperate it, except at a very heavy expense and inconvenience," proclaimed Congressman John Covode of Pennsylvania. "Every pulsation of slavery is against the law of production," stated Representative Oliver Morse of New York. "It can only flourish by expansion; but expansion over fertile and beautiful virgin lands, in like manner to curse and blight them, is an alternative which the voice and arm of the North and of the nation will never permit." By the terms of this critique, national priorities were clear. Slavery was counterproductive and sought to expand out of weakness; therefore, it should be contained.

The free states, the Republicans stressed, had been more than fair in the past regarding distribution of the public domain. As a matter of fact, noted Representative Justin Morrill of Vermont in 1860, the South had benefited the most from expansion. As a result of the Louisiana Purchase and the acquisitions of Florida and Texas, the South possessed two-thirds of all the fertile land in the United States during the 1850's and a much larger proportion of unimproved acreage than New England or the Middle Atlantic states. "These facts," Morrill concluded, "show how baseless is

the claim of the South for more territory—and, if not baseless,
how much greater the occasion for arresting an institution whose
demands are so imperious and increasing." At a time when, in the
words of Seward, "Free labor has at last apprehended its rights,
its interests, its power, and its destiny, and is organizing itself to
assume the government of the Republic," the South could not
justifiably cry foul. Her rationale, that she needed more territory
to avoid unprofitable and unmanageable slave concentrations,
was attacked as spurious. If not, then why did the South seek to
obtain yet more slaves through a reopening of the African slave
trade or to annex Cuba, whose population density was five times
that of the American South? Such measures appeared to aggravate the very evils of which Southerners complained.

For the Republicans, the goal of Southern expansionism could
only be political aggrandizement—an effort to maintain the
stranglehold over national offices and legislation enjoyed by
the slaveholders as a consequence of the three-fifths clause of the
Constitution. This clause, granting the South three congressional
seats and electoral votes for every five slaves, was denounced as
just one device by which the slaveholding minority constantly
neutralized, and often overruled, the national majority. Congressman Charles Hoard of New York saw the Slave Power behind the
Kansas troubles. He interpreted the contest as involving far more
than the abstract question of slavery; the very principle of majority rule was on trial. An "*organized, disciplined,* and *politic* MI-
NORITY" had attempted to subvert this principle by seizing the
Kansas government from the majority "for the purpose of ele-
vating a sectional institution which is at war with the rights, the
dignity, and the material interests of the MAJORITY." Morrill
warned that the South desired Cuba not to strengthen American
capabilities against European intrigues in the Caribbean but as
a means of building up sectional political power and creating
"that notable equality in the Union through which eight million
people shall balance and check-mate twenty million."

Despite their blunt appeals to Northern racism and self-
interest, the Republicans' ideology contained an idealistic core
rooted in moral reform. Morrill put it well when he said of slavery: "There is no veil thick enough to hide the stain on the face

of the Republic." The breakdown of class deference in Jacksonian America had been related to a widening of moral horizons. A new evangelicalism, freed from Calvinist conceptions of original sin, preached individual regeneration. The lives of the truly converted would be a testimony to their faith through their warfare on all manifestations of sin, including institutionalized forms such as slavery. Gone was the gradualism of the earlier emancipationists and the easy social acceptance of slavery. The reform spirit was most intense in the rural belt of Yankee culture, which had spread from New England across New York and Pennsylvania and along the shores of the Great Lakes into the upper Midwest. These rural folk had two main choices in combating slavery: They could either join an abolitionist society or vote Republican. Many did both.

By the nature of its political approach, Republican antislaveryism was more moderate and tolerant of imperfections than what many abolitionists demanded. Nevertheless, its moral commitment was clear-cut, though undeniably flawed by racism. Whereas the radical abolitionists wanted to extirpate slavery where it existed, the Republicans preferred the more orderly and constitutional program of containing slavery and placing it on a slow, but certain, course to extinction. "Confine this malady within its present limits, surround it by a *cordon of freemen,* that it cannot spread, and in less than twenty-five years, every slaveholding State in the Union will have on its statute books a law for the gradual and final extinction of slavery," proclaimed Thaddeus Stevens of Pennsylvania. He was probably overly optimistic in predicting the demise of slavery within a generation, but all Republicans were certain that slavery was too wasteful and unproductive a labor system to survive without fresh accretions of land. Their program posed no racial threat to America, the Republicans hastened to add. It was assumed that the free states would not permit any significant number of freedmen to come north, and the South would be relieved of the blacks by government-subsidized migration and colonization abroad.

The obvious corollary of slavery restriction was the settling of the territories with free white labor, and here the Republicans revealed their skill at integrating and reinforcing the separate themes of their ideology into a comprehensive, self-sustaining moral vision of America's mission in the world. The crux of this vision was the belief that America was divinely ordained to reveal to the world man's ability to govern himself under free democratic institutions. The image of America as the repository of mankind's hopes and dreams had motivated the Revolutionary generation, and the Republicans adapted it to the expansionist drive and moralistic fervor of the mid-nineteenth century.

Since America was to teach other nations by example, and since her continued expansion was considered inevitable, the march of freedom could not be halted by slavery. As Oliver Morse of New York explained, slavery must be excluded from the territories in order to "hasten the civilization of the continent, and the redemption of man from the thraldom and barbarities that have hitherto beset him." Senator Daniel Clark of New Hampshire conceded that the United States probably could reduce to slavery the states of Central America, but he recoiled from such a national destiny. "I ask no such future for my country, because I remember, and it will ever prove true, that 'the nation that sinneth shall die.'" Another Republican from New Hampshire, T. M. Edwards, sketched the higher purpose for which Providence had permitted the Anglo-Saxons to dispossess the aborigines of the American continent. The national domain was decreed by God

> . . . to be a great inheritance for the support of freemen, by free labor, under free institutions; and that, as it shall be overspread by an industrious and intelligent population, cultivating all the useful arts, and in a later period the ornamental, it is destined . . . to be the scene on which is to be exhibited the most perfect condition of human society that the world has yet known; and they [Republicans] would feel that they were participating in a violation of this trust, if they did not protest against and resist its abuse.

Republican ideology presented an unavoidable challenge to Southerners. Seward promised an unceasing assault upon slavery in his 1858 declaration that free labor "will henceforth meet you boldly and resolutely here; it will meet you everywhere, in the Territories or out of them, wherever you may go to extend slavery." The South could not seek refuge in tropical America.

"Even there you will found States only for free labor to maintain and occupy. The interest of the white race demands the ultimate emancipation of all men."

The dominant response in the cotton states was that espoused by the Breckinridge Democrats, an aggressive and forthright defense of slavery expansion as a condition essential to the continued prosperity and security of slave society. This defense summarized all the racial and class motifs developed in earnest by Southerners since the 1840's. But, to maximize their political appeal, the Breckinridge party had to shape an ideology that would meet the needs of their constituency while simultaneously rebutting the Republican charge that slavery degraded white labor. This was achieved by combining a constitutional argument in favor of expansion with the insistence that the diffusion of slavery would benefit all white Americans through increased racial control and economic gains.

As the minority section, the South clung to states' rights as the sheet anchor of her safety. The Breckinridge Democrats followed in this tradition by claiming constitutional legitimacy for their cause. A typical campaign refrain was that of the Norfolk *Southern Argus*: "One would suppose the country was about to vote for *Union* or *Disunion*, instead of voting for Constitutional State Rights and Equality, against Northern aggression." Specifically, they pointed to the Dred Scott decision as confirmation that slaves were property, recognized as such in the Constitution, and that slaveholders were entitled to take them into the territories as they would other forms of property. By declaring the Missouri Compromise to have been unconstitutional, the Supreme Court gave Southerners a tremendous moral boost. Now they could use legal precedent against the Republicans. Senator Robert Toombs of Georgia crowed: "We tore off your restriction, trampled it under foot in Congress, condemned it by the people, and had our action approved by the judiciary." But the Court had hardly ended the territorial debate. The Republicans contemptuously rejected its decision as one that nationalized slavery, and the Douglas Democrats evaded it through the concept of popular sovereignty, entrusting only the actual settlers of a given territory with the power to decide on slavery.

Frustrated by such an empty victory and still trying to find a constitutional formula that would open the territories to slavery, some Southern Democrats argued that the right to carry slaves into the territories implied the additional right to claim protection for that property. Since "the mere naked Constitution does not afford that adequate protection which the nature and description of the property requires," Brown of Mississippi demanded that Congress pass protective legislation whenever necessary or compel the territorial legislatures to do so. The South may have no immediate use for these measures, Brown added, but the outposts of constitutional liberty had to be secured. "Yield not an inch of ground," he urged fellow slaveholders. "It is better to die defending the door-sill than admit the enemy and then see the hearth-stone bathed in blood." Neither Brown nor Jefferson Davis succeeded in having Congress pass what their opponents assailed as slave-code legislation. Many Southerners justly complained that such a step violated Calhoun's cardinal tenet that the admission of any congressional control over slavery was unacceptable. But, by focusing attention on the issue, Brown and Davis helped to popularize the ideological ultimatum that split the National Democracy at Charleston. Once the Douglas forces refused to accept a slave code as part of the party's platform, the Southern Democrats bolted and subsequently nominated Breckinridge after a last abortive attempt at reconciliation in Baltimore six weeks later.

The Breckinridge Democrats tried to convince all Americans that the extension of slavery was to their economic advantage. They reasoned that the slave-produced staples of the South were indispensable to the American economy; for, not only did these staples form the basis of U.S. exports, but planters, by specializing in them, created a home market for the surplus agricultural production of the West and furnished the raw material that provided jobs for Northern workers. Moreover, without a constant enlargement of their markets through the spread of the plantation, Western farmers would face an unprofitable glut of foodstuffs. The agrarians of the West and South should unite against their common enemy, the Republicans. The real objective of this party, alleged the Tallahassee *Floridian & Journal*, was "to get

possession of the offices of the Federal Government, and dis-
tribute the rich spoils of their conquest among their greedy followers in the shape of high salaries and lavish expenditures of
taxes levied upon the agricultural classes of the country by the
means of discriminating duties."

This call for a Western alliance was ignored, except in the
lower Ohio Valley. The economies of the Midwest and Northeast
had become integrated during the 1850's as the railroads shipped
an ever-higher percentage of grain and meat to Eastern markets
for consumption or export and as the prosperous West absorbed
a growing volume of manufactured goods. This symbiosis was
expressed in a common political program of homesteads, land
grants to railroads, some tariff protection, liberal immigration requirements, and free soil. The South, by opposing all of these
policies, had only increased her political isolation.

To most Northerners, the Breckinridge men's attempts to pose
as the friends and guardians of white labor rang as hollow as the
pretentious assertion of L. Q. C. Lamar "that God's sun does not
shine on a nobler, prouder, happier, more prosperous, and elevated class of people, than the non-slaveholders of the South."
The Republicans scoffed at these claims and referred Southerners
to their own descriptions of the ignorant and bedraggled poor
whites who worked in the cotton mills. The average Northern
farmer had had no contact with blacks, and he could reasonably
conclude that the Republicans' stand on free soil offered him the
best chance of maintaining that separation and protecting his
own welfare in the territories. Nevertheless, in the South, where
black competition was always a potential threat, the Breckinridge campaign could effectively counter Republican ideology by
substituting race for class as the most crucial social distinction.
This approach shrewdly recognized that rights and privileges of
any sort meant more to the poor than to the rich, since the former
had no access to the amenities and prerogatives of those in
power. As Jefferson Davis remarked of the poor: "Their all is suspended upon their *superiority* to the *blacks*—their all of equality,
in a political and social point of view—the social equality of their
wives, daughters, and sons, are all suspended upon, and involved
in this question." For the Southerner, the Republicans' insistence

that all men were endowed with the inalienable right of liberty was fraught with social danger. "Is there any one silly or wicked enough to deny that they mean to include the *negro*" among the men so endowed? asked the *East Floridian* in 1860. The paper dredged up the statistic that, within the past year, 72 white women in Massachusetts had married black men. This, plus the admission of blacks to jury duty in the same state, was proof to the editor that the Republicans "aim at no less than a general emancipation of the slave, and extending the mulatto colored principles of Massachusetts to the State of Florida." The victory of these principles would make slaves out of white men and freedmen out of the Africans. Most whites would be forced by the rich to perform the involuntary and menial tasks previously done by the slaves.

The socio-economic profiles of the Breckinridge politicians and their followers mesh at several points and help to explain the party's radicalism on the territorial issue and its political use of racism. Of the three sets of politicians who competed in the South in 1860 (the Republicans were permitted to enter an electoral slate in only a few pockets of the Upper South), the Breckinridge men were consistently the youngest and the most likely to be lawyers or natives of the Deep South. There were no sharp contrasts among the politicians along the lines of slaveholders versus nonslaveholders or planters versus yeomanry. Nearly all owned slaves. As a result of his heavy majorities from the slaveholders in the newer plantation areas and the poor whites in the pine barrens, Breckinridge carried the lower South.

An outline of the vote in Georgia and Virginia illustrates the pattern in two states representative of the major regional subdivisions in the South. In Georgia, Breckinridge won half of the black counties—those in which slaves outnumbered whites. His vote was concentrated in the fresher cotton lands of the southwestern part of the state and the isolated rice regions along the coast. The black areas that he lost comprised the old plantation belt of central Georgia. Whether measured by flows of white and slave population, cotton production, or land usage, the Breckinridge counties experienced significantly higher rates of economic growth than the Whiggish areas. The same factors differentiated the counties of the small cotton farmers—those in which slaves comprised about a third of the population. Breckinridge rolled up his heaviest majorities in the poor white counties; he ran weakest in areas where urbanization and industrialization had begun to make inroads. Aside from Savannah, he lost the cities, and, of the 19 counties with a manufacturing output in excess of $200,000, he carried but four.

With allowance for the greater stability and industrial orientation of the Virginia economy, the same voting model held there. Breckinridge lost the major cities and the ten leading manufacturing counties. Tobacco culture made a sharp comeback in Virginia in the 1850's, and the Breckinridge black-belt vote was centered in the areas where tobacco production had expanded the most. The moderately prosperous, general-farming counties, where about 40 per cent of the families owned slaves and where tobacco was a second crop, were Whig strongholds. Breckinridge's rural strength was in southwestern Virginia, a region of poor whites still in a semifrontier condition in 1860. This had been the one extensive rural area of the state with room for a large influx of white settlers in the 1850's.

The most outstanding characteristic of the Breckinridge campaign was its appeal to newer social elements actively engaged in acquiring land and slaves. Among the Breckinridge politicians, this was indicated by the higher percentages of lawyers and of young planters and slaveholding farmers. For those not born to wealth (and, in the South, wealth always meant land and slaves), law was the customary means of climbing the social ladder. The ambitions of the young lawyer became proverbial. Since the profession was unstructured, with the most rudimentary licensing procedures, virtually anyone with a smattering of education could hang out a shingle. The lawyer had several options: He could enter politics and use any of innumerable local offices to learn of his county's wealth and opportunities; or he could seek out and acquire patronage; or, by moving to a frontier region, he could assist in the sale of the public lands and, with an insider's knowledge, amass land for himself.

The young Breckinridge planters and slaveholding farmers had come to political maturity in the 1850's. Social and economic developments during the decade had hindered their chances for success and prestige. The prices of everything that was needed to stock a plantation or just to begin in commercial agriculture— land, slaves, provisions—rose sharply, while the price of cotton, the major cash staple, remained steady. Even more galling was the antislavery crusade. The moral condemnations of the North must have seemed especially inflammatory to the young South- erners, whose recently acquired slaveholding status had not yet been economically secured or encrusted with the defenses of time and tradition. It was tempting and easy for these men to blame the North, specifically the abolitionists and Republicans, for many of their problems. The antislavery forces would never permit any additional slave territory or any loosening of the prohibition against the African slave trade. Thus, no relief in the form of fresh land or cheaper slave prices was to be forthcoming. All the slaveholder wanted, so the argument went, was an equal oppor- tunity to compete in the territories; but even this would be de- nied him by the free-soil North.

Economic pressures and status anxieties were major factors in radicalizing young slaveholders, particularly in the cotton South. They brought their vitality and frustrations to the Breckinridge campaign and helped shape an ideology tailored to similar groups in the recently developed slave regions. The frontiers of cotton agriculture in the 1850's had been opened up by the rail- roads. Small slaveholding farmers flocked into regions previously unable to compete with the planter-dominated river valleys in production and marketing. By slashing transportation costs from interior areas, the railroad further democratized cotton culture, as the cotton gin had done at the turn of the century, and en- larged the economic opportunities of a generation of Southerners. The Breckinridge Democrats spoke to the hopes and fears of these new cotton entrepreneurs, promising them that, if the Yankees refused to stop insulting them or putting a brake on their progress, then an independent South would do them justice.

The issue of slavery in the territories had no direct economic relevance for the poor whites. Trapped in a vicious cycle of pov- erty and ignorance, they had no floor beneath their lowly status except the presence of enslaved blacks. The color line did give them a certain self-respect, and they would fight viciously to keep that line from being blurred. The Democrats had always been masters at exploiting this racial pride. The Breckinridge men, declaring that only the victory of their candidate could ensure racial stability, charged that Bell and Douglas, by refusing to defend Southern rights, were contributing to the abolitionists' eventual triumph. These tactics were effective and reinforced the normal Democratic voting behavior of the poor whites on the periphery of the black belts.

The Crumbling Center

The Bell Whigs and Douglas Democrats were in an untenable position. The Whig ticket was headed by the "two coldest men in America," according to one conservative. The Whigs wanted to bring an end to the slavery agitation by removing the issue from politics and to preserve the existing order. These negative objectives were incurably tainted with the dull and stale smugness of an elite that confused stability with leadership. The nonplatform of "Constitution, the Union, and the Enforcement of the Laws" offered to meet the burning question of the expansion of slavery by ignoring it. But evasiveness solved nothing. Stephen Douglas had the charisma that John Bell lacked, but Douglas's party was split irreparably after Charleston. Douglas, one of the few genuinely tragic figures in American political history, devoted his entire career first to forging and then to leading a political center based on a Southern-Western axis, only to discover, in 1860, that his attempts had failed—the center no longer existed. His formula of popular sovereignty, designed to localize the problem of slavery in the territories and take the issue out of national politics, was denounced in both the North and South as a deceptive and indecisive device that prolonged the agony of arriving at a final decision. In trying to satisfy both sections he succeeded only in alienating both.

Whigs were openly dismayed by the state of public affairs in 1860. In their correspondence and speeches, they bemoaned what they saw as the loss of public virtue, intelligence, and patriotism without which the Republic could not survive. It was only in

moralistic terms that they could interpret the changing world
around them. "The people by nature are prone to error," wrote
Alexander Stephens. "Their inclinations in politicks are that way
as in morals they are to sin." A republican government was possible only when statesmen, by appealing to truth and virtue, persuaded the people to do right despite their natural desires. But
now the American republic, like similar experiments in the past,
was about to fail, because the people had been corrupted by
demagogues.

The Whigs saw confirmation of this world view all around
them. Selfish demagogues abounded in both sections. Stephens
blamed the Democratic split entirely upon the Southern bolters.
"They ran not from a platform but from a man. The platform was
a pretext. The whole rupture originated in personal ambition,
spite and hate." These were the "bad men bent upon mischief,"
who would drag the South into a revolution. Their concern was
not the public good, said Stephens, but personal gain. "Their
game is that of the demagogue, always a low, mean and base
one."

The Republicans were also condemned as unprincipled and
the Northern equivalent of the fire-eaters. One of the top Whig
newspapers in Georgia, the Augusta *Chronicle & Sentinel,* stated
that there was no valid reason for the Kansas-Nebraska Act to
have aroused Northern hostilities. In fact, the Republicans had
"seized upon it as an instrument whereby to excite the dark passions, the unreasoning prejudices, of a fanatic populace. . . ."
Around the nucleus of antislavery fanaticism they built a party
pandering to "all the vile isms of this generation," a party that

> stands forth to-day, hideous, revolting, loathesome, a menace not
> only to the Union of these States, but to Society, to Liberty and to
> Law. It has drawn to it the corrupt, the vile, the licentious, the
> profligate, the lawless, and is the embodiment not only of anti-
> slavery, but of communism, of agrarianism, of free-loveism, and
> all the abominations springing from a false society.

The worst fears of the Whigs had come true. All the constitutional safeguards intended to preserve order and balance in government had proved helpless in checking the Republicans. For

here was a strong, sectional party that was a veritable "fiend, the type of a lawless Democracy, a law unto itself, its only Lord, King Numbers, its decrees but the will of a wild mob."

That public morality and standards of statesmanship had so degenerated did not surprise the Whigs. It was the inevitable result, they felt, of the establishment of the party system. For the Whigs, political parties were a necessary evil. At best, they could serve as a device for selecting honest and capable gentlemen to exercise control from above. But this elitist idealization of the party could not survive the dictates of a modern party structure that funneled and shaped mass demands into a political program. From the Whigs' viewpoint, partisan loyalty had replaced fealty to the Constitution as the criterion for public advancement. The spoils system spawned by the Jacksonians, rotation in office, the establishment of a party press, had all apparently contributed to demoralization in public affairs. Even the sanctity of the ballot box had been invaded, as the parties catered to the immigrant rabble by giving them the vote.

The evils of the party system were thought to be aggravated by uncontrolled expansion. Ever since the Texas-annexation issue, the Whigs had argued that the nation was already large enough, and that time was needed to administer and assimilate the gains. By the 1850's, they worried that the limits of an efficient and manageable empire had been breached. Corruption was fed by an empire grown too large to punish wrongdoers and too fat to try. In 1859, Bell argued that "every irregularity, every abuse, every corruption, likely to grow up in the Government . . . [has] been increased and multiplied pretty much already in proportion to our expansion." This same unrestricted growth had stimulated unhealthy and unwarranted demands for ever more land. Senator Thompson of Kentucky complained that "our people have been so petted and so spoiled upon this subject, again and again surfeited, like a great child whose appetite is vitiated by sweetmeats, that they are eternally whining because their stomach is not as big as their eyes, and they cannot swallow everything they see." He had the courage to emphasize that expansion brought out the worst in the American character. The effects of Americanization on other peoples, Thompson said, could be compared to the invasion of a barn by a pack of voracious Norwegian rats that scattered and ate the weaker blue rats. The American settlers would lie, cheat, steal, and kill until they had what they wanted. Continued expansion, asserted the Whigs, would result in anarchy or in military despotism. The absorption of foreign races "without sympathy, without congeniality of sentiment, without appreciation of the blessings of freedom," would destroy constitutional government. A huge army and federal bureaucracy would be required to control the bloated empire.

The Whigs admitted that they had no economic self-interest in expansion. Northern Whigs catered to the shipping, importing, and textile interests of the Eastern seaboard, which maintained close economic ties with the South; they had little contact with the expansionist agrarians. In the South, the party was strongest in the Border states and settled plantation regions, which would be hurt economically by the acquisition of more slave territory. "I recollect well the effect upon the old States of the opening of Alabama and Mississippi," said Senator Anthony Kennedy of Maryland. "The State of Virginia has not yet recovered from it." She had been bled of her labor, free and slave, and, although some capital was generated by slave sales, far more, Kennedy contended, had been lost through the emigration of thrifty, enterprising citizens and the drop in land values. Some 15 million acres had been abandoned in Virginia because cultivation would have been unprofitable. Labor costs were high because of the demand from the Southwest, but grain prices, an increasing source of Virginia's agricultural income, were low owing to competition from the Midwest and a depressed home market.

The economy of the entire Upper South was caught in a bind. Whereas the cotton states had an assured export market for their cotton, the grain states, with a larger white population, had to vie on unequal terms with the free-labor, and more fertile, lands of the Western states for their share of the export market in grain and provisions. The solution was Henry Clay's old program of stimulating the home market by offering tariff protection for industries weakened by foreign competition. This would increase the purchasing power of industrial labor and raise grain prices. Industrial diversification within the South would be fostered, and population would grow more dense. "The tendency of these [measures]," explained Kenneth Rayner of North Carolina, "is to make *land* more valuable—as the home market is encouraged, and exchanges of the products of labor prevail all around us locally, as they prevail among nations, on a more extended scale."

The Whigs, then, had no use for the Breckinridge demands for the protection of slavery in the territories. They agreed that the South needed an outlet for her slaves, and that, if she were systematically denied that outlet, she had every right to expect congressional guarantees to reopen the territories for slavery. But, since the Whigs felt that Southern rights were adequately protected, they saw no immediate need for a slave code. The Kansas-Nebraska Act had abolished the Missouri Compromise restriction and given territorial legislatures all the power over slavery the Constitution allowed them to exercise, pursuant to appeals to the Supreme Court; and the Court in the Dred Scott decision had decided that Congress could not prohibit slavery in the territories. The South had thus won all she could reasonably desire. In addition, the Whigs suspected that the enactment of a slave code would spark another expansionary surge. From their experience, this would further damage the economies of the Upper South and, by accelerating the drain of slaves from these states, hasten the destruction of slavery on the Southern periphery. They felt more than justified, therefore, in accusing those who favored a slave code of placing their ambitions above the best interests of the South.

The appeal of the Douglas Democrats hinged on the willingness of the voters to put off a decision on the slavery question. This was the traditionally safe political approach, but it no longer sufficed by 1860. The doctrine of popular sovereignty was too elastic and indefinite. Politics as the art of accommodation had already been ruled out, once each section had begun to coalesce around its own candidate. Douglas was too intelligent a politician not to recognize this fact, but he had no choice but to pose as a sectional broker. This was the role he had nurtured in the 1850's and the only one that gave him any chance, however slim, of gaining victory.

In a political campaign with sharp moral overtones, the compromiser is suspect. This was Douglas's misfortune; neither section trusted him. The Republicans accused him of avoiding his moral responsibility by admitting that slavery had a right to the territories. On the other hand, Southerners feared that popular sovereignty would exclude slavery just as surely as would the Republicans' doctrine of congressional prohibition. Indeed, many felt that Douglas represented an even greater threat, because his position smacked of dishonesty and deceit. "Lincoln says—you have no right to take slaves to the territory—but if you have a right, you have a right to protection. Douglas says—squatters have a right to drive out slaves; that [you have] a right to go there with slaves, but no right to protection," reasoned one Southerner to Jefferson Davis. "What choice is there between the two? Lincoln is consistent and logical. Douglas the reverse." The South could not compete under the Douglas terms. Slaveholders were generally reluctant to enter a new territory because of the value and vulnerability of their slave property. Particularly in a period of sectional agitation, free labor would be certain to control the territorial governments and to vote slavery out before it had had a chance to come in. This was blatantly unfair, charged the Breckinridge Democrats. "History has taught us," noted the Norfolk *Southern Argus,* "that the South may successfully battle with Wilmot provisoism on the floors of Congress, while it is helpless before Squatter Sovereignty on the plains of Kansas."

These attacks accentuated the ambivalence of the Douglas ideology. In the North, the party often professed to be more opposed to the extension of slavery than were the Republicans; whereas, in the South, the expansionary potential of popular sovereignty was touted. "The only safe doctrine, for the South, was *non-intervention* by Congress," contended Judge Hiram Warner, a Douglas elector in Georgia. He pointed out that, under this policy, slavery was protected in Utah and New Mexico. Admittedly, the rest of the present territories would be free, but that was a natural result of laws of production and climate, not the working of popular sovereignty. The settlers would opt for slavery once territory to the south was acquired. If the voters considered "our future acquisitions—Cuba, Mexico, and Central America—the ultimate outlets for our redundant population, and the natural

home of the negro, a moment's reflection would convince any one
that our safety, our equality, our very salvation depended upon
the maintainance of the doctrine of non-intervention."

Since the demands of the pro- and antislavery factions were
irreconcilable, Douglas tried to placate them by allowing each
to read into popular sovereignty what it wanted. For the sake of
party harmony, this approach was the only recourse, but logically
it tended to drive both wings toward the more consistent ideological positions of the Republicans or Breckinridge Democrats. The
one substantial group ideologically satisfied by popular sovereignty was the constituency for which it was first formulated—
the farmers of the lower Midwest. Many of these Democratic
agrarians had migrated from the Upper South, some in search of
better land and others to get away from slavery. They were both
antislavery and Negrophobic. A few were attracted by the Republicans' commitment to free soil, but far more were repelled
by the Republicans' stand on black civil rights and their conception of a positive role for government in public affairs. The Republicans were the carriers of Yankee culture in the Midwest.
Not only did they view public questions as ultimately moral issues, but they also demanded that the morally and socially fit,
who by definition were one and the same, should lead and guide
their communities. Thus, they wanted to use government as a
means of enforcing their own value system and social norms.
Democratic farmers of Southern stock were not only raised on a
states'-rights philosophy that posited a very limited role for government, but they also rejected a party that posed as their moral
and social betters. Despite their opposition to slavery, they felt
more comfortable under the Douglas banner, which was more
congenial to their negative conception of government as well as
to their hatred of the planter and the black man.

Douglas still offered his Western supporters the vision of an
empire. George Pugh of Ohio, a top Douglas lieutenant, favored
the annexation of Cuba on the ground that "the expansion of our
Federal system, as one emergency after another shall require, is
the law of our development; it is the sign of our national vitality;
the pledge of our national endurance." The popular Ohio congressman Samuel S. Cox referred to a so-called law of interna-

tional relations by which *"Nationalities of inferior grade must surrender to those of superior civilization and polity!"* This expansion should benefit only whites, but the Midwestern Democrats stressed that, out of fairness to the slaveholders and in recognition of the fact that blacks were incapable of successful colonization, the South should not be rigorously barred from all the territories. If she were, and if the Republicans had not previously emancipated the slaves, the South would be forced to save her own civilization by expelling her excess blacks to the North. Declaiming against the alleged Negro-equality principles of the Republicans, Representative W. H. English of Indiana warned that, if these principles were ever victorious, "the peace of the whole country shall be endangered, the guarantees of the Constitution violated, and these free States overrun with free negroes, to eat out the substance of the white man, compete with his labor, and trespass upon his political rights."

This link between racism and acquiescence in the spread of slavery was an old one in the lower Midwest, and no one explained it better than had Congressman William Sawyer of Ohio in 1847. He "was opposed to enslaving mankind; but of the two evils he preferred the least; if he must either take this surplus black population into the bosom of his own State, or let the South have territory on which to send them, he chose the latter." Not aversion to slavery expansion but anger over having been placed in a hopeless political position by Southern demands characterized the mood of most Douglas politicians in the Midwest. W. W. Wick, an Indiana Democrat, warned Senator Hunter not to wreck the Democracy on an abstraction. He reasoned that the South had a slave shortage and would not risk her slaves in the present territories, even if they could carry them there. Be patient, he advised. "When Tamaulipas and Vera Cruz shall be ours, our people will find a way to favor the views of the South."

The poor showings made by Bell and Douglas were the political manifestation of their ideological weaknesses. Bell carried only the Border South and Douglas the single state of Missouri, plus a share of the New Jersey electoral vote. With the exception of Arkansas, the Whig share of the vote throughout the Deep South had dropped since 1856. The Southern vote for Bell was concentrated in cities, towns, manufacturing centers, and older plantation areas past their economic peak. He also ran well in planting counties with an exceptionally high concentration of agricultural wealth, such as the Mississippi Delta and the Louisiana sugar bowl. Among Southern Democratic voters, the Douglas candidacy was competitive only among the upland farmers and the foreign-born. What little support he received from planting areas came from those in economic decline. For example, in only 15 rural counties of Georgia did he poll 20 per cent or more of the vote. Most of these were old plantation regions that, during the 1850's, had experienced steep losses in white and slave population, cotton production, and farm acreage.

In contrast to the Breckinridge politicos, the greater age of the Bell politicians and the heavier representation of business groups reflected an appeal to an older generation and a different social milieu. With more of their ambitions satiated or blunted, the Whigs were more inclined to conserve what they had. Many of the planters could remember an era in which they were the leaders, when Democrats were often regarded as social upstarts and the vulgar demagogue was kept within bounds. It was then that many Whigs had acquired their wealth and status. Their principal allies continued to be small-town merchants and urban factors, who marketed their crops and advanced them credit. The entire party was imbued with the good tastes of the Virginia gentleman and the national outlook of those with business and personal ties to the North. The main weakness of the party in the Deep South was its narrow and stagnant political base. The established plantation regions gradually lost their pre-eminence as newer areas were opened up and as political egalitarianism stripped the planter elite of its few remaining privileges. Since the Lower South was overwhelmingly rural, Whig strength in towns and cities could be more than neutralized by the predominantly Democratic rural vote.

The Douglas Democrats were the remnant of the Jackson-Benton wing of the party. Some of its Southern leaders were men whose first political enemy had been not an abolitionist but a Federalist or a National Bank man. These old party warriors resented the pretensions and the arrogance of the younger Breckinridge forces. The strength of the Douglasites was in the cities, among the foreign-born and Democratic businessmen, and, to a lesser extent, in the diversified farming districts among the yeomanry. Hence, the movement had little sympathy with the demands of the expanding cotton frontiers. The leaders tried to work with the Northern branch of the party on the slavery issue, and they invoked the memory of Jackson as a nationalizing force uniting the sections. Hampered by a weak organization and by lack of funds, their candidate ran a poor third in most of the South.

JOHN BROWN'S GHOST

No issue so galvanized white fears or engendered such blind hatred of the North as did the rumors of slave uprisings that swept over the South in 1860. The fear cut across class lines and drove whites together in self-defense against the common enemy —the abolitionists. Although the first signs of panic had appeared after John Brown's raid on Harpers Ferry in the fall of 1859, a measure of calm had been restored before the Breckinridge Democrats flagrantly capitalized on the rumors for their partisan effect. The dangers in this cynical exploitation were evident to those who cared to see them. Concerning the actions of Governor Wise of Virginia, who used Harpers Ferry for his own political advantage and then assured Brown's martyrdom by refusing to stay his execution, a fellow Virginian warned that he had "conjured a Devil neither he nor perhaps any one can lay, and, arraying the roused pride and animosities of both sections against each other, has brought on a *real crisis* of imminent peril to both."

The greatest source of the purported slave plots was Texas. In early August, newspapers across the South ominously announced the discovery of a fiendish and well-organized plan to lay waste the whole of northeastern Texas. The instigators and leaders were said to be two Northern preachers, upon whose order the slaves were to strike on the first Monday in August. Provisions were to be destroyed, communications cut, arms and ammunition seized, and entire towns burned to the ground, until the whites were helpless and at the mercy of the avenging blacks.

A disastrous fire in Dallas in early July sparked the investigation that revealed this central "plot." Once the populace was put on the alert, conspiracies sprang up everywhere. Two thousand abolitionists were spotted organizing in Anderson County. An attempt to fire Austin in late July failed, but Henderson was leveled by arson on August 5. The Galveston *Citizen* cited Henderson as a terrible lesson for other towns. "The citizens put no faith in the reported conspiracy, and neglected to appoint a patrol or set a watch." The village of Athens had been more careful. "The negroes were taken up and whipped, and to the astonishment of many, the fact [of a revolt] was disclosed," wrote a resident. Strychnine and other poisons were allegedly found that were to have been poured down the wells and sprinkled over food. Several whites and blacks were hung or shot.

Vigilance committees were formed throughout the state to ferret out the enemy. What passed for evidence was usually adduced to establish the abolitionism of the accused before he was punished. On other occasions, as when a man was found hung on the outskirts of Fort Worth, the citizenry met and endorsed the lynching after the fact. Reports in out-of-state papers portrayed Texans as living in a virtual state of siege. The Charleston *Mercury* told of crowds gathering in Dallas, "anxious and eager to lend their assistance, and ready to quell every disturbance that threatens the peace of the State." Since any Texas emigrants passing through might be expelled abolitionists, Southern towns were advised by an Alabama paper to organize patrols whose duty "should be to drive from their midst all stragglers, and suspicious characters."

The facts of the Texas slave uprisings, however, were a great deal less exciting than the tales trumpeted in the Breckinridge press. Governor Sam Houston, the head of the state Bell campaign in Texas, repeatedly told Texans that the numbers of arrests and hangings had been wildly exaggerated, that no vial of poison had ever been found, and that what fires had occurred were accidental. Conservatives stressed that the populace was in desperate straits and therefore susceptible to agitation, because Texas had suffered more than any other state from the general drought that had hit the South in 1860. One observer noted that

Texas farms were in pitiful condition—"the corn is withered and destroyed, the grass on the prairies is burnt to a crisp, and the stock everywhere is famishing for food and water." Further embittering the settlers were food shortages. Staples had to be shipped in by rail, and prices, as a consequence, skyrocketed. In some localities, water was selling at 25¢ a gallon. Under such conditions, conservatives contended, extensive fires were inevitable, and "some houses, and even towns, may have been burnt." "But," added the Griffin (Georgia) *Union*, "that burning and hanging has been carried on to the extent reported, we have no idea."

Another plausible explanation for the Texas excitement was offered by the pro-Douglas Mobile *Register*. Allowing for exaggeration, the paper still felt that there had been serious troubles in Texas. But it blamed the disturbances on "gangs of desperados from the prairies, perhaps also from south of the Rio Grande, whose object is plunder, and who use the negroes as tools for their nefarious purposes." Efforts at restoring calm, however, failed; land values dropped; and settlers abandoned the state. Some, explained Houston, left "for fear their negroes would be falsely accused of incendiarism, and hung; and others for fear they, as not being slaveholders, might be charged with being Abolitionists and lynched."

The distortions and fantasies of the Texas episode characterized nearly all the reports of abolitionist conspiracies. On August 9, for example, the Rome (Georgia) *Courier* stated that an insurrectionary plot had just been uncovered. At first, the details were hazy, but a card nailed on the post office door in Rome a few weeks later specified Sunday the 26th as the day for the revolt and referred the citizenry to the confessions extracted from the plotters in the neighboring town of Adairsville. After a messenger from that town addressed a meeting in Rome and divulged all the details, the men in Rome formed a vigilance committee and marched on Adairsville. They found nothing more suspicious than a white man, recently discharged from the penitentiary, passing a spurious bank note to a black. He was arrested on the charge of attempting "to instil wrong notions in the mind of a negro," received 39 lashes, and had half of his head shaved.

Elsewhere, the white mobs engaged in more than cruel pranks. In Currituck County, North Carolina, a white group, led to believe from a slave about to be whipped that slaves had run away with Irish canal workers, attacked the Irish encampment. Two Irishmen were killed, several others wounded, and the rest jailed along with the blacks found in their camp. Just across the state line, in Princess Anne County, Virginia, a free black told authorities, while under arrest, that an uprising had been maturing for months. He told of another free black who had written to friends in the North to hire men to land a boat loaded with arms. Spurred by these revelations, patrols scoured the woods and swamps south of Norfolk. The twenty-odd suspects rounded up were quickly released for lack of evidence, but an Irish canal ditcher who allegedly approached them from his camp with gun in hand was killed.

The story was distressingly similar throughout the South—wild rumors, frightened slaves confessing to "plots," dragnets pulling in nothing but more frightened slaves and poor whites living on the fringes of respectable society, beatings, and occasional lynchings. Although it soon became obvious to conservatives that Southern papers had been carrying farfetched stories of insurrectionary movements, "most of which turned out, on examination, to be totally false, and *all of them* grossly exaggerated," Breckinridge editors nevertheless rarely corrected their reports when errors were brought to their attention or even bothered to print retractions. Journalistic standards were quite low; and some of the abolitionist tales were undoubtedly mere fabrications. In 1859, a St. Augustine editor admitted to a secret agent of the Interior Department investigating the slave trade that he had intentionally blurred the date on an 1804 agreement between the captain of a Rhode Island slave ship and a slave firm off the African coast so as to give the impression that the contract was contemporary. He published the false story "to bamboozle the Northern abolitionists."

Bell and Douglas editors exercised some discretion and often refused to print sensational stories they felt would shock the people and lead to personal and property destruction. But playing on the common fears was too effective an electioneering gambit to be disregarded by the Breckinridge press. "The excitement growing out of these matters has killed off all conservative feeling in Texas," reported the correspondent of the New York *Herald* in September. "You may now note down every Texan as a disunionist." Breckinridge was righteously depicted as a true democrat, with the courage to publicize all the facts and trust the will of the people. The opposition, however, "true to their theory of keeping the people in ignorance . . . not only seek to divert attention from our warnings, by bringing us into disrepute as disunionists; but wherever an opening occurs, they spring up some side issue, which is no sooner fairly in the field than one of them mounts it, and seeks to ride into office thereon." Pointing to the attacks already made upon slavery while the South was still theoretically an equal in the Union, the Breckinridge forces asked how slavery could ever be safe in a government ruled by the Republicans. To prevent Texas from serving as a prelude to another Santo Domingo massacre, they pushed their candidates as the only ones "who can, if elected, stem the current of Abolition and retard the progress of their ruinous doctrines."

The irresponsibility of the Breckinridge press should not be discounted, but the near trauma produced in some regions by the abolitionist scare was a result of more than political opportunism. By reacting so violently against what was more often than not an imagined threat, Southern whites were able to focus their group hostility on a stereotyped enemy and thereby project onto a hated outsider the anxieties and repressed desires of a beleaguered society. During the first half of the nineteenth century, slavery was abolished throughout most of the Western Hemisphere, the key decision being that of England in 1833 to end slavery in her colonial possessions. The South's increasing isolation was magnified by the rise of Northern abolitionism and its political counterpart, the Republican party. Outstripped in economic and political growth by the free states, the South became conscious of the growing weakness of her position. Adding to her frustration were Republican taunts over her impotency.

"You who advocate the perpetuity of slavery," said the Illinois Republican Owen Lovejoy, "are like a set of madcaps who should place themselves on the top of an iceberg which had disengaged itself from the frozen regions of the north, and begun to float downward, and downward, through the warm climates." The South could have expected no other treatment. In 1850, Alexander Stephens had anticipated the derision that awaited her. "In the halls of Congress, nothing but debates about the crimes and the iniquity of slavery, and the duty of the General Government to withhold all countenance of the unholy institution of human bondage." To an honest and proud Christian like Stephens, as well as to countless other Southerners, the unforgivable insult of such legislation as the Wilmot Proviso was its "expression to the world of the deliberate opinion of the Federal Government that institutions tolerated in the South deserve public censure and national odium. . . ." The pressure on Southern leaders and institutions by the 1850's was incredible. It generated a pervasive sense of insecurity, an anxiety over whether slavery could be maintained against the onslaughts of its enemies.

The abolitionists were the most visible enemy. Southerners never knew quite what to make of them. Since their dedication and zeal were above reproach, Southerners concluded that they were religious fanatics who, in the words of James Orr, "like fanatics in every age of the world are guided neither by religion, morality, nor justice." In an appeal to the nation's strong streak of nativist anti-Catholicism, Richard Bowie of Maryland denounced abolitionism as "a species of Protestant Jesuitism, an attempt to ingraft on our political system spiritual dogmas. . . ." The abolitionists, Southerners insisted, could not be fair or reasonable social critics, since they would either subject the South to a bloodbath by forcing the violent overthrow of slavery or precipitate a race war by denying slavery room to expand. From the Southern perspective, talk of peaceful emancipation was mere cant, since the races could not live together in peace without slavery. The danger posed by these devoted, though deluded, men stemmed from their fearlessness. Senator Chester Ashley of Arkansas granted that they were prepared to go to the gallows in defense of their principles. What's more, they "would suppose, could they set every slave free to-morrow, or possibly cut the throat of every slaveholder in all the South, that they were doing God service." Many also believed that abolitionism was permeated with radicalism. All forms of labor were involuntary, contended the proslavery forces, and the abolitionists, by striking at the specific form of slavery, were endangering labor-capital relations everywhere. Whereas the true fanatic was motivated by a misguided love of the slave, the agrarian abolitionist was driven by hatred of the master and the wish to level Southern society for his own benefit.

Yet, the existence of the abolitionist movement fulfilled certain Southern needs. It gave Southerners a means of dispelling any nagging doubts they might have over their failure to emancipate their slaves or treat them better. Joseph Lumpkin, Chief Justice of the Georgia Supreme Court, wrote in 1848 that, had it not been for the abolitionists, the South might "have been guilty . . . of political and social suicide by emancipating the African race, a measure fatal to them, to ourselves, and to the best interests of the Confederacy and of the whole world." In defense against the "violent assaults of these fiends," Southerners examined their peculiar institution and gamely concluded that it was a positive good. The duty of the South was clear. As Hammond once elaborated to Calhoun, she had "to deprive the Abolitionists of the Clap-trap of the 'Golden Rule of Christ,' 'the laws of nature and natural rights' and to make them enure to our cause—to show that the 'Compact' between master and Slave is just and to the advantage of the Latter and to trace 'Southern decay' to other causes than Slavery which in fact is all that saves us." In Southern mythology, the typical slave was happy and carefree, and he would have been allegedly even more so had the South been left alone. Jefferson Davis told the Senate that the liberalizing measures the Virginia planters of Jefferson's generation had allegedly introduced had to be scrapped with the advent of abolitionism. If present slaves were not educated, allowed more personal freedoms, or manumitted, then blame yourselves, he told Northerners.

The most fiendish of all abolitionists were those who invaded the South to overthrow slavery by force. Exposing and punishing these men assumed a ritualistic purpose, involving whole communities, and functioned to promote Southern unity. The problem of internal loyalty, always crucial to Southern leaders, became an obsession after the mid-1830's. Despite their public portrayal of the South as a classless, united society anchored by immutable racial differences, they were not so naive as to believe that slavery could survive free discussion in an open society. Resentments of lower-class whites, doubts over the economic efficacy of slavery, and the persistent burden of internal security could, potentially, be expressed in attacks on slavery, not so much in moral terms, however, as in terms of its social and economic costs for the majority of whites. To stifle any criticism, or even debate, from within, Southern leaders imposed rigid censorship on all printed material entering the slave states as well as on all public communication, spoken or written, within them that in any way touched upon the slavery question. This course was generally approved by the Post Office Department, but, whenever conflicts arose, the South refused to back down. When, in 1856, the postmaster at Yazoo City, Mississippi, was ordered by the first assistant postmaster general to deliver the Cincinnati *Gazette* to a local resident, he ignored the command. Citing Mississippi law, he said: "It is now the only safe mode by which we can protect ourselves from the vile and incendiary abolition sheets, with which our country is flooded, and which are already having their effect, if the Newspaper reports of the disaffection among the Slave population be true." The dictates of security also took precedence over matters of conscience. An article in the religious creed of a society could hold that slavery was inconsistent with Christianity; but the printing and circulation of that article, even among the society's members, was enjoined on the ground that all Southern religious groups admitted slaves, whom the article would tend to make dissatisfied with their servitude.

No matter how closed a society she became, the South could become neither secure nor united. The blacks were an obvious threat. Again, the South's public posture was one of bliss and serenity. "Our doors are unlocked at night," Jefferson Davis assured a political gathering in New York City; "we live among [the slaves] with no more fear of them than of our cows and

oxen. We lie down to sleep trusting to them for our defence. . . ."
The slave patrols that roamed nightly through the countryside
told a different story, as did the bristling defenses in cities, leading Olmsted to remark of Charleston that one might "imagine
. . . the town was in a state of siege or revolution." The hyper-
sensitivity to rumors and to the slightest hint of outside interference with slavery belied the fears that could not be dismissed.
After her two-year stay on a Georgia plantation, Frances Kemble
observed that "a slave population, coerced into obedience, though
unarmed and half fed, *is* a threatening source of constant insecurity, and every Southern *woman* to whom I have spoken on the
subject has admitted to me that they live in fear of their slaves."

Still, the image of the contented slave was not just an ideological barb to be hurled at the North. Southerners desperately
wanted to believe that their slaves were truly content, for the
psychological burden of admitting to being surrounded by a
savage and vengeful alien race would have been crushing. The
fiction could be maintained, and the danger somewhat abated,
by blaming outsiders for disturbing a naturally well-ordered and
safe society. Since public safety was of vital concern to every
Southerner, all could unite against the abolitionist invader as
the fear of insurrection bridged the gap between classes.

The influence of the outsider could, theoretically, be minimized by isolating the slave. This principle applied to all facets
of the slave's life, including his religious instruction. In attempting to enlist the support of the South Carolina planter Wade
Hampton for a missionary among his slaves, a Methodist preacher
cleverly argued that the "slaves on each large plantation would
form a congregation of themselves, and would not be in danger
of corruption by being bro't together with those on the neighboring plantations." Nevertheless, the slaves could not be wholly
insulated from Southern life. Religious gatherings, holiday cele-
brations, and political barbecues were all occasions for slaves
to come together and exchange the latest news and rumors.
There were always some unscrupulous whites willing to risk the
wrath of a vigilance committee by illegally trading with slaves,
exchanging liquor for stolen goods. The slaves themselves, in the
meantime, whether by overhearing the conversations of whites

or by exposure to the public discussions of slavery at election time in the papers and on the stump, gradually became aware of the subversive idea of the vulnerability of slavery. "The slaves hear and comprehend much more of the speeches and letters, which are delivered and written, than is generally supposed," stressed a Mississippian to Calhoun in 1848. Alluding to the free-soil movement, he added that "it is very generally understood among the slaves, that a great movement is now being made on their behalf; the objects to be accomplished not precisely defined, but by which their condition is to be affected." Four years earlier, Hammond had told Calhoun how "astonished and shocked" he was to discover that some of his slaves actually knew of the actions of the abolitionists and the opinions of the Presidential candidates. Hammond linked the recent fires in the lower part of his district with the dangerous knowledge acquired by the slaves. This insubordination was "fearful—horrible. A *quick* and *potent* remedy must be applied. *Disunion* if *needs* be."

The suspected white sources of disunity were Southern non-slaveholders and Yankees residing within the South. The allegiance of the former to slavery could not be taken for granted, but ties of race and kinship with the planters made them appear less of a threat to domestic stability than did the presence of Northerners. The guile and deceit of the Yankees made them cunning adversaries. Edward Pollard cautioned that they deliberately ingratiated themselves with their Southern hosts by professing admiration of slavery, then gratified their real hatred of Southern institutions by tampering with the slaves and publishing anonymous antislavery letters in the Northern press. They required careful scrutiny. "The man who would devise a safe opportunity to publish what he knew to be false and libellous of those whose good will he had won by another lie," proclaimed Pollard, "might, with the same hope of impunity, venture on a grander revenge, and secretly conspire with the slave in a rebellion."

The lesson frequently drawn from John Brown's raid and the Texas troubles was that all newcomers were suspect. The *East Floridian* pointed out that, before he embarked on his murderous designs, Brown was apparently just another quiet resident of the community going about his own business. The Texas plot *"was gotten up through the agency of apparently honest settlers from distant States, who until its development were above suspicion."* Southerners, then, could never be quite certain just who their enemies were. To resolve this dilemma, declarations of loyalty were demanded from everyone. "We regard every man in our midst an enemy to the institutions of the South who does not boldly declare that he or she believes African slavery to be a social, moral, and political blessing," announced the Atlanta *Confederacy* in February, 1860. "Any person holding other than these sentiments, whether born at the South or North, is unsound, and should be requested to leave the country."

The constant anxiety over internal security had to be relieved. One response was to project onto the North all the calamities and degradation associated with the feared collapse of slavery. "If our slaves must wrongful[ly] be taken from us," argued William Duval in 1849, "we will try and settle them in the North, we will give them freedom and let them conquer our enemies, and give them their cities and country that they may win by their arms." The tables would be turned. "Able leaders, discipline and arms will carry that destruction and ruin to our enemies that they are preparing for us. The fancied security of the North may be shattered by a volcano—over which they little dream they are preparing for themselves." Another comforting fantasy was provided by total commitment to a divinely ordained racist world view. Such a belief postulated that God would not punish the South for upholding racial purity and cultural order through slavery. Hammond calmed his own fears by reassuring Calhoun that Southerners were not destined "to bow our heads to the destroying Angel. . . . We have not merited it. Its consummation [i.e., slavery's destruction] would throw civilization backwards a century or more."

The most positive outlet for this anxiety was to seize and expel all abolitionists who dared to enter the South. Entire communities were encouraged to root out the enemy. His mere presence was sufficient proof that the established authorities had failed to protect the South. Extralegal groups, sometimes just mobs, but often well-organized vigilance committees with officers and by-

laws, were formed. Drawing on both the vigilante justice common to the frontier areas of the South and the tradition of step-
ping outside the law to punish those deemed guilty of tampering
with slaves, these committees were frequently a law unto themselves. Although their ostensible function was to capture abolitionists, they actively sought to purge their communities of all
possible threats. The members of the Bamberg, South Carolina,
committee were typical in their determination "to arrest and examine all persons suspected of any designs against the peace or
good order of the neighborhood." Committees in Texas were
urged to draft lists of all suspicious persons. There was talk of a
black list to include those who were to be exterminated by immediate hanging. The result of this frenzy was a ruthless drive
for social conformity. The subversives most often uncovered
were transient or recently settled, semiskilled laborers of Northern or foreign birth. These men had no place or status in their
communities and were convenient scapegoats for the outside
world that maligned Southern values and threatened social chaos.

Community hostility was directed against those outsiders who
deviated in any way from Southern customs and taboos. Ethnic,
class, and religious differences were exploited. Irish railroad and
canal workers were considered potential abolitionists, and, in
Texas, insurrectionary rumors provided the Anglo-Americans with
a convenient excuse for arresting Mexicans en masse and deport-
ing them from given areas. Newcomers, especially if they were
poor, were vulnerable to charges of abolitionism. In June, 1860,
Peter Pent, a German-born cabinetmaker who had settled in
Lake City, Florida, was dragged out of bed and savagely beaten
by the local vigilantes, hired by one H. B. Elder who coveted
a town lot owned by Pent. The German received little public
sympathy, since he was accused of having uttered such subversive sentiments as blaming slavery for depressing his wages. One
who did support Pent, a Mr. Ellinger, was publicly denounced
by Elder for being poor, German, and Jewish. He was "one
whose race crucified the Saviour and parted his raiment among
them, and have ever since been trafficking in old clothes; a fellow
loafing around town without any regular occupation for a liveli-
hood."

Northerners suspected of abolitionism were generally travelers foolish enough to have expressed a preference for the Republicans or to have been caught talking with slaves. Those who resided in the South were left alone, unless they appeared to their neighbors to be nonconformists. After living in Southampton County, Virginia, for over a year, Edward Hedley, a New Yorker, was ordered to leave in the fall of 1860. He was accused of working for the underground railroad. His first crime seems to have been settling "in an obscure out of the way place styled Nottoway Mills, through which not even a public road runs." Here, he was free from public scrutiny, and, after his neighbors had boycotted the local post office for fear of being associated with him, he supposedly used the office "to carry out his own intrigues and designs upon our community." He was accused of voicing dangerous ideas at Sunday school and of teaching blacks, both free and slave. To clinch the case against Hedley, the vigilance committee labeled him a cheat and a scoundrel who had one Republican friend who subscribed to the New York *Tribune* and another who consorted with black women.

Although virtually all the reported abolitionists were isolated and helpless individuals when arrested, Southerners persisted in imagining that their enemies were part of a gigantic and incredibly efficient organization. This belief in a giant conspiracy rendered plausible the many reports of insurrections by relating them back to a single central plot, masterminded by John Brown and, after his execution, systematically carried out by his followers. The conspiratorial theory also helped to explain why the abolitionists had been able to enter the South undetected and to make contact with the slaves. Sworn to secrecy, communicating only by mysterious signals, and aided by a network of spies and informers, they were able to breach Southern defenses. At times, their powers bordered on the omnipotent. They could enter and leave communities at will, make intricate plans months in advance, and whisk slaves away to freedom. It may even be that Southerners identified with this exaggerated stereotype of the enemy who not only could criticize and attack slavery as few Southerners would ever dare to do but also could get away with it. Such identification would have been a socially acceptable means of expressing one's own doubts or frustrations over slavery and was perfectly safe so long as the enemy was converted into a fiend who ultimately would be punished.

The abolitionist as fiend clarified Southern values by contrast. If the abolitionist mocked the freedom and openness of American society by joining a secret organization, the Southerner appeared ever more loyal to democratic institutions. The Southerner was also shocked to hear of what had supposedly been planned on the state election day in Texas, the key to the abolitionist plot in that state. While the men were away at the polls, the blacks allegedly had been ordered to kill the defenseless women and children, seize all weapons, fire the homes, and ambush the returning white males. Standards of decency had no meaning for the abolitionists. They were said to have encouraged the male slaves to choose beforehand what fair Southern women they desired and to spare them, while slaughtering the rest together with the children and old folk. In view of these abominable tales, Southerners asked, how could such a foe even claim to be Christian? So inhuman were these fiends, so perverse their inclinations, that they would wantonly desecrate the Sabbath by planning insurrections for that holy day. "Neither the Sabbath nor the precincts of the sanctuary, nor the defenceless condition of the people, the hopelessness of women or the cry of infancy could plead with [the] ruthless savages, but were rather incentives to their thirst for blood"—this was the lurid image of what a Sunday revolt in Virginia might have resembled had the plot not been discovered at the last minute. The authors of this terrifying projection, the Minute Men of Princess Anne County, warned that the populace could expect "a butchery with axes, hoes and spades, prosecuted amidst corpses and flaming dwellings and with all the revelry of hellish hate." Measured against the imagined conspiracies and monstrous cruelty of the abolitionists, the white Southerner naturally emerged as a more honest democrat and a more humane Christian.

Whatever Southern needs were fulfilled by the existence of the abolitionists, the legacy of the abolitionist panic of 1860 was hatred and visceral fear. Goaded by the terrifying thought of losing racial control, the Southern temper turned ugly and vi-

cious. "I have just learned that a white woman was shot by a
slave, twelve miles south of this place, and afterwards was rav-
ished," wrote a Texas resident in a public letter. "The negro, I
presume, was burned at the stake on that night." The efforts even
of conservatives to moderate tensions were frequently accompanied by a clamor for lynch law. All suspicious white vagabonds
should be seized, advised the Augusta *Chronicle & Sentinel*, and
the whole matter examined "cool[l]y and dispassionately, by the
oldest and best citizens, and when adjudged guilty, swing the vagabonds to the nearest tree, and say nothing about it." The enemy
could be anywhere, and the sources of danger were bounded only
by the imagination of the plotters. Northern free blacks reportedly
were selling themselves into slavery so as to aid their brothers
by stirring up revolts. Some slaves in Texas allegedly poisoned
a batch of gingercakes and nearly succeeded in killing several
whites. Besieged from all sides, Southerners resolved to defend
themselves at whatever cost.

No matter how much Southerners disagreed as to how immediate or distinct a threat a Republican victory would present,
they were united in the belief that racial integrity and control
must be maintained. Since emancipation was unthinkable, the
mere existence of an antislavery federal administration pledged
to restrict slavery was a menace to Southern civilization. In this
crisis atmosphere, with emotions so close to the surface, even
conservatives were forced to insist on the South's right to resist a
Republican victory. Once Southern political opinion coalesced
on the need to resist, no matter how much the conservatives desired a passive resistance, the momentum had shifted to the secessionists.

5. The Illusion of Security

After Lincoln's election, the Breckinridge politicians immediately assumed control of the secession campaign. They had the backing of nearly all the Southern governors. Ideological changes from the Presidential election were chiefly ones of emphasis—the prospects of an independent South grew rosier, and the consequences of submitting to Republican rule grew gloomier. Secession would be peaceful, of course, and with minimal social disruption. In marked contrast to the crisis of 1850, the South was not congratulating herself on her prosperity but was worried over a commercial panic triggered by the Republican victory and aggravated by a year-long drought. A free-soil administration was no longer a potential danger but a menacing reality, and it was coming to power simultaneously with the peaking of Southern fears over internal security. In exploiting these advantages, the radicals offered not only the tactics by which Southerners could free themselves from the incubus of the hostile Union but a secessionist ideology that promised both prosperity and an end to the agitation over slavery.

RADICALISM REDEEMED

So complete was the radicals' triumph, first with the secession of the cotton states and then, after the firing on Fort Sumter and Lincoln's call for the militia, with the withdrawal of the Border South, that conservatives were convinced the crisis of 1860–61 was part of a carefully engineered plot to destroy the Union by disrupting the Democratic party and thus assuring a Republican victory, which would be used as a pretext for secession. Gover-

nor Letcher of Virginia expressed the prevalent attitude toward
Rhett and Yancey when he told Senator R. M. T. Hunter in
June that their "purpose is the disorganization and overthrow of
the Democratic party, and the country must see it, and understand it." As the campaign wore on, Whigs could scarcely contain their disgust and anger. W. W. Paine of Georgia felt that
the Breckinridge men were rank disunionists who should wear a
red flag, "emblematic of civil war, and carnage." There was no
excuse for their disunionism, he fumed; "it is treason both against
God, and man. This cry of protection, is a masked battery behind
which the disunionists have rallied to concoct their dark plots.
. . . Are not such men moral traitors? And will not the vengeance
of Heaven overtake them?"

This indictment was based on the conservatives' reading of the
motives behind the demands for an unambiguous guarantee of
the protection of slavery within the territories. Since Southern
Whigs and Douglas Democrats in general had no direct interest
in the expansion of slavery—indeed, would economically suffer
from it—they traced the intransigence of the Breckinridge Democrats to individual ambition and greed. Their elitist outlook predisposed them to interpret political affairs in terms of leaders
directing the masses. Hence, the extremism of the Breckinridge
forces should be blamed on the scheming and selfish politicians
at the head of the party. In particular, conservatives knew that
Douglas had become positively distasteful to many Southern
Democrats. Jefferson Davis once referred to him as "our little
grog-drinking, electioneering Demagogue." Clearly, personal
rancor complicated efforts to reach a compromise at Charleston.
As Robert Toombs reported to Stephens: "The real difficulty at
Charleston was that a large number of Democrats North and
South had committed themselves so far against Douglas that they
were lost if he was nominated, and they therefore preferred
ruining the party with themselves than ruining themselves without the party."

Moreover, it was evident that the pressure for a slave code was
not coming from the Southern stalwarts of the Democratic party.
National leaders such as Cobb in Georgia and Davis in Mississippi (whose own protectionist resolutions in the Senate were

introduced only as a moderate counterweight to the more doctrinaire stance of Albert Gallatin Brown) were willing to let the issue ride, working, instead, to unite the party against the Republicans. The firebrands were not part of the Democratic inner circle, and the problems of maintaining a national coalition were none of their concern. They could enhance their own power base by forcing into the open divisive sectional issues popular with the voters back home. Most Southern editors applauded any bold defense of slavery, and the most expedient course for the typical politician was a hard line on Southern rights.

South Carolina, the state with the most tenuous ties to a national party, produced the most consistent brand of radicalism. Rhett reasoned that all national party organizations had to be destroyed before the South's true revolutionary ardor could be developed. Especially in South Carolina, Alabama, and Mississippi, the people were willing to strike for independence, but they were constantly held back by "the spoils men and unionists," the natural offspring of a party system that sacrificed principles for place and power. No party could be loyal both to the nation and to the South, since, for Rhett, the needs of the two had become mutually exclusive. "So long as the Democratic party, as a 'National' organization, exists in power at the South, and so long as our public men trim their sails with an eye to either its favor or enmity, just so long need we hope for no southern action for our disenthralment and security. The South must dissever itself from the rotten Northern element." Knowing that the Southernrights faction could not control the Charleston convention, Rhett had foreseen back in January "the importance of obtaining the secession of the Alabama and Mississippi delegations, on the issue of squatter sovereignty and the construction of the Dred Scott decision." After the bolt, states'-rights groups could rally round men of true Southern principles, and two vital goals would be secured: "This will ensure the defeat of the double-faced 'National' Democracy so called—and make up the issue between the sections, with a resistance party already formed to meet the event of a Black Republican President elected by the North."

Rhett, the philosopher of revolution, was proved correct. Other radicals, such as the Beaufort planter William Lawton, agreed that the best President would be "the most ultra Black Republican abolitionist to be found. . . ." In the event of his election, Lawton hoped "the Southern States may be forced, or kicked into an organization of such a Government, as I wish to see established."

The conservatives' belief in a plot was not just the fabrication of a frustrated political faction, but to view secession from only this perspective is an oversimplification and distortion of the national crisis. No one could be certain what effect two Democratic candidates would have on the Republican chances for victory. The initial expectation of a surprisingly large number of Southerners was that the election would be thrown into the House after no candidate had received an electoral majority. It was known, for example, that Lincoln would not pick up support from the South; moreover, some combination of the opposition might deprive him of enough electoral votes in the North to cost him a majority. Although most politicians were privately conceding Lincoln's election by early September, J. Henly Smith, a Washington newspaper correspondent, was assuring Alexander Stephens as late as October that fusion tickets would defeat Lincoln in Rhode Island, Pennsylvania, Indiana, and Ohio. Most newspapers held out the possibility of an electoral stalemate until the state election returns from the North in late October foretold a Republican sweep in November.

The calculations had gone awry because of a general overestimation of Douglas's strength in the North and an underestimation of the antagonism between the Buchanan and Douglas wings of the Democracy. Douglas had repeatedly declared that he could beat the Republicans on the issue of noninterference with slavery. If this were true, argued the radicals, why not give the Little Giant a fair chance to prove himself by allowing him to run in the North unencumbered by the need to placate Southern interests? The South would have her own candidate, Northern Democrats could rally behind Douglas, and Douglas would actually be strengthened in his contest with Lincoln. Nevertheless, the Democratic rupture, by denying Douglas the united backing of his party, hurt him more than it helped him among the Northern voters. Pro-administration forces, mustering money and patronage against him, were more interested in defeating him than in preventing a Lincoln victory. The proposal not to run a Breckinridge ticket in states where Douglas appeared strong and vice versa never crystallized into a definite plan because of the jealousy and hatred between the two factions. The Breckinridge forces claimed Pennsylvania and New Jersey in addition to all of the South and argued that they were competitive with Douglas in the rest of the North. Not until fall were serious efforts made to unite Democratic strength in crucial Northern states. By then, however, it was too late. Blaming this disunity upon the anti-Douglas policies of President Buchanan and Howell Cobb, his Secretary of the Treasury, Smith told Stephens that both these Democrats had misjudged the Republican's vote-getting potential. Bitterly, he added, "Their treachery deserves a *rope's end.*"

Contrary to the conspiratorial theory, most radicals were driven by a need to vindicate themselves and their society. Their major goal was not so much an independent South as a secure one. Young men with their careers mostly still ahead of them, the radicals spoke for a generation that demanded an end to the recriminations and moral condemnations provoked by the slavery question. They had never known a Union in which half of the nation was not damning their values and institutions, and they had come to political maturity in a decade of nearly constant sectional agitation. Convinced that the South lacked the labor resources to keep pace with the rapid progress of the North, disgusted by her dependence on Northern markets and manufacturers, and distressed about her increasing moral isolation, the radicals saw a society rapidly losing self-confidence and self-respect. They feared that the South, weakened by party questions and bereft of political prestige, was on the brink of doom. In 1859, Pollard proclaimed:

> [H]er peculiar institution has to bear a burden of censure, under which, even the best men of the South think it must sink, unless strengthened by new measures; the common territories of the Republic are being steadily closed to it; the black lines of free-soilism, in which it must languish and die, are being drawn around it, and the dregs of the poison cup are at our lips.

The anguish of men like Pollard, combined with the expansive
thrust of the cotton frontiers, energized the Breckinridge movement and made the party's aims and membership nearly synonymous with radicalism.

To preserve the South was to preserve slavery, and this, insisted O. R. Singleton in a standard radical argument, could be
accomplished only when "the people of the North shall put down
this Republican party, open the territories to us, protect slavery
when carried there, enforce the fugitive slave law, and give us
the full measure of our rights under the Constitution." For the
radicals, it was both absurd and hypocritical to expect these goals
to be furthered by supporting Douglas. The South had placed her
trust in national Democratic administrations throughout the
1850's and had seen her position steadily eroded. She had acquired no additional room for slavery and the free-soil forces
had grown ever stronger. Buchanan's administration had been
the major disappointment. If not committed to Calhoun's idea of
strict sectional equality, Buchanan was eager to meet Southern
demands for more territory. Yet, not only did the South make no
headway in Mexico or Cuba, she was shut out of Kansas. These
failures, when added to the unprecedented boldness of John
Brown's raid, confirmed for many Southerners the pessimism expressed by the radicals in 1856. The large Northern vote of the
Republican nominee, John C. Frémont, "shows that the *immediate* future . . . is big with peril," confided H. J. Harris of Mississippi to Jefferson Davis. "Besides this, the few northern States
that went for Buchanan were carried by considerable giving way
on principle, and the signification of our victory is greatly weakened. . . . As it is, the democracy have the offices four years
more, and that is all."

Nothing could be gained by backing another Northern Democrat in 1860, and certainly not one so deceitful as Douglas. Moreover, explained a "States' Rights Man" in the Richmond *Enquirer*
on the eve of the bolters' Richmond convention, the "defeat of
the South, under the lead of Mr. Douglas, upon the Squatter Sovereignty platform, does not present the Southern issue. To vote
him down is not [an] insult to the South. —To vote down the
'Squatter Sovereignty' candidate, nominated as he will be against

the protest of the States' rights party, will not present an issue upon which we can resist the abolitionizing of the Government." For the radicals, this was the crucial weakness of a Douglas candidacy. As the Mississippi editor and politician Ethel Barksdale phrased it, Douglas was not right on "the articles of faith, and here I fear will be the rock upon which our party will split."

From the radicals' persuasion, the prime goal in 1860 had to be a South prepared for resistance and aroused to the dangers of remaining within the Union without further guarantees for safety. Complete unity was out of the question; but, if the South ran a true states'-rights candidate, she could accomplish several objectives: To begin with, she might prevent any of the candidates from receiving a majority of the votes, thus throwing the election into the House, where she would be in a strong position to bargain. Failing in that, the South would have, at least, discovered the identity and strength of her friends and foes. Above all, however, the issues of the campaign would be so sharply and clearly defined that Southerners would be shaken out of their lethargy and submissiveness. The more sectionalized the issues, the better, reasoned the "States' Rights Man." The South would vote as a unit and would "show the Northern people that we are in earnest." Her ticket, "by the very process of the election, [would] create an organization to resist with force the free negro policy of the Black Republican President." Win or lose, the South would know where she stood. If Douglas were proved wrong and the Republicans did represent a clear majority of Northerners, "Our Southern ticket would then become the rallying cry for a movement which would leave the Abolitionists the simple duty of ruling only over the Northern States, because our people would be united in the common object of resistance."

The radicals were concerned less with plotting to break up the Union than with creating a set of conditions that would force a resolution of the question of the rights and security of slavery within or without the Union. Their mood of belligerent righteousness was founded on their unalterable determination, as Singleton put it, to "have an expansion of slave territory in this Union if you will allow it, or outside of the Union, if they must." They sought followers on the explicit issue of slavery's morality. Arguing that only a sectionalized South could stop the aggressions of a sectionalized North, and willing to accept party defeat before party demoralization, the radicals predisposed Southerners to interpret the election of 1860 as a challenge not to be ignored. "If the South fails [in the election], and does not redeem herself, she loses every thing—equality—security—liberty—life itself," warned the Charleston *Mercury*. The stakes could not have been higher. If the Republicans triumphed, the radicals insisted, secession would have to be the price of the South's salvation.

The crisis atmosphere produced in the South by Lincoln's election was a response to a particular image of the Republicans projected by the radicals' ideology. They were depicted as an implacable foe with whom compromise was impossible. Never certain whether the Republicans were madmen or just greedy, the radicals condemned them as both. Their party was "organized fanaticism led by organized venality," said Congressman L. M. Keitt of South Carolina in a public letter. When pushed to explain Republican successes, however, the radicals usually blamed "fanaticism." In a letter to Hammond in late October, Keitt wrote that no other factor could account for the Republican victories in New England, Pennsylvania, and the Midwest. All these areas had different and often opposing interests, and they shared close economic ties with the South; yet, they were united against slavery. "Must not the fanaticism be strong, which breaks through habit, party, discipline, and material interests? The Republican party may die, but its principles will survive. If Lincoln is elected I can see no refuge but disunion." Rooted in the conviction that slavery was a sin and should be restricted, the ideas, principles, and politics of the party, the radicals charged, were inherently hostile to the Constitution and the rights of the South. If the Republicans were right, what was there to discuss? "If slavery be a crime against God, and against humanity, if it be a curse to society, if it contain the fruitful seeds of irremediable woes," then, asserted Congressman J. L. M. Curry of Alabama, "it is as idle to talk of moderation and non-interference with the rights of the South, as it would be to attempt to propel a skiff up the surging cataract of Niagara."

In the racicals' critique, slavery could not survive a Republican administration. The Republicans allegedly would ignore, if not actually encourage, John Brown–type raids into the South. Comparing the Texas outrages to Santo Domingo, the *East Floridian* warned that the frequency of these plots, while Southerners were "*still* equals in the confederacy, foreshadows the condition of affairs which may be anticipated, when the reins of government are entrusted to the hands of their bitter enemies." The radicals also emphasized the indirect means by which a Republican government could undermine the institution. Slave property was said to be already insecure in the Upper South because of the ease with which the slaves could escape into the free states. Under the Republicans, the number of fugitives would so increase that the owners would be forced to sell off their remaining slaves to the Lower South. With federal offices, contracts, and money at their disposal, the Republicans would build up an antislavery party within the South. All the latent enemies of slavery—immigrants, the poor, and nonslaveholders—as well as "men of easy virtue, who will be seduced by Federal favor into the embrace of Republicanism," would have a vehicle for their resentment and a weapon with which to destroy slavery. The post offices would be opened to abolitionist literature, and even military officers might become subversives. The Border states were most susceptible to this threat. As one worried Democratic politician from Clarksburg, Virginia, put it in February, 1860: "We have some trouble to keep a proper sentiment on the slavery question." The Richmond *Enquirer* asserted that, by taking a "gradual and insidious approach, under the fostering hand of federal power, Abolitionism will grow up in every border Southern State, converting them into free States, then into 'cities of refuge' for runaway negroes from the gulf States." Within four years of the Republicans' gaining complete control of the government, Toombs predicted, a free-labor party would exist throughout the entire South. The radicals cautioned that, if the Republicans decided to enact a plan of gradual emancipation after having established a political base in the South, it would be too late for resistance. "And wouldn't posterity, divided, and distracted have to submit?" worried Keitt. "Patronage, power, divisions at home would do the work."

To forestall any possible attraction to an antislavery party, the

radicals intensified their efforts to equate Republican doctrine
with black equality. In his letter of resignation from the Senate,
Clement C. Clay of Alabama served notice on the nonslaveholders that the purpose of the Republicans was "to make the
negro [the white Southerner's] equal in political and social privileges—going to the polls, the witness stand, the jury box, the
representative hall, as the peer of the white man, and claiming
his daughter in marriage, as is now done according to law in
Massachusetts." This insistence on the Republican threat to racial
order was basic to the secessionist ideology. Southerners interpreted the Constitution as a document formulated by the white
race solely for the benefit of the white race. One of the chief blessings it was intended to secure was the protection of black slave
property. White unity, stressed the secessionists, had been broken
by the Republicans, "whose misplaced sympathies for the negro,
and lust for political domination, have made them unmindful of
their obligations to their partners of the white race." To vindicate the pervading theme of the Constitution—the essential difference between the races and the consequent subjection of the
blacks—the South had to secede.

Secession was touted as being in the best interests of the nonslaveholders, in that it would save them from the degradation of
a forced racial and class equality with the blacks. The secessionists predicted that, after the Republicans destroyed slavery, the
wealthy would either leave the South or invest their remaining
capital in land, thereby monopolizing all the acreage worth cultivating. Labor would be plentiful and cheap, consisting of the
blacks, who would be forced by Northern prejudices to remain
in the South, and the poor whites, who would lack funds to leave.
Wages and sharecropping arrangements would not rise above the
subsistence level, since they would be determined by black laborers inured by slavery to working hard with only food, clothing,
and shelter as compensation. The majority of whites would be
landless tenants living under the specter of amalgamation, at best,
or a racial war of extermination, at worst. Therefore, support
secession now, the radicals urged nonslaveholders, or resign yourselves to a future in which you will not escape exchanging places
with the black man.

Even if the Republicans in power proved passive, the radicals preached that the demise of slavery could not be averted. They reminded Southern whites of their terrible vulnerability to the free-soil doctrine of encirclement and confinement and egged them on by exploiting their sense of helplessness in the face of impending ruin. Remaining within a Republican-controlled Union would be inviting racial suicide. Keitt told the Republicans:

> You will admit no more slave States, that you may curb the power of the South; and you would confine slavery within its present area, that it may perish through suffocation. You would build a wall of fire around the South, and wait for the time when the increase of population will press upon the means of subsistence; when competition will pauperize labor, and society will shudder from famine into the embrace of servile war.

In contrast to the debasement of submitting to Republican rule, the radicals offered the peace and prosperity of secession. Contradicting their own characterization of the enemy as unreasoning zealots, the radicals contended that the North would not attempt to coerce the South back into the Union, since the Yankees had no economic interests that would be served by war. England would be a staunch friend of an independent South, for she would not risk losing the primary source of her raw cotton supply. Cotton was king, and the economy of England, as that of the North, could not survive without the staple. If cotton were held back, predicted one South Carolinian, "not all the ruin which relentless war has ever brought upon a stricken people, will rival the desolation which that single event will spread through the great manufacturing and commercial States of Europe and America." Were the North foolish enough to fight, her whole paper system of credit would collapse. Congressman William Boyce of South Carolina declared that the "first gun fired in civil war will cost them five hundred million dollars, and strikes . . . will become epidemic." As the financial crisis deepened and Northern capitalists heard "the curses of their unemployed mob, demanding bread or blood . . . ," they would come to their senses and sue for peace.

The radicals had consistently maintained that the Northern

economy lived parasitically off the South. The greater prosperity
of the North was not a tribute to its free labor or a condemnation
of slavery; it was solely a result of the unfair fiscal and economic
policies of the federal government, which diverted wealth from its
natural channels and enriched the North at the expense of the
South. After all, reasoned the radicals, Southern planters produced
the agricultural staples that were the mainstay of American exports and the basis on which Americans received foreign exchange
to pay for their imports. Yet, little of this wealth remained in the
South, and her material growth increasingly lagged behind that
of the North. The only sensible explanation, wrote "Disunion Per
Se" in the Charleston *Mercury*, was "that 'the blight' which it
has been contended . . . rests upon the Southern States, is not
'the blight of slavery,' but the blight of a Union in which we are
cheated and swindled out of the legitimate fruits of our own
industry. . . ."

Back in 1850, Muscoe Garnett, a Virginia States'-Rights Democrat, published a popular pamphlet in which he concluded that
the South paid seven ninths of the federal taxes and received but
two ninths of federal disbursements. The figures were juggled
anew in 1860, until one writer, George Gardner of Georgia, exclaimed that the "advantages of secession [from] a pecuniary
point of view, are almost incalculable." He cited the same economic villains as had Garnett: the federal tariff, which constrained Southerners, an agricultural people, to pay artificially high
prices for manufactured items, whether imported from abroad or
purchased from protected Northern industries; the navigation
laws and federally mandated domestic monopoly of the coastal
and indirect trade by American vessels, which deprived the non-
shipping South of the opportunity to enjoy freight rates lowered
by foreign competition; and the excess of public expenditures in
the North over the South. Gardner concluded that the South
would save herself $75–$100 million annually by secession.

Once freed from her colonial dependency, the South could
market her cotton on her own terms and import goods directly
from Europe. Cotton earnings would remain within the South to
finance a burgeoning economy. Nascent industries could be protected by a revenue tariff. If, however, the free-trade faction of

County bar associations pledged not to enforce the collection of debts due a Northern firm. Southern mobs turned on Yankee salesmen. A correspondent from Granville County, North Carolina, reported to the Norfolk *Argus* in November that "wonderful to relate I have not seen or heard of a Northern drummer [i.e., traveling salesman], but one, since I came into the State, and he was collecting and closing up his business—and was run off from Franklinton yesterday morning—with the promise of tar and feathers if found there in the evening."

STALEMATE IN THE BORDER SOUTH

The conservatives had a sensible, rational reply to most of the radicals' doctrines. They treated the theme of peaceful separation with contempt. No one could accurately gauge the potential power of the free states, and the condition of the regular army was pitiful, with many Southern officers resigning, but the Whigs had little doubt that the North would fight. Cotton was certainly crucial to the outside world, the conservatives admitted, but the South eventually had to sell her cotton, and England knew it. The British would be hurt by a disruption in the cotton flow, but they would suffer through it rather than lose their profitable and expanding trade with New York, one of their best markets. New York would not permit any restrictions on her trade as a result of a Southern free-trade policy and would go to war to protect her interests. She would have the backing of the Western agrarians. Even if the prime markets of these farmers had been in the South, rather than in the East, they still would never consent to having the lower Mississippi Valley controlled by a foreign power.

Secession would expose the South to all the uncertainties and sacrifices of war. Her prosperity would be ruined, and every right ever claimed in her contests with the North would be surrendered. Absolutely nothing could be gained. "Are we to brave at once the derision and contempt of the world for destroying this government upon such frivolous pretexts?" wondered D. G. Cotting, a Georgia unionist. "Are we to . . . undergo the horrors of civil & servile war—to impoverish & demoralize by the event the thousands of happy and quiet families in Georgia, already dis-

tressed & panic stricken, by the apprehension of it happening?"
The fighting would be remorseless and would result in "revolu-
tion, anarchy, and desolation," prophesied the Macon (Georgia)
Journal & Messenger.

In contrast to the Democrats, who viewed government as a
process for releasing individual energy, the Whigs saw it as a device for controlling this energy for the sake of the common good.
The balance between anarchy and stability was a fragile one,
especially in a democratic society, and would be destroyed, perhaps forever, in a civil war. "Revolutions are much easier started
than controlled," stressed Alexander Stephens in a public letter,
"and the men that begin them, even for the best purposes and
objects, seldom end them." The masses would be unleashed. "Human passions are like the winds; when aroused, they sweep everything before them in their fury." Of all peoples Southerners
especially should prize order, reasoned the conservatives. As
slaveholders, their very lives depend upon tight security and the
maintainance of a respect for authority. The laws and military
protection of the Union provided a form of order that should be
cherished, not destroyed.

It was held that slavery could not survive disunion. "Pinckney"
noted, in the Augusta (Georgia) *Constitutionalist*, that, for all
the antislavery sentiment in the North, a fugitive was truly free
only when he reached Canada and thus escaped federal jurisdiction. Secede, he told his fellow Southerners, and you in effect
make Canada border on the Ohio. The vastly greater insecurity of
slave property along the border would cause a gradual recession
of slavery until it was either completely extinguished or cramped
into a thin band along the Gulf Coast, where the weather was too
hot for whites to work. Others predicted that the slaves would
be freed by the advancing Northern armies. "We could not by
any earthly power maintain them," wrote one Kentuckian to
Stephens.

Conservatives were also dismayed by the South's lack of economic progress, but they attributed it to the absence of agricultural and industrial diversification. Who were the real
friends of the South, they asked, those who prattled about Southern rights and preached disunion but did nothing to build up the

Southern economy; or those who would create a truly independent, powerful, and flourishing South within the Union by patronizing home industry and a more balanced agriculture? Had the latter course been heeded, assured the Augusta *Constitutionalist*, the South would have been strong enough to win all her rights without resorting to threats of disunion. The New Orleans *Commercial Bulletin* asserted that the Whig policy would have attracted skilled labor, "adding to our State revenues, and making us independent, to a great extent, of the North for many of those articles which we must have, and which we can make just as well as they can, thereby keeping our capital at home for investment and reinvestment, and consequent perpetual augmentation."

The conservatives showed that Northern tariffs and bounties did not always work to the disadvantage of the South. These measures obviously favored American over foreign industries, but eventually they fostered competition, and some U.S. goods, such as homespuns and calicoes, were cheaper in 1860 than comparable British goods ever could have been. Sectional politics did not explain New York's middle-man role in cotton shipments. That was determined by the world balance of trade, capital flows, and marketing facilities.

Since the radicals' diagnosis of Southern ills was wrong, so was their remedy. Free trade, far from being a panacea, would only compound problems. The South had no ships; nor did she have the capital and material to build any. If she spurned Yankee carriers, therefore, she would be completely dependent on the price-fixing policies of European shippers. It was easy enough for South Carolina to talk about free trade, but the Upper South, where most of the industry was located, would demand some sort of protection. If the rash act of striking for independence did not impoverish the South through huge military expenditures, stressed the conservatives, it nevertheless would weaken the economy by increasing the expenses of government and adding the costs of what formerly had been free trade relations with the North.

No one dared suggest that the Republicans did not present a grave menace to slavery, but conservatives were convinced that the South was overreacting to Lincoln's triumph. What was needed, they said, was time, moderation, and the strength and resolve that could come only through unity. A Southern convention should meet to hammer out an ultimatum based on common grievances. The conservatives recommended that, in selecting delegates, the party leaders be discarded, since their partisanship and agitation had brought on the crisis. They could hardly be expected to be fair and competent now. Cool-headed, wise, and discreet men should be chosen, unconnected with politics, if possible. The minimum demands of the convention should include recognition of the perfect equality of slavery within the territories and repeal of all the personal liberty laws (statutes in some of the Northern states that absolved citizens from failing to comply with the Fugitive Slave Act).

Some conservatives demanded that the North should redress these grievances before March 4, the date of Lincoln's inauguration; but others, noting that the Republicans did not have a majority in Congress or on the Supreme Court, would permit Lincoln to assume office. These men, in particular, scoffed at the alarm over a Southern Republican party. The poor whites would be loath to join a party pledged to destroy the institution that gave them their sole claim to pride and independence. Furthermore, how many Southerners would be brave enough to declare themselves Republicans, and how many Northerners would be foolhardy enough to fill a federal office under Lincoln in the South? "If it is death for a traveler to express doubts of the righteousness of slavery," reasoned one paper, "what would the maddened people do when a friend of an Abolition President should undertake to sway the sceptre of Federal power on southern soil?"

Denied entry to the South and checkmated in Washington by a united South and her allies, the Republicans would be powerless to damage slavery seriously in a period of just four years. The South could block all antislavery legislation and, by threatening to "lock the wheels of government," could penalize with the loss of congressional representation all recalcitrant states that refused to enforce the Fugitive Slave Act. The South, finding herself in no immediate danger and with the option of secession open at any time, could afford to be patient. "But with concert of action at the South, the victory of Southern Rights is already ours," reassured the Milledgeville (Georgia) *Southern Recorder* in late November. "No man of sense will deny it."

The advice of the conservatives was heeded only in the Upper South, and then only until the firing on Fort Sumter. Conservatives were calling for a holding action, and this temporizing meshed perfectly with the mood of a Border state such as Virginia, torn between her increasing ties to Northern markets and a free economy, on the one hand, and her commitment to slavery as a way of life demanding undivided allegiance, on the other. During the winter of 1860–61, Virginians clung to the hope that somehow a centrist position could be staked out within the Union.

Initially, Virginians rejected secession more decisively than they had Breckinridge. The Bell and Douglas press had branded the Breckinridge leaders as disunionists, whose real aim was the creation of a Southern confederacy in order to reopen the African slave trade and reduce slave prices. This had to be their goal, the anti-Breckinridge opposition contended; otherwise, the rhetoric of the Breckinridge campaign, which asserted simultaneously that the South was suffering from a labor shortage and yet was in dire need of expansion, appeared to be self-contradictory. As D. H. Hoge, a Douglas elector, explained: More slave territory "in the present condition of things, would increase the demand [for slaves], raise the price, and thus make it more difficult for [the cotton states] to get a supply." This greed for cheaper slave labor with which to cultivate cotton lands could be satisfied only outside the Union. Secession, followed by African imports and insecure slave property all along the South's northern rim, would ruin the economy of Virginia. The Whigs estimated that slave prices would drop at least 50 per cent. Since Virginia had been selling an average of 10,000 slaves a year to the Lower South at $600 apiece, she stood to lose about $3,000,000 annually in slave sales. Judge R. H. Field, a Whig from Culpeper County, pointed out that the price of land would fall in proportion to the depression in slave values, "and all persons who are much in debt, will be broken up entirely and ruined." White labor and those who relied on the profits of hiring out their slaves would be impoverished. Who would employ laborers at the present daily wage of $.75 to

$1.50, asked Hoge, if blacks could be bought for $150 or hired for a year at $30? Laborers are now the friend of slavery, he added, "but, if reduced, as by this system they would be, to beggary, and starvation, is there not reason to fear that they would turn upon the slave institution and sweep it from the face of the earth? And who could blame them?"

A Southern confederacy, conceived and controlled by the cotton states, had serious disadvantages for the Upper South. Assuming that the prime goals of this confederacy would be cheap slaves, free trade, and expansion, Virginia unionists stressed that each of these measures clashed with the economic interests of the Border region. "Free trade and direct taxation are to incipient manufactories like those of Virginia, what joint worm is to the wheat crop, or Asiatic Cholera to the feeblest of the human race." The ability of this republic to defend itself and win recognition would be contingent on her cotton diplomacy. She would expand both to protect her cotton monopoly and to satiate the ambitions of the young slaveholders in the Deep South. Since cotton production—the source of her wealth and power—would be limited only by the availability and price of slave labor, unionists concluded that this government naturally would "insist upon having negro labor cheap, either from Africa by direct importation, or from the border slave States, at prices but little, if at all, greater than those paid for the native African." The expansion that would so damage her economy could probably be achieved only through war, argued the conservatives, and here Virginia would also have to sacrifice men and arms. An anonymous "Unionist," writing in the Alexandria *Gazette*, pleaded that Virginia really had no intelligent choice. Either she could join a cotton confederacy whose expansion would make her "but a mere insignificant border member," or she could defend the Union "consecrated in her affections as eminently the work of her illustrious sons, at once a monument of her glory, and a pledge of her future prosperity."

The Upper South hung back and voted down secession in their legislatures or in specially called conventions. Secessionism was largely limited to the Breckinridge planting districts. Led by Virginia, the Border states tried to act as mediators, notably in the abortive Peace Conference that met in Washington in Febru-

ary of 1861. Radicals doggedly attempted to shake the region out
of its uneasy limbo. Predicting a splendid future for Virginia in a
Southern republic, they invited her to become the South's Ruhr
Valley, the industrial center that would serve the new nation. Virginia, they promised, would inherit the Southern markets previously dominated by New England, and Norfolk would emerge as
a great commercial port rivaling New York. Glossing over the hard
facts—that the South as a whole simply did not have the home
markets to sustain any significant industrialization, and that her
industries could grow only behind tariff protection, which the
cotton states would be reluctant to grant—the Virginia radicals
also ignored the implications of their own argument. If the Upper
South ever succeeded in becoming a reasonable economic fac-
simile of New England, then the slave states were laying the foundations for the same bitter differences in political economies that
they argued had been instrumental in destroying the harmony
and mutual cooperation of the original Union.

The radicals were more forceful and effective in stressing racial
themes. In a widely distributed public letter, Senator Hunter told
Virginians that, if they remained with the free states, "their slave
population would indeed be 'penned in' and 'localized' within
their own borders." The Lower South would not want Virginia's
slaves for two reasons, he warned: They would aim to maintain
slavery in Virginia for as long as possible in order to have a political ally in the North and to create a buffer zone for their own
fugitive slaves. Eventually, however, emancipation would certainly follow. As the slave surplus built up, wages would fall and
white labor would leave. After the blacks became the dominant
element of the population by their sheer density, Virginia and the
other Border states would lose what little political influence they
had exerted in the Northern confederacy and be helpless to prevent abolition.

None of these dangers, of course, would exist in a Southern confederacy. Virginia could find an outlet for her excess slaves among
her sister states or in whatever territory might be acquired. In
addition, white labor would benefit immeasurably, since, according to Hunter, any oversupply in the slave market would be
smoothly eased by transferring the blacks to an area where their

labor would be more productive. The "labor market which he leaves is thus gradually relieved from the pressure, and the white man remains in the land of his birth, to enjoy the profits of remunerating operations."

As Lincoln's election came and passed, the pressure on the Upper South to commit herself irrevocably grew more intense. The threats from the cotton states to close off the domestic slave trade were translated into an article of the provisional constitution of the Confederacy that gave the Southern Congress discretionary power to prohibit the trade with those slaveholding states that remained in the Union. Furious on first hearing of this intimidation back in December, the Lynchburg *Virginian* attacked the Deep South for its spiteful shortsightedness. Penning up their slaves would only precipitate emancipation "in the course of a few years" and convert Virginians into the resentful enemies of the slaveholders farther south, who would "assign us the post of danger, making a rampart of Virginia, to enable them to 'preserve their domestic peace.'" On the other hand, Virginia had no assurance that the North would permit her to engage in the slave trade with a Southern republic. Slave trafficking with a foreign country was illegal, and any trade with the ex-states presumably would come under the same ban that applied to Brazil and Cuba. The entire question would be academic if the free states in the truncated Union attained a three-fourths majority and decided to amend the Constitution and free the slaves.

Virginians seemed damned whichever way they turned. Their allegiance was an individual matter and often rested on their reading of the role of blacks in Virginia's future. William C. Rives, Jr., son of a prominent Whig planter and politician, inherited his father's staunch unionism. Worried that Virginia might be too white for a slave confederacy but too black for a Northern one, he toyed with his father's idea that a central confederacy, consisting of the Border region plus the more moderate states from both sections, might yet save the Union. This proposal never progressed beyond the talking stage, but it appealed to young Rives as an alternative to committing his state permanently to slavery. His father had been gradually phasing out slave labor in his agricultural operations, and this gave William firsthand confirmation

of his belief that slavery was an unprofitable and unwanted institution in the Upper South that should be slowly dismantled. "We
should never forget in Virginia that our concern with slavery is
a temporary one," he told his father in mid-December. "Our
permanent interests are identical with those of Maryland &
Pennsylvania." He accepted the racial consequences of emancipation with equanimity, assuming that some place would be found
for the freed slaves.

His brother Francis, on the other hand, was hardly so sanguine.
"You say that no interests in Virginia could be permanently identified with those of Slavery," he wrote to William. "If you accept
my amendment & insert 'negrodom' in the place of Slavery I
agree with you." Francis, who was then living in New York City,
asked William how he would like it if the North had the same
ratio of blacks as Virginia, and if "every third house in Beacon
Street & in the Fifth Avenue, was inhabited by negroes! The
thought is too disgusting to any sane caucasian to pursue." To
avoid this degradation, Virginia had to side with the cotton
states. Contending, as had Hunter, that Virginia would be inun-
dated by blacks if she failed to secede, and that these blacks
would be banned from entering the North, Francis foresaw the
whites' being "driven either to hybridization on terms of equality,
or flight from disgusting swarms of odorous, leprous decaying
black lazzaroni." Only the anticipation of transforming Virginia
into a white society by sending her slaves into the territories about
to be acquired by a Southern republic could quiet his fears of
racial disaster.

The stalemate represented by the conflicting views of the Rives
brothers was finally broken by the mass indignation over the
fighting at Sumter and Lincoln's call for troops to quell the
rebellion. No such indecision had occurred in the Lower South.
There, the radicals had successfully exploited the simple fact
of Lincoln's election by portraying it as the overriding issue
that could not be ignored—as a challenge to Southern civilization
that had to be met by immediate secession. In both sections, the
conservatives had been forced to react to external events beyond
their control, except that, in the Deep South, this weakness was
already crucial by the late fall of 1860.

Secession Accomplished

Tutored by their failure in 1850, the radicals were prepared with a positive, aggressive strategy in 1860. They knew, as James Seddon of Virginia expressed it in 1859, that, if a Republican were elected President, "the first impression of indignation and dismay at the South must be seized. A few and the boldest either of private men or of the States must at once *strike* and then there will be no chance but for the others to rally and unite." Secession was to be accomplished as soon as possible through individual state action not contingent upon the decision of any other state. Convinced that a better chance for secession would never present itself, and that acceding to Lincoln's inauguration would establish the fatal precedent of submitting to Republican rule and forever blunt the spirit of resistance, the radicals attacked all efforts at delay. Plans to unite the South before secession were denounced as too slow and cumbersome and as divisive schemes that would revive unionism. No prior cooperation was essential, insisted Rhett's Charleston *Mercury*; only the expectation that, "by the action of one or more States, there shall be the *reasonable probability* that a Southern Confederacy will be formed."

Precedent was on the side of the secessionists. The cooperative approach, haltingly tried in 1850 and again after John Brown's raid, had misfired, leaving frustration and humiliation in its wake. The last straw for many had been the South's inability so much as to organize a convention to protest the butchery of Brown's men and to demand additional safeguards from the North. Christopher Memminger of Charleston, a moderate by the standards of his state, had been commissioned by the South Carolina legislature in late December, 1859, to travel to Richmond and recommend the calling of such a convention to the Virginia legislature. Leery of reopening old wounds and fearful of any plan that smacked of disunion, Virginia rejected the Carolina proposal. Writing from Richmond, Memminger confessed to William Porcher Miles that his lingering hopes for cooperative resistance had been shattered. "It seems to me that we should finally be brought to the point of making the issue alone and taking our chance for the other States to join us, whenever a Black Republican has the rule over us." Miles needed little convincing, and, in August, he told Hammond: "I am sick and disgusted with all the bluster and threats, and manifestoes and 'Resolutions.' . . . Let us act if we mean to act without talking. Let it be 'a word and a blow'—but the blow first."

By November, the *Floridian & Journal* could reason with some plausibility that secession was really the last conservative remedy left to the South, since repeated *"threats made in the absence of Secession"* had merely exposed Southern weaknesses and emboldened the North to worse aggressions. A reconstructed Union with new constitutional guarantees for Southern protection was still possible, the paper continued, but only if the South bargained outside the old Union. She had cried wolf too often to be heeded otherwise. When Virginia tried to implement the convention policy, the Charleston *Mercury* scornfully reminded her that this was the same Carolina approach she had repudiated back in January. "It was hooted down, and rejected as a disunion measure. . . . The times have now passed beyond it. Virginia may now call, but the South will not answer." According to the *Mercury*, the cotton states finally realized that they could not entrust the Upper South to protect slavery. With the latter, slavery was a matter of convenience, not of necessity. "They may possibly live and thrive without slavery; and with them slavery, or its abolishment, is a question of mere expediency, as a choice of different instrumentalities of prosperity. To us the institution is vital and indispensable. We must maintain ourselves in this struggle or be utterly destroyed."

From the onset of their campaign for secession in November, the radicals enjoyed two immense advantages that the moderates and conservatives were powerless to overcome. In the Lower South, the secessionists controlled nearly all of the governorships and state legislatures. They were able not only to force the calling of state conventions to consider the question of secession but to set the dates well in advance of Lincoln's inauguration. As military commanders, the governors could order the state militia and volunteer companies to seize federal forts and arsenals. Radical domination also extended into the ranks of the political machinery, where the editors and county leaders of the victorious

Breckinridge party stumped for secession. Additional machinery
for disseminating propaganda and reinforcing the crisis atmosphere was furnished by the "1860 Association," a South Carolina
group that published and circulated secessionist pamphlets, and
by paramilitary companies, such as the Minute Men and the more
rabid vigilance committees. Breckinridge politicians assumed the
leadership of all these groups.

With this organizational strength, the radicals could mobilize
mass unrest and apprehension in the Deep South behind their
program of immediate secession. They goaded Southerners into
action by first ridiculing them for their humiliating impotency
and then appealing to their pride. "None but the fawning spaniel
loves the rod that smites him or the foot that kicks him," scoffed
Fitzhugh. After sanctifying slavery as "this 'great gift of God,'" an
anonymous writer in the Charleston *Mercury* asked Southerners
whether they would permit it to be destroyed by giving in to
abolitionist rule. "You cannot, for your safety forbids it—you dare
not, for your manhood forbids it—you *dare* not, for your *honor*
forbids it!" The cult of Southern womanhood, that asexual by-
product of the Puritan conscience shamed by the loose sexual
relations between white men and black slave women, was invoked. Enshrined as a paragon of virtue and purity, the innocent
and defenseless women reminded their male protectors that the
highest ideals of Southern civilization could be debased at any
moment by the libidinous blacks. "Should the dark hour come, *we*
must be the chief sufferers," noted a "Southern-Rights Lady."
"Enemies in our midst, abolition fiends inciting them to crimes the
most appalling, our little ones torn from our arms, perhaps tor-
tured to death before our eyes, and *we* degraded beneath the
level of brutes."

Frightened whites responded to the secessionists' call for decisive action. The pace of attacking social outsiders and alleged
Southern enemies accelerated. The mayors of several cities, after
publicly denouncing roving bands of vigilantes, offered rewards
for the arrest and conviction of those who led lynch mobs. The
urban vigilance committees were fully organized by late November, and the papers carried warnings for all persons to be careful
of their language. In New Orleans, Northern businessmen were

ordered to leave for making pro-Lincoln statements, and local residents were threatened for subscribing to Northern newspapers. George Forester, a German-American editor in the city, fled to St. Louis as soon as he heard that some old antislavery letters of his had been translated into English for a group calling itself the "Southerners of the Blue Cockade." According to Forester, the "Southerners" employed "a cloud of spies in every district of the town, and a whole army of those bloodthirsty and reckless rowdies and thugs, ready to do anything at a moment's notice." A drunk vagrant, arrested for sleeping in a public park, was detained in chains for several days in the New Orleans jail before being commanded to leave the city. He had angered the police by wearing a Lincoln campaign button from Missouri and by mockingly calling himself a Black Republican.

Terror tactics were also used in rural districts. The Barnwell correspondent of the Charleston *Mercury* commended the vigilance committee from Midway precinct for doing a fine job. "Not a suspicious person, or event, escapes their notice, and the offender is brought up with a short turn, and is made to feel that eyes are upon him which he cannot elude, and that hands are ready to be laid upon him at any hour of the day or night." The young men on the Bamberg committee, the correspondent added, would as soon shoot an abolitionist as a squirrel, "though there will be this difference between [the] game—that they can eat the latter themselves, but must turn over the former to buzzards." Accounts of Northerners' being whipped or tarred and feathered were commonplace.

A letter written by a Southern businessman, Samuel J. Halle, in early December from Friar's Point, Mississippi, detailed one of the more grisly episodes of community vengeance. Halle described a near-pogrom directed against Northern residents of the village after a spectacular fire on the evening of December 10. The blaze, which involved two cotton gins and the slave quarters, was the fifteenth that had damaged cotton gins in the county within the previous six weeks. A week earlier, the enraged citizenry had already found one scapegoat, an abolitionist, who was hung, "barrelled up and rolled into the river at this point." Suspecting that the most recent gin fires had been set by the abolitionist's cohorts to avenge his death, the vigilance committee immediately fell upon three Northern carpenters "and hung them to the first tree, and afterwards cut them down and burned them." The next morning, the remaining Northerners were seized and, before they were shipped up the river on a steamer, "some of them were branded with the letters G.B. (gin burners)." The testimony of a black (which, by Southern law, would normally not have been admissible in court against a white man) had implicated those who were hung. "He said they had told him all the negroes were to be free next March, when Lincoln becomes President, and that there will be a general rising of the negroes then." In closing his letter, Halle noted that the "vigilance committee have sworn to hang every Northern man who comes here from this time until the 4th of March, and all such had better be in h—l than Friar's Point."

A less destructive outlet for Southern frustrations than this blind rage was unbounded enthusiasm over the prospects of secession. Whole communities, men and women, banded together in spirited and reckless defiance of the Northern enemy. Young men were urged to join corps of Minute Men, since "Our homes are being invaded. Our parents, whose heads are blooming for the grave, are being foully insulted, and their proud honor ranked among the lowest, vilest possessions on earth. The virtue of our beloved sisters is being slandered." While the men marched, hunted down abolitionists, and patrolled the black districts, the women contributed by organizing fairs to raise funds for arms and banners. No military parade was complete without the presentation to the commanding officer of a resplendent flag sewn by the local women.

Joyous celebration erupted as secession approached. When news of the passage of the Florida convention bill reached Jacksonville, the citizenry flocked to a mass meeting, heard speeches, and cheered a 15-gun salute, one for each slave state, plus an extra volley for Florida. Typical of the carnival atmosphere that greeted South Carolina's secession was the reaction in the cotton town of Eufaula, Alabama. As soon as the telegraph reports came in, early in the afternoon of December 20, the town's cannons were fired. At sunset, a 100-gun salute was accompanied by the ringing

of all the town's bells. When dusk settled, the town was illumi-
nated by candles placed in windows, by bonfires, and by torches
carried in a mass procession which met the county's volunteer
companies at the town hall. Everyone marched to the mayor's
home, to be regaled by the oratory of ex-Congressman Eli S.
Shorter. "At the conclusion of his speech the ladies on the porch
sung the Southern Marseillaise in splendid style, the chorus was
joined in by hundreds, and at the conclusion of each verse, shout
after shout went up for 'Southern Independence in a Southern
Confederacy.'"

Many Southerners who might have been attracted to a more
moderate position were awed and often frightened by this dis-
play of frantic enthusiasm. In early November, Hammond, whose
radicalism had mellowed considerably during the 1850's while
he was a Senator, told his close friend, novelist William Gilmore
Simms, that the "Reign of Terror" had arrived. "The wild mob
headed by the Mercury seems to have taken the bit in their teeth
& defied the rein." After noting that he had heard on "good authority" that the Minute Men of Columbia had threatened to
hang an upcountry cooperationist if he were elected to the state
convention, Hammond confessed: "I should be afraid to go to
Columbia, though I am as much in favor of dissolving the Union
as any one. I advise you not to go there." A few days later, Hammond exclaimed: "People are wild. The scenes of the French
Revolution are being enacted already. Law & Constitution are
equally & utterly disregarded." Despite the terrorist excesses of the
secessionists, Hammond's alarm was clearly exaggerated; it was
nevertheless echoed by others until it became a litany. Cowed
and divided, conservatives remained in the background for their
own safety and rarely mustered a fraction of their strength. In
contrast to their enforced lethargy was the fierce energy of the
radicals. "I have never, in all my public life, met with so much
recklessness, so much violence and tyranny, as I have here this
winter among the disunionists," reported a North Carolina unionist
to William C. Rives in mid-January.

Unconditional unionism was out of the question in the cotton
states, and any attempt to force it, admitted one conservative,
"would have done no good, but on the other hand would have

created a strife among the people that all would deprecate."
The only viable alternative open to unionists was a cooperationist
or conditional unionist position tied in with the demand that any
prosecessionist decision of the state conventions be referred to
the people for their final judgment. The former course, based on
the premise that in unity there is strength, would have delayed
secession until a given number of states had agreed to withdraw
as a bloc. The latter option of conditional unionism would have
given the North one last chance to redeem her promises to recognize Southern rights. The slave states, gathered in convention,
would present an ultimatum, the rejection of which would signal
the end of the Union.

As weak and vacillating as these positions appeared to many
aroused Southerners, and however convenient a refuge they offered the more timid secessionists, the unionists had no choice if
they were to mount any counterattack against immediate secession. The dilemma facing conservatives was epitomized by a
mass-resistance meeting in Savannah on the night of November
8. A friend of Alexander Stephens informed him that he had
"never before seen such an uprising of the people of all parties."
With the vast crowds, haranguing speakers, and fireworks competing for attention, the rally "was emphatically a *demonstration*
of the popular feeling upon the recent election. There was no
stemming the current, though during the day we succeeded in
modifying its violence & bringing the leaders somewhere in the
neighborhood of reason." The organizers of the meeting had intended to pass immediate-secession resolutions, but the conservatives succeeded in confining these demands to only a declaration
never to submit to Lincoln's election and a call for a state convention to determine the proper means of redress. "The people
are wild and driven to desperation, and the only hope of influ-
encing them is to unite in the movement, modified as it is (for
the resolutions specify no particular line of action), in order that
it may receive the proper direction after the excitement of the
hour shall have passed away." This Savannah type of compromise was the best the conservatives could achieve throughout
much of the Deep South. Their dread of living in anarchy or under the dogmatic rule of the radicals had induced many to join

the secession movement in an effort to mitigate the worst consequences of the inevitable revolution.

The conservatives' plea for time to weigh once again the value of the Union was of small comfort to those Southerners concerned over internal security and weary of the seemingly endless crises over slavery. By harping on the North's determination to destroy slavery and on the growing political power of the free states, the secessionists easily undercut the conservatives' appeal. "It is not the Constitution and the laws of the United States which need amendment, but *the hearts* of the northern people," argued Howell Cobb in a printed circular to the "People of Georgia." "To effect the first would be a hopeless undertaking, whilst the latter is an impossibility."

The initially weak unionist position became hopeless when Congress was unable to agree on any compromise measures. The discussion of even apparently negotiable issues, such as repeal of the personal liberty laws, set off acrimonious debate. Would their repeal, asked Jefferson Davis, "renew good offices, or restrain raids and incendiarism, or prevent schools being founded to prepare missionaries to go into lands where they are to sow the seeds of insurrection, and, wearing the livery of heaven, to serve the Devil by poisoning wells and burning towns?" Congressmen from the Border region grasped at the admission of New Mexico as a slave state as a harmless measure that would restore a semblance of good will between the sections. Slavery did exist in the territory, but holdings were small and confined chiefly to personal servants; few, therefore, expected the institution to thrive or expand. Nevertheless, most Republicans rejected the admission as a violation of the party's faith, and most Southerners denounced it as mere tokenism. C. C. Washburn, a Republican Representative from Wisconsin, correctly noted that the establishment of slavery in New Mexico or any of the other existing territories would not satisfy the South. "The question you will have to meet is, whether you will guarantee slavery in all territory hereafter to be acquired. Southern gentlemen will in a moment yield up everything else that they clamor about, if we will only consent to that."

The specific plan that Washburn had in mind was the Crittenden Compromise, a package of six proposed constitutional amendments presented to the Senate on December 18, 1860. The crucial amendment would have permanently institutionalized the principle of the Missouri Compromise by guaranteeing to the South that slavery would be recognized south of 36°30′ in all present territories, as well as those "hereafter acquired." Southern leaders indicated that this blank check for the future expansion of slavery was the one plan that might possibly forestall secession. Senator Toombs of Georgia announced that he would accept it, along with other satisfactory concessions, "so that the whole continent to the north pole shall be settled upon the one rule, and to the south pole under the other."

Precisely because of such expansionist visions, however, the 36°30′ plan never had a chance of passage. Northerners also assumed that the United States would continue to acquire more territories and that, as Washburn once put it, "annexation [to the Isthmus of Panama] is as certain as the march of time, and cannot be prevented unless you radically change the character of our people." Aware that they were the stronger party, Northerners saw no reason to allow slavery to monopolize so much of the anticipated acquisitions. Senator Milton Latham of California, a Democrat, invoked Manifest Destiny to explain why the people of his state would accept no rein on their progress. After all, "they have been looking eagerly to the acquisition of the State of Sonora, Lower California, in order that we might have complete control, not only of the Gulf of California, but of the entire trade and commerce of the Pacific coast. The adoption of this amendment would forever dissipate any such hopes." Latham was convinced that the Republicans would reject any southern annexation rather than permit slavery to expand. Republican approval of the Crittenden 36°30′ amendment would have been an act of political suicide, a negation of the party's ideological core. Acceptance, exclaimed James Wilson of Indiana, "means the dismemberment of Mexico. It means Cuba. It means Central America. It means an empire of slavery, such as the world never before witnessed." Urged by their constituents not to yield an inch, the Republicans unanimously voted against the Crittenden Compromise. Pointing to this action as the latest example of the

Republicans' bad faith, Southern Democrats likewise renounced the Compromise.

Congress had accomplished nothing. As the Southern Manifesto of December 13 had declared, "The argument is exhausted." The Republicans were defiant and confident and the Southern radicals anxious not to be cheated out of their impending victory by any last-minute bargain. Reporting back to Alexander Stephens from Washington, J. H. Smith described the radicals as "active and vigilant. They anticipate and thwart nearly every plan of conciliation that is mooted. They aggravate instead of soften and ameliorate the alarming symptoms, and let not an opportunity pass to throw obstacles in the way of an adjustment."

As everyone had anticipated, South Carolina took the lead in secession. There was none of the hesitancy of 1850. "This State I think will have to lead. The absence of party spirit enables us to do so," Keitt had told Miles back in early October. Yancey did not command enough respect in Alabama, and Davis might prove to be overcautious in Mississippi, so "we must rely on ourselves in moving off." On October 5, William Gist of South Carolina confidentially informed the other cotton-state governors that he would ask his legislature to call a special convention in the event of Lincoln's election. Since the legislators would be assembled in Columbia in early November for the choosing of Presidential electors, Gist could easily follow through on this initiative. To ensure that the unionists would have virtually no time to organize, the radicals took advantage of the popular enthusiasm generated in Charleston by the resignations of Judge Magrath (a respected conservative) and other federal officials and by the announcement that Governor Brown of Georgia had recommended the immediate calling of a convention in his state. A delegation demanding prompt action reached Columbia on November 10. After hearing their report of a mass rally in Charleston on the previous evening, attended by several prominent Georgians, the legislature decided to advance the dates for the election and assembling of the state convention by a full month over the times in the original bill reported out of the senate. The radicals' victory was complete; by December 20, South Carolina was out of the Union. "When the Ordinance was passed the bells rang, cannon fired, men shouted, women waved their handkerchiefs, the shops were shut up, and almost every body got drunk," recounted one onlooker.

The example of South Carolina was all the incentive needed by the southernmost tier of slave states. By February 1, they had all seceded. In the elections for delegates to the state conventions, the pine barrens and expanding cotton regions, Breckinridge's two strongholds, went solidly secessionist. The yeoman farmers provided the backbone of the opposition. The major defections from the Breckinridge-secessionist camp came from this group, especially in the isolated mountainous districts, where Douglas's candidacy had never taken hold. Since they owned land and had an economic stake in Southern society, the self-respect of these farmers was not so exposed as that of the poorer whites living in the piney woods; hence, they were not quite so susceptible to racist propaganda. These yeomen, with few slaves in their midst, were also not so vulnerable to rumors of slave uprisings as the whites in the black belts.

The Whigs, confused and disheartened, and half-hoping that whatever settlement was reached would be a final one, put up a feeble resistance in the Lower South. As a result more of apathy than of active support for secession, many Whig planting areas and towns were carried by the secessionists. Their tactic of cooperative secession was ridiculed as do-nothing submissiveness and was further undermined by the radicals' disingenuous assertion that it violated the constitutional prohibition against states' entering into treaties with one another. Moreover, the governors, by appointing rabid secessionists as commissioners to visit other state conventions to confer on the relative timing of secession, were able to argue that the only safe and honest cooperative policy was being carried out. Even the moderate demand that the actions of the conventions should be ratified by the people was ignored in every cotton state except Texas. The Whigs had a strong case here, especially since the secession elections had attracted only a very light voter turnout. The time allotted for campaigning had been very short, and in many counties only the secessionists were sufficiently organized to prepare an electoral ticket.

Publicly, the secessionists reasoned that the people had already spoken in the election of delegates, but privately many admitted that the masses could not be trusted. "I do not believe the common people understand it, in fact I know that they do not understand it," confided A. P. Aldrich, a South Carolina legislator, to Hammond: "but whoever waited for the common people when a great move was to be made[?] We must make the move & force them to follow."

All that the Whigs could salvage was a larger representation in the secession conventions than their strength in the Presidential election would have warranted. Confident of victory and eager to present the façade of a united, nonpartisan South, the Breckinridge secessionists invited Whigs to join them on platforms pledged to secession, either immediately or within a reasonable length of time. Flattered and anxious to exercise some influence, many Whigs accepted this offer. Most, however, rejected immediate secession or boycotted an election in which they had no real choice.

After the withdrawal of Texas on February 1, the secession movement appeared to be arrested. The Upper South—specifically, Virginia, North Carolina, Tennessee, and Arkansas—remained in the Union until the spring and the fighting at Sumter. Few men were so relieved by this hiatus in revolutionary activity as President Buchanan. Buchanan, a career politician of limited vision, crushed by the realization that the Presidency was about to become not the glorious monument to his life's work but its humiliating epitaph, wanted nothing more than to leave the White House on March 4 with the nation still at peace. A cautious politician by nature, he was also hamstrung during the secession winter by his lame-duck role. He justified his own indecision and lack of power by the constitutionally comforting theory that, whereas no state had the right to leave the Union, no federal authority existed to force it back in. Such sophistry satisfied very few, but it did provide a legalistic framework within which Buchanan could finish his term without having to recognize the seceded states or plunge the country into bloodshed.

The best that can be said for this evasiveness was that it

helped to buy time during which a restructured Union, built around new constitutional guarantees for the South, might have been fashioned. This was the lingering hope of Whigs in both sections, a false optimism fed by pro-Union rallies in several Northern cities and by the Washington Peace Conference, which met in February. The financial and shipping interests of the Eastern cities wanted a settlement along the lines of the Crittenden Compromise, but they could exercise scant leverage without support from the rural heartland of Republicanism. Although Border-state unionists tended to exaggerate the willingness of the North to compromise, their misreading was minor compared to the fundamental misjudgment of the Republicans. The pause in secession deluded the Republicans into an overestimation of Southern unionist strength. This misconception spawned Seward's policy of "masterly inactivity," a nonaggressive course whereby the incoming administration would sit back passively and allow Southern unionists first to roll back the secessionist tide and then to contribute to a voluntary reconstruction of the Union by convincing the cotton states that they were helplessly isolated. Buchanan's policy of benign neglect had no such catchy title, but it amounted to the same thing.

The radicals also felt that to delay too long in creating a Southern republic might spark a popular groundswell for reunion. On January 14, Miles informed Howell Cobb "that on this latter point [of reconstruction] I have had some nervous anxiety lest after we are all out there may be a disposition to reform the old Confederacy." Far sharper fears were expressed by ex-Congressman J. L. Pugh of Alabama to Miles on January 24: "I am oppressed by the apprehension that we are in great danger from the reconstructionists." If the Republicans ever agreed to the Crittenden plan, Pugh predicted that "the border states will present an unbroken front & my fear is we shall be overwhelmed." Of course, he added, this calamity could be avoided by war. "Now pardon me for suggesting that South Carolina has the power of putting us beyond the reach of reconstruction by taking Fort Sumter at any cost."

Pugh was half-correct. An uneasy peace persisted during the winter, not because the Republicans or secessionists were inclined to compromise, but primarily for lack of an issue that would force a confrontation. Almost by a process of elimination Fort Sumter became this issue. Lincoln's decision to resupply this physical symbol of federal authority was a challenge that the secessionists could not avoid and an opportunity they could not resist. It would be unfair to contend that either side started the war, for, in fact, both sides readily accepted it as the moral equivalent of their ideological commitments.

An End to the Agitation

In retrospect, secession appears as a headlong rush into self-destruction, just as the Whigs had foreseen. Yet, the eagerness of Southerners in the cotton states to embrace secession was not just an emotional binge in which they were heedless of the possible consequences. Although the radical leaders were not so blind or foolish as to have ignored the possibility of military defeat, they constantly minimized the dangers. From their perspective, slavery, the cornerstone of Southern civilization, was already doomed within a Republican-controlled Union, so that the South had nothing to lose by gambling on independence. If a war did result—and most radicals privately conceded that this was probable—the secessionists did not expect the fighting to be either prolonged or socially destructive. Of course, as the Border states pointed out, the radicals in the Lower South could afford these illusions, since, initially at least, their homeland would be spared the brunt of the fighting. At the same time, however, neither section fully anticipated the grim realities of the war. The congressmen who flocked to picnic at First Bull Run with their wives while the battle unfolded beneath them were as disillusioned by the rout of the Union troops as were the Rhetts and Ruffins by the expanding output of the Northern economy, which they had assumed would collapse into class warfare without cotton to sustain it.

The myths of peaceable secession and "Cotton Is King" reassured Southerners that slavery could survive secession; but, in themselves, they were too passive to have energized the secession movement or account for its appeal. Representative Martin Crawford of Georgia, characterized by J. H. Smith as "crazy" and "insane" on the secession issue, had said (in Smith's words) that

> he would prefer to see the whole South from the Delaware to the Rio Grande, one charnel house of destruction, to submitting a single day to Lincoln's administration, upon any terms that any body could imagine, and that, So help him God, if Georgia did, under any sort of circumstances, submit or remain in the Union one day, if he could possibly get enough of ground to stand on, in any land on earth that was not so degraded, he would at once leave the State.

Crawford's rage and anger were typical of secessionist leaders. Regardless of the risks, they were determined to strike for independence. This passionate dedication was the culmination of the South's efforts to cope with an outside world that rejected her values and ideals.

For an individual, the core value of any ideology is a function of how well it idealizes the institutions under which he must live and the type of person those institutions constrain him to be. Thus resentful and frustrated over the North's moralistic attacks on slavery, and ever more isolated in world public opinion, Southern whites were easy prey for an ideology that not only promised an opportunity to manage their own affairs free from outside interference but also provided a positive reinforcement of their maligned value structure. This was the radicals' greatest accomplishment. Slaveholders, generally younger than their moderate and conservative opposition, they could relate more easily to Southern anxieties, since they constantly had to vindicate their ambitions and life-styles in the face of the abolitionist offensive confronting their generation. Hesitantly at first, but with increasing confidence in the late 1850's, they projected for their fellow Southerners a bold image of an independent Southern nation that would become the best of all possible worlds—a perfectly secure slave society that would earn the moral respect of others and would revel in the glories of an imperial destiny. This was racial and class home rule with a vengeance. Far from hastening her destruction, the radicals proclaimed, secession was the South's only chance to assert her self-esteem and to claim the power that ought rightfully to be hers.

On the eve of secession, Southerners yearned for domestic
peace and tranquillity, but they feared the worst. A. B. Longstreet, President of South Carolina College, asked, in "An Appeal
to the South": "Is there any thing on this earth, not to say in this
Union, which could compensate me for one week's alarms of the
tender ones of my household? And yet it has been the undis-
guised aim of the Abolitionists to stir them in every family in
the South, not for a week, or a year, but interminably!" The
prevalent sense of desperate insecurity had been fed by the terrifying rumors spread during the Presidential campaign. Lawrence
Keitt could barely express his sense of horror in a September
letter to Hammond. "See—poison in the wells in Texas and fire for
the Houses in Alabama—Our negroes are being enlisted in politics
—With fire and poison how can we stand it?" Never before, he
exclaimed, had the abolitionists gotten so close to the slaves. "If
northern men get access to our negroes to advise poison and the
torch we must prevent it at every hazard." On November 5, Congressman John Ashmore of South Carolina wrote to Horatio
King, a high-ranking Buchanan Democrat, that the "Treason, insurrection & murder" perpetrated upon innocent Southerners
during the past year had convinced him "for the *first time*" that
the South could not be safe within the Union. Anything was preferable to submission. "The blowing of 100,000 cannon & the
slaughter of an hundred Waterloo's would be music to my ears &
gladness to my sight rather than see S.C. the victim of Lincoln,
Seward." Warning King not to underestimate the Southern resolve, he portrayed a society willing to risk everything.

> Our women & children are ready & eager for the conflict & would
> kick us out of our homes if we basely & tamely yield again. Our
> young girls—Daughters—from 12 to 15 years of age are entreating us
> —their Fathers—to train them in the use of fire arms & daggers. . . .
> We *will arm them,* & if dire necessity drives us to thus expose them,
> we will carry them to the battle field with us. Better for them that
> they encounter the horrors & chances of war, than endure "negro
> equality," & "emancipation" & its logical result "amalgamation."

The radicals told the South that secession would achieve permanent internal security at the same time that it prevented the

dreaded racial apocalypse. A free South, having her own armies and navies, would be able to cow the slaves and resist any outside efforts to free them. As an independent people, Southerners would have complete authority to screen all foreigners who wished to cross her borders. No longer would abolitionists, disguised as friends and fellow citizens, be free to enter the South at will and go among the slaves plotting insurrections. As one Georgian explained to Stephens, we should "make an impassable wall between the North & the South so that negroes could not pass over to the North or an abolitionist come to the South to annoy us any more." The secessionists also predicted that the number of fugitive slaves would drop. For, they contended, the North, desirous of having her trade with the South placed on the level of a most favored nation, would have the good sense to see that runaway slaves were returned promptly or paid for in full.

Even more reassuring was the radicals' assertion that all slavery agitation would cease once free and slave states constituted two distinct, independent nations. This remarkable achievement, noted George Gardner in a published article, would prove secession to be "the only remedy, the only panacea for the evils of Abolitionism." The movement would collapse, because the North would no longer have the power to emancipate the slaves. More important, the will to do so would be gone. Northerners would feel no more moral responsibility for the existence of slavery in a Southern Confederacy than they currently did for its presence in Cuba or Brazil. The slavery question would "be entirely withdrawn from their politics, where, in the hands of designing demagogues, it has heretofore exercised such a potent and controlling influence. Its agitation, therefore, would soon die out for want of the pablum to feed it, and friendly relations would speedily be established between the two Governments."

Once the agitation was stopped, Southerners could again enjoy peace of mind. "Let it be remembered," stressed Longstreet in the *Southern Guardian,* "that disquiet has made its way into our families, and has been increasing for some time past, while we are in the Union, and where it will end, if we remain in it, God only knows." The anxieties were renewed with every Presidential election. It was stump speaking that naturally led to indiscreet table talk concerning slavery, and reprints in the Southern press of antislavery speeches and editorials that "bring uneasiness into our families—not the things said and done by fanatics afar off." Believing that "all this ends where the separation begins," Longstreet agreed with Gardner that the moral and political power of the North to interfere with slavery would be removed forever by secession. But he also dwelled on the domestic bliss which awaited a free South. Slave discipline would be no problem. "Get us away from Republican influences, and we [master & slave] shall dwell together in peace on earth, and mingle hymns in heaven." Since the source of slave disorders was the connection with the North, the blacks would be a quiet and orderly labor force if left alone. The South's paternalistic racism dictated that "no peasantry in the world are better suited, by nature, to the agricultural vocation in which they are employed, and no peasantry are better supplied with all the necessaries of life." The possibility of internal divisions would be nil, because slavery would cease to be a topic of public discussion—unheard of in the Southern Congress and never mentioned in the press or during elections. "No question would arise about slavery in the abstract. . . ." The Northern fanatics would be aliens, as harmless as the abolitionists of England. "Our press—our literature—our legislatures—our religious and charitable institutions—our churches and our homes—would be free of them." Longstreet's harmonious slavocracy offered the security of a controlled environment from which antislavery ideas would be rigorously excluded. By thus protecting the slaveholders, it also assured the poorer whites that the existing racial accommodations would be maintained.

Although independence would supposedly enable the South to seal herself off from her enemies and from subversive ideologies, the radicals realized that the new nation would atrophy without expansion. The core of their indictment of Republican rule had been the inevitable loss of class and racial control that the restriction of slavery would precipitate. The continued profitability of plantation agriculture, white supremacy, the gradual diffusion of blacks out of the South, the ability to command respect from others, and the radicals' version of Manifest Destiny, whereby the white master race eventually would rule tropical America for the benefit of all mankind, all were predicated on the spread of slavery.

Contemporaries had no doubts that an independent South would plot an expansionist policy. This was a central theme in the Northern image of the Slave Power and the stated goal of the secessionist leaders. "We shall have an empire sufficiently large for *our* purposes and for empire during the next hundred years," announced the Charleston *Mercury*. "In the meantime, we shall colonize Texas throughout, and Chihuahua [Mexico] and a few more good Southern States. We shall have all the Gulf country when once we have shaken ourselves free of the Puritans. . . ." In expanding, the South would be fulfilling her destiny. After proclaiming that "Expansion is the peculiar necessity of the southern people," the Augusta *Constitutionalist* sneered at the argument that Spaniards, Creoles, Indians, "*et sic de similibus*" would block the southward march of slavery; "for the dominant race will supplant all others, and slavery will expand South to Brazil, and from her till stopped by snow. It may be an evil, but like cholera, no power can check it but frost."

This anticipated empire would be far stronger than any other. For, by monopolizing the productions of the tropics, without which, in the words of Keitt, the "civilized world would avert her face, the advance of nations would be arrested, and every throne in Europe would be reduced to dust and ashes," the South would become invincible. With the Gulf of Mexico as their inland sea, and with slavery established throughout the West Indies and Central America, Southerners would direct a mighty confederation equal to any military challenge. We cannot fail, asserted one secessionist, to "form the most splendid and powerful empire in the world."

By responding to and accepting these illusions of grandeur as a model for the future, Southerners were able to compensate for the growing sense of inferiority and helplessness that had characterized their relations with the free states after the Mexican War. No longer would they have to be concerned about the hopeless task of winning their fair share of the territories or about slipping further behind the North in population and economic development. An empire awaited them, assured the secessionists, if only they had the courage to grasp it. Of even greater satisfaction to their persecuted sensibilities was the projection of Southern nationalism as a vehicle that would earn respect for their institutions while at the same time exposing the weaknesses and hypocrisies of Northern society. By freeing herself, the South was told, she would be punishing the North.

Of course, no one respected Southern values, railed the secessionists, since the South invited the contempt of the rest of the world by her degraded association in a common government with those who plundered and insulted her. The first step in redeeming Southern honor must be independence. Southerners would show the world that they were not so spineless as to be incapable of ridding themselves of outsiders who incited slave rebellions, swindled them in business transactions, and, most galling of all, decried Southern morality in their prayers and curses while "disdain[ing] to preach the gospel to or feed the degraded starving [free] negroes in their very midst."

A truly civilized people, argued Fitzhugh, must have not only the attributes of refinement but the ability to supply all their own needs. Measured against this criterion, the South was only half-civilized, being shamefully dependent on the North for her commerce, manufactures, and, to a great extent, the education of her children. "We must learn to walk alone, and disunion alone can teach us. . . . Talk of negro slavery—it is not half so humiliating and disgraceful as the slavery of the South to the North." A self-sufficient and prosperous South would settle the debate over slavery in the most effective and practical manner. "The world will never believe slavery to be right, until it sees the civilization of slave States as high as that of free States," insisted Fitzhugh. In Keitt's poetic vision, the greatness of an independent South would ensure her an honored place in history: "Civilization will gather round her banner, as bright and beautiful as morning round the mountain spread."

This vindication of slavery would be all the sweeter because of the humbling of the North. While the South added more territory than made up the present Union, the free states would stagnate, hemmed in as they would be by the jealousy of Great

Britain and crippled by the loss of the Southern trade. Their economy, "built up from robbery upon the South," would soon come crashing down. The radicals boasted that the unemployed masses would roam Northern cities like packs of wild, starving animals crying for "bread or blood." The vengeance of the masses would be all the more appalling because they had been tutored in the Higher Law doctrine of the abolitionists. Having disregarded repeated warnings from slaveholders to stamp out this revolutionary heresy, Northerners would have to pay the price. Jefferson Davis had told a New York City audience as much in 1858. "What security have you for your own safety if every man of vile temper, of low instincts, of base purpose, can find in his own heart a higher law than that which is the rule of society, the Constitution, and the Bible?"

The fury of the poor would be directed against businessmen no longer able to use slaveholders as scapegoats for the frustrations and injustices of a free capitalist society. "At the North [slavery] has served as a vent for fanaticism, communism, and those secretions of a morbid sentimentality, which, without this safety-valve, would long since have resulted in a social explosion; and which will be as cruel to the pure and the good, when it does come, as it is certain in the future," said Representative Preston Brooks of South Carolina in 1854. During the winter of 1860–61, the secessionists declared that this explosion was at hand. When Northerners "come with their piteous whines and with meek and humble protestations of future good behavior, [and] beg to be taken again into the Confederacy," the debt owed the South would have been cancelled. Having repented of their false doctrines only after suffering a terrible retribution, Northerners would finally see the error of their ways. "By their own licentious acts they will have fallen," prophesied the Charleston *Mercury*, "—and they will fall never to rise again, but as a broken, needy and humbled people."

Initially a cathartic experience, secession eventually led to a numbing disaster. Hopes of glory and safety were soon dissipated, since so much of the appeal of Southern nationalism was based merely on an illusion of security embraced because of a widespread desire and need to share in the secessionists' dream of power, security, and self-respect. The Upper South, Whig planters, urban groups, and the upland yeomanry were reluctant secessionists who saw that the image of an invincible South was just a mirage. But they could not offer a compelling vision of their own, for many of their preconceptions were the same as those of the outright secessionists. Nearly all Southerners were hostile to the Republicans, abhorred abolitionism, and believed that slavery alone could maintain racial control. Above all, they were united by their common vulnerability to the social consequences of emancipation. Very few Southern unionists ever disagreed with the dogma that the South should defend slavery to the last man, but many felt that the timing of immediate secession was too hasty and they were not yet convinced that slavery could not be protected within the Union. Once the war began at Sumter, however, the question of timing became immaterial, and the Union loomed as a distinct military threat to slavery.

THE IRONY OF DEFEAT

That a civil war would destroy slavery was not a foregone conclusion. Southern conservatives feared that it would do so, and abolitionists fervently hoped so. Nevertheless, on the eve of the war, a disturbingly large number of Northerners would have concurred with the 1848 declaration of Northern anthropologist Lewis H. Morgan that "The unity of our race under the same government and institutions, is of more consequence to the welfare of humanity at large, than the perpetual bondage of the whole African family." Until he was forced by military exigencies to issue the Emancipation Proclamation, Lincoln told the South again and again that the sole war aim of the North was the restoration of the Union—with slavery, if need be, without it, if necessary. Ultimately, Southerners had no one to blame but themselves for at least the speed with which emancipation came.

Most Southerners never wanted a final confrontation on the slavery issue so much as to be left alone. The majority accepted slavery with resignation and did not even bother to defend it as a positive good until constrained to do so by the moralistic attacks of the abolitionists. Even if their critics were correct and slavery was wrong, the slaveholders asked what difference it made. "There are many evils in the condition of men which we would be glad to remedy," conceded Jefferson Davis; but, as with disease and poverty, "not being able, we permit them to exist as less than those which would follow an interference with them." Keitt put it more forcefully: "But, even if slavery be the product of rapine and violence; even if it be the hideous wrong the Abolitionists declare it to be, still the South is wedded to it in eternal union."

But the South, of course, was not left alone. Although Richard Meade of Virginia was probably correct when he told Northern congressmen in 1850 that "There is not a southern man who would ever open his lips on the subject of slavery or disunion, if you would cease your assaults," his observation was beside the point. By the 1850's, the abolitionists or Republicans were always there to mock the Southerners over the unavoidably close and intimate racial relations in their slave society. As an infant, the slaveholder was cared for and suckled by a black; as a child, he played with black companions. And, as Owen Lovejoy delighted in relating, "when he reaches manhood, he invades the nigger quarters to place himself in the endearing relation of paternity to half-niggers. Finally, if he should be ambitious, it may occur that he will come to Congress to represent a constituency, three fifths of whom are niggers. . . ." In addition to stripping Southerners of their pretensions to racial purity, Republicans focused on the morality of slavery. "I am right, or the fire-eaters are right," exclaimed Lovejoy in 1860. "If slavery is right in Virginia, it is right in Kansas. If it is wrong in Kansas, it is wrong everywhere." This moralism could best be politicized by the policy of confining slavery, a constitutional program that recognized the evil of the institution while blocking the growth of a slave South, which a majority of Northerners by 1860 had come to perceive as a threat to their self-interest. The South seceded rather than await what she felt would be the inevitable social chaos triggered by permanently damming up the blacks.

In their efforts to defend slavery and to keep the option of solving their racial dilemma through the gradual diffusion of the blacks, Southerners quickly learned how gravely they had miscalculated. The fire-eaters were the first to be disillusioned. As early as February, 1861, L. W. Spratt of South Carolina was insisting that the failure of the Provisional Congress to adopt a clause reopening the African slave trade had aborted the revolution. He reasoned that slavery would never be safe until there was a slave in every household. The South must avow and affirm its faith in the institution "as a living principle of social order." By refusing to reopen the African trade, *"our whole movement is defeated.* It will abolitionize the Border Slave States—it will brand our institution. Slavery cannot share a government with democracy—it cannot bear a brand upon it; *thence another revolution. It may be painful, but we must make it."*

The fire-eaters were in no position to carry out Spratt's threats. The broad middle spectrum of Southern political opinion could be won over to secession only if the hard-core radicals were repudiated. From the beginning, the fire-eaters were denied positions of power within the Confederacy, and they reverted to their familiar role of outsiders carping at the established party structure. Only DeBow, in his promotion of war bonds, was able to work effectively with the Confederate Government. Yancey failed as a special ambassador to Britain and had an undistinguished record in the Confederate Senate, marked as it was by the same personal animosities that had characterized his earlier forays into politics. Rhett's programs were rejected. He spent most of the war lashing out against the centralizing tendencies of the Davis Administration and denouncing those whom he suspected of favoring a reconstruction of the Union.

Saddest of all, however, was the fate of Edmund Ruffin. He was a sick, pathetic figure during the war. Permitted to fire the first official shot on Fort Sumter, he traipsed around the Virginia countryside during the early summer of 1861 looking for a fight. He fired a cannon during First Bull Run and, the next day, was on the bridge he had hit searching for bodies. He found only three. "This was a great disappointment to me. I should have liked not only to have killed the greatest possible number but also to know if possible which I had killed and see and count the bodies." The need for approval had degenerated into a compulsion to prove how many Yankees he had killed. The prospect of a Southern defeat was literally unthinkable to Ruffin. In April of 1865, the now-bankrupt old man converted his suicide into the final act of political defiance. "And now with my latest writing and utterance, and with what will be near my latest breath, I here repeat and would willingly proclaim my unmitigated hatred to Yankee rule—to all political, social and business connections with Yankees, and the perfidious, malignant and vile Yankee race."

Most other Southerners turned to the Cult of the Lost Cause as consolation for their poverty and defeat. Their greatest solace, however, would be the discovery that, if they had lost slavery, they nevertheless had retained racial control. The racial, and not the economic, function of slavery had ultimately defined the antebellum South. The proslavery ideologists, who would have been satisfied with nothing less than a hierarchical society based on the rule of planters and the idealization of slavery as a proper and permanent ordering of social relations, were a reactionary minority. The bulk of Southerners were racist egalitarians who fought desperately not to preserve this conservative, paternalistic vision of their society but to ensure the dominance of white over black. Southerners mistakenly assumed that the blacks could be controlled and segregated only through slavery; Northerners knew better. Lovejoy, in telling the South, in 1860, that she could have as much time as she wished to emancipate her slaves, added: "You must transform them from slaves into serfs, and give them homes, and protect and guard the sanctity of the family." The black serfdom that would have satisfied the Republicans in 1860 was the eventual lot of the freedmen in the postwar generation. The passage of the rights guaranteed to all Americans in the Fourteenth and Fifteenth Amendments was a remarkable tribute to Republican idealism and the new concept of nationhood born of the war years; but enforcement was deferred indefinitely by the Compromise of 1877, which acceded to Southern demands for complete home rule on racial matters.

Slavery did not survive the war, but the racial and class exploitation of the blacks did. Had Southerners been assured of this fact in 1860, much of the impetus for secession, especially among the masses, would have been drained. Nevertheless, the suspicion lingers that most Southerners would never have forgiven themselves had they not fought to preserve slavery. Aside from the tremendous economic loss, emancipation meant living with blacks who, if they were less of a physical threat free than they were enslaved, would be even more of a social menace when freed. At least, out of their military defeat Southerners could fashion the Cult of the Lost Cause, the perfect vehicle to enshrine the highest ideals of their antebellum society and to condemn the North for accomplishing what the South never could have done for herself—the abolition of slavery.

Important Dates

1817   American Colonization Society founded.

1820   Missouri Compromise: Maine admitted as a free state, Missouri as a slave state; slavery barred in the territories south of the 36°30′ parallel, from the Mississippi to the Rockies.

1822   Denmark Vesey slave plot in Charleston, S.C.

1831   First issue of Garrison's *The Liberator* published. Nat Turner insurrection in Virginia. Heightened security precautions throughout the South.

1832–33   Nullification Controversy in South Carolina. American Antislavery Society organized.

1835   Southern states pass laws barring abolitionist literature.

1836   Texas wins independence from Mexico.

1837   Congress adopts the "gag rule" to prohibit introduction of antislavery petitions.

1839   Liberty party founded as abolitionism begins to be politicized.

1844   Bluffton movement in South Carolina.

1845   Texas, annexed by Congress, and Florida become the last slave states to be admitted to the Union.

1846   War with Mexico begins. Wilmot Proviso first proposed.

1848   Treaty of Guadalupe Hidalgo ends Mexican War: in return for $15,000,000 and assumption of $3,250,000 in Mexican claims, United States receives present states of California, Utah, Arizona, and New Mexico. Free Soil party established. Discovery of gold in California.

1849   Calhoun's "Address to the Southern Delegates in Congress."

1850   Sectional crisis over compromise package of 1850: California
          admitted as a free state; territories of New Mexico and Utah
          free to legislate on slavery subject to review by Supreme
          Court; slave trade abolished in District of Columbia; new
          Fugitive Slave Act widens federal jurisdiction. Failure of
          Nashville Convention. South unable to extend 36°30′ line to
          the Pacific.

1852   *Uncle Tom's Cabin* popularizes antislavery cause.

1854   Kansas-Nebraska Act: popular sovereignty instituted for
          territories where slavery previously had been barred by the
          Missouri Compromise; Republican party founded; disintegra-
          tion of national Whig Party accelerated; Ostend Manifesto
          dramatizes U.S. interest in Cuba.

1856   "Bleeding Kansas." John Frémont, first Presidential candidate
          of Republicans, runs a strong second to James Buchanan.
          Slave conspiracies reported throughout the South.

1857   Dred Scott decision: Supreme Court declares unconstitu-
          tional the slavery restrictions of the Missouri Compromise on
          ground that Congress cannot bar slavery in any territory;
          blacks ruled ineligible for citizenship—decision rejected out-
          right by the Republicans and denounced as inapplicable to
          popular sovereignty by the Douglas Democrats. Publication
          of Hinton Rowan Helper's *The Impending Crisis of the
          South*, a bitter antislavery polemic by a native Southerner.
          Overthrow of the filibusterer William Walker in Nicaragua.

1858   Lincoln-Douglas debates. Seward's "Irrepressible Conflict"
          speech. African slave traders gain complete control of South-
          ern commercial conventions. Southern efforts to acquire Cuba
          continue to be blocked, and Kansas voters reject Lecompton
          Constitution after it is sent back by Congress.

1859   John Brown's raid.

1860   *January*
          Virginia rejects South Carolina's plan to call a convention to
          protest Brown's raid.
          April
          Delegates from cotton states bolt the national Democratic
          convention at Charleston on issue of territorial rights of
          slavery.

May
Bell and Lincoln nominated.
June
Breckenridge and Douglas nominated after Democracy fails
to reunite at Baltimore.
July–December
Southern crops badly damaged by drought. Constant rumors
of slave conspiracies and abolitionist emissaries.
November
Lincoln elected. Economic panic.
December
South Carolina leads off secession.

1861   *January*
Lower South secedes. Last chance at compromise collapses
when Republicans refuse to allow slavery south of 36°30′ in
present territories and all those "hereafter acquired."
February
Formation of the Confederacy at Montgomery.
March
Inauguration of Lincoln.
April
Civil War begins, and Upper South secedes after firing at
Fort Sumter.

Bibliographic Essay

The literature on the slave South, quite apart from that dealing with the coming of the war, is enormous. The following, highly selective, bibliography is intended to acquaint the reader with the works that most influenced my outlook on the coming of the war, as well as to suggest sources for further investigation of the major themes discussed in this book.

For a perspective on Civil War historiography, one should begin with Howard K. Beale, "What Historians Have Said About the Causes of the Civil War," Social Science Research Council Bulletin 54, *Theory and Practice in Historical Study: A Report of the Committee on Historiography* (New York, 1946). An updated treatment will be found in Thomas J. Pressly, *Americans Interpret Their Civil War* (New York, 1965). The several volumes in Allan Nevins, *The Ordeal of the Union* (New York, 1947–50), supplemented by the early chapters in J. G. Randall and David Donald, *The Civil War and Reconstruction* (Boston, 1961), give a detailed and well-organized account of the nation in the 1850's. Arthur S. Link and Rembert W. Patrick, eds., *Writing Southern History: Essays in Historiography in Honor of Fletcher M. Green* (Baton Rouge, La., 1967), provides both bibliographies and assessments of the major studies done on the South. Much of this research has been gracefully synthesized in Clement Eaton, *The Growth of Southern Civilization, 1790–1860* (New York, 1963), a work remiss only in its failure to convey the anguish and social pressures within the South.

SLAVERY, EXPANSION, AND RACISM

Ulrich B. Phillips, *American Negro Slavery* (Baton Rouge, La., 1966; reprint of the 1918 edition), and Kenneth M. Stampp, *The Peculiar Institution: Slavery in the Ante-Bellum South* (New York, 1955), are departures for an understanding of slavery. Phillips, a Southern paternalist, stresses the social consequences of the institution and minimizes its brutality, while Stampp reminds us of the harsh discipline and entrepreneurial ambitions of the slaveholders. Southern fears concerning town slaves and the decline of bondage in urban areas are amply documented in Richard C. Wade, *Slavery in the Cities* (New York, 1964). Robert S. Starobin, *Industrial Slavery in the Old South* (New York, 1970), is a major and long-overdue study. The prohibitively high slave prices of the late 1850's are reviewed by Phillips in "The Economic Cost of Slaveholding," *Political Science Quarterly*, XX (June, 1905), 257–75; their political manifestation, the agitation to reopen the African slave trade, is handled by Ronald T. Takaki in *A Pro-Slavery Crusade* (New York, 1971). Takaki contends that the agitation was central to efforts aimed at enforcing moral unity within the South on the slavery issue, but his argument is overdrawn, particularly in its tendency to identify all defenses of slavery with repressed moral guilt over the institution.

Douglas C. North, *The Economic Growth of the United States, 1790–1860* (New York, 1966), and Stuart Bruchey, *The Roots of American Economic Growth, 1607–1861* (New York, 1965), succinctly analyze the Southern economy in its national context. Still unsurpassed for its integration of economic with political themes is Robert R. Russel, *Economic Aspects of Southern Sectionalism, 1840–61* (Urbana, Ill., 1924). The dominance of the plantation is explained by Lewis C. Gray in "Economic Efficiency and Competitive Advantages of Slavery Under the Plantation System," *Agricultural History*, IV (April, 1930), 31–47, and by Phillips, "The Origin and Growth of the Southern Black Belts," *American Historical Review*, XI (July, 1906), 798–816. In their pioneering article, "The Economics of Slavery in the Ante Bellum South," *Journal of Political Economy*, LXVI (April, 1958), 95–130, John R. Conrad and Alfred H. Meyer statistically demonstrate that the economic viability of slavery in the Upper South was dependent on the profits generated by the internal slave trade. The social side of this trade and its repercussions for both master and slave are deftly treated in Frederic Bancroft, *Slave-Trading in the Old South* (Baltimore, 1931).

The conclusions reached by Fabian Linden on the elitist holdings of wealth, reported in "Economic Democracy in the Slave South: An Appraisal of Some Recent Views," *Journal of Negro History*, XXXI (1946), 140–89, have been verified and extended by Gavin Wright in " 'Economic Democracy' and the Concentration of Agricultural Wealth in the Cotton South, 1850–60," *Agricultural History*, XLIV (January, 1970), 63–93. The connection among this elitism, soil exhaustion, and mobility is made clear in W. H. Yarbrough, *Economic Aspects of Slavery in Relation to Southern and Southwestern Migration* (Nashville, Tenn., 1932). Stanley Elkins and Eric McKitrick, "A Meaning for Turner's Frontier: Democracy in the Old Northwest" and "The Southwest Frontier and New England," *Political Science Quarterly*, LXIX (September and December, 1954), stress that the frontier experience in the old Midwest eventually led to a host of small towns and a business-oriented booster politics; in the South, it resulted in more plantations and the perpetuation of planter dominance and cotton agriculture. The frontier slaveholder was a parvenu, and no one has captured him better than W. J. Cash, *The Mind of the South* (New York, 1941).

In revealing the limits and paradoxes of Southern efforts at agricultural reform and industrialization, Eugene Genovese, *The Political Economy of Slavery* (New York, 1965), reopened the debate on the economic factors underlying the expansion of slavery. Chauncey S. Boucher, *"In Re* That Aggressive Slavocracy," *Mississippi Valley Historical Review*, VIII (June–September, 1921), 13–79, has shown that there was no unity on a policy of aggressive expansion, but he misjudged the extent to which nearly all Southerners agreed that more room would eventually be necessary. The outward thrust of the nation in the generation before the Civil War, as well as Southern designs on Mexico and the Caribbean, are discussed in Albert K. Weinberg, *Manifest Destiny, A Study of Nationalist Expansionism in American History* (Baltimore, 1935), and Frederick Merk, *Manifest Destiny and Mission in American History* (New York, 1966), a shorter but often more perceptive study. The quest for markets by both free and slave states is the theme of the early chapters in William Appleman Williams, *The Roots of the Modern American Empire* (New York, 1969).

Although historians have underestimated the racial motivations behind Southern demands for more territory, the pervasive racism of antebellum society has increasingly come under study. William Stanton, *The Leopard's Spots: Scientific Attitudes Toward Race in America, 1815–59* (Chicago, 1960), traces the intellectual development of the belief that the races were distinct species. Leon F. Litwack, *North of Slavery* (Chicago, 1961), describes Northern prejudice against free blacks. His findings have been related to the free-soil movement by Eugene H. Berwanger, *The Frontier Against Slavery* (Urbana, Ill., 1967), and to Northern opposition to emancipation by V. Jacque Voegeli, *Free But Not Equal: The Midwest and the Negro During the Civil War* (Chicago, 1967). The essays in C. Vann Woodward, *American Counterpoint, Slavery and Racism in the North-South Dialogue* (Boston, 1971), are suggestive, and the synthesis achieved by George M. Frederickson, *The Black Image in the White Mind* (New York, 1971), especially in his treatment of the racist egalitarianism of Southern whites, is striking and convincing.

The main concern of Donald L. Robinson, *Slavery in the Structure of American Politics, 1765–1820* (New York, 1971), is with an earlier period, but I found his comments on Southern arguments for diffusing slavery to be suggestive; they helped to clarify my own thinking. The failure and ambivalence of efforts to rid the nation of its black population are examined by P. J. Staudenraus, *The African Colonization Movement, 1816–65* (New York, 1961). Two short articles, Paul H. Buck's, "The Poor Whites of the Ante-Bellum South," *American Historical Review*, XXXI (October, 1925), 41–54, and W. O. Brown's "Role of the Poor Whites in Race Contacts of the South," *Social Forces*, XIX (December, 1940), 258–68, reveal how racist appeals were used as an exploitive tool of class rule.

Southern Radicalism and Sectional Crisis

There is no comprehensive study on antebellum Southern radicalism, but works on individual leaders suggest the outline of the story. Avery Craven, *Edmund Ruffin, Southerner* (New York, 1932), and Laura A. White, *Robert Barnwell Rhett: Father of Secession* (New York, 1931), offer many insights into extremist leadership; but Ottis C. Skipper, *J. D. B. DeBow, Magazinist of the Old South* (Athens, Ga., 1958), is a bit thin. J. F. H. Claiborne, *Life and Correspondence of John A. Quitman,* 2 vols. (New York, 1860), and John Du Bose, *The Life and Times of William Lowndes Yancey* (Birmingham, Ala., 1892), are adequate, though uncritical; their chief value lies in their collection of letters and speeches. For Yancey's early career, I drew upon Ralph B. Draughton, Jr., "The Young Manhood of William L. Yancey," *Alabama Review*, XIX (January, 1966), 28–40; for my interpretation of the radical leaders as social outsiders, I am indebted to the points raised by David Donald in "The Proslavery Argument Revisited," *Journal of Southern History*, XXXVII (February, 1971), 3–18, in which he describes the rabid proslavery advocates as alienated men unable to find a niche in Southern life commensurate with the elite status of their fathers.

The crisis of 1850 was the direct product of the nation's success in the Mexican War. Otis A. Singletary, *The Mexican War* (Chicago, 1960), is a fine short study of the politics and military campaigns of the war. Its divisive repercussions for sectional relations constitute the theme of James C. N. Paul, *Rift in the Democracy* (Philadelphia, 1951). Holman Hamilton's *Prologue to Conflict: The Crisis and Compromise of 1850* (Lexington, Ky., 1964) is a model of succinct historical scholarship. Cleo Hearon, "Mississippi and the Compromise of 1850," *Publications of the Mississippi Historical Society*, XIV (1914); Chauncey S. Boucher, "The Secession and Co-operation Movements in South Carolina, 1848–52," *Washington University Studies*, V (1918); and Richard H. Shryock, *Georgia and the Union in 1850* (Durham, S.C., 1926), stand out among the state studies.

Debate over the motivations behind the Kansas-Nebraska Act, the single most explosive political event of the 1850's, has produced a flood of literature. Roy F. Nichols, "The Kansas-Nebraska Act: A Century of Historiography," *Mississippi Valley Historical Review*, XLIII (September, 1956), 187–212, is an essential guide. The uproar over the Act destroyed the Whigs as a national organization: Arthur C. Cole, *The Whig Party in the South* (Washington, D.C., 1913), and W. Darrell Overdyke, *The Know-Nothing Party in the South* (Baton Rouge, La., 1950), survey the wreckage in the slave states. Roy F. Nichols, *The Disruption of American Democracy* (New York, 1948), remains a classic study of the breakdown of the Democratic party in the late 1850's. In his study on Republican ideology, *Free Soil, Free Labor, Free Men* (New York, 1970), Eric Foner analyzes how the Republicans integrated moral and economic themes into a world view that attacked the slave South as a threat to the ambitions and values of Northern society. He also demonstrates the idealism that permeated much of the Republican crusade.

Particularly helpful for the election of 1860 are Allan Nevins, *The Emergence of Lincoln*, vol. 2 (New York, 1950); Nichols, *The Disruption of American Democracy*; and, for the South, Ollinger Crenshaw, *The Slave States in the Presidential Election of 1860* (Baltimore, 1945). The essays and comments in Norman A. Graebner, ed., *Politics and the Crisis of 1860* (Urbana, Ill., 1961), and George Harmon Knoles, ed., *The Crisis of the Union, 1860–61* (Baton Rouge, La., 1965), summarize recent scholarship and interpretations. The Southern malaise over internal security, which often bordered on panic, is related in Steven A. Channing, *Crisis of Fear: Secession in South Carolina* (New York, 1970); Ollinger Crenshaw, "The Psychological Background of the Election of 1860 in the South," *North Carolina Histori-cal Review*, XIX (July, 1942), 260–79; and Donald B. Kelley, "Har-pers Ferry: Prelude to Crisis in Mississippi," *Journal of Mississippi His-tory*, XXVII (November, 1965), 351–73. A brilliant essay by David Brion Davis, "Some Themes of Counter-Subversion: An Analysis of Anti-Masonic, Anti-Catholic, and Anti-Mormon Literature," reprinted in Edward N. Saveth, ed., *American History and the Social Sciences* (New York, 1964), 175–89, alerted me to the patterns implicit in the projection of group hostility in a mobile, egalitarian society and fur-nished me with a conceptual framework within which to measure the Southern fear of abolitionists against the conspiratorial phobias of other Americans.

Of the monographs dealing with secession on the state level, Chan-ning, *Crisis of Fear*; Roger W. Shugg, *Origins of Class Struggle in Louisiana* (Baton Rouge, La., 1939); Percy Lee Rainwater, *Missis-sippi: Storm Center of Secession, 1856–61* (Baton Rouge, La., 1938); and Henry T. Shanks, *The Secession Movement in Virginia, 1847–61* (Richmond, Va., 1934), best combine narrative and interpretation. The role of the Republicans during the secession winter of 1860–61 has been examined by David M. Potter, *Lincoln and His Party in the Secession Crisis* (New Haven, Conn., 1942), and Kenneth M. Stampp, *And the War Came* (Baton Rouge, La., 1950). Whereas Potter empha-sizes the possibility of compromise, even at this late stage of the crisis, and faults the Republicans for their inflexibility, Stampp quite cor-rectly points out that the extension of slavery as guaranteed by the drawing of a new 36°30' line to the Pacific was a fundamental issue on which neither section could compromise and still remain true to its values and interests.

PUBLISHED SOURCE MATERIALS

The sense of immediacy they alone can create makes contemporary articles, speeches, and correspondence an indispensable source. Al-though often less accessible than most of the works cited above, they should be consulted wherever possible. The following very brief list includes only those major works that were of most value in this study and that also can serve as a departure for research in Southern and na-tional politics in the late antebellum era.

DeBow's Review, the leading journal of the slave South, provides a convenient and extensive sampling of Southern opinion. Sectional ten-sions, legislation, and political discussion on a wide range of topics can be followed in the *Congressional Globe,* an annual compilation of congressional debates. Of the many collections of published correspondence, three are pre-eminent for their breadth of coverage: J. F. Jameson, ed., "Correspondence of John C. Calhoun," *American Historical Association Annual Report,* vol. 2, 1899; Ulrich B. Phillips, ed., "The Correspondence of Robert Toombs, A. H. Stephens, and Howell Cobb," *ibid.,* vol. 2, 1911; and Charles H. Ambler, ed., "Correspondence of Robert M. T. Hunter, 1826–76," *ibid.,* vol. 2, 1916. Of more limited interest but still extensive are: Dunbar Rowland, ed., *Jefferson Davis, Constitutionalist: His Letters, Papers, and Speeches,* 10 vols. (Jackson, Miss., 1923); M. W. Cluskey, *Speeches, Messages, and Other Writings of the Honorable Albert Gallatin Brown* (Philadelphia, 1859); J. G. Hamilton, ed., *The Papers of Thomas Ruffin,* 4 vols. (Raleigh, N.C., 1918); and J. G. Hamilton, ed., *The Correspondence of Jonathan Worth,* 2 vols. (Raleigh, 1909).

The coverage in Dwight L. Dumond, *Southern Editorials on Secession* (New York, 1931), and Howard C. Perkins, *Northern Editorials on Secession,* 2 vols. (New York, 1942), is thorough and representative. Finally, for the student interested in the tempo and mores of Southern life, as well as in the living conditions of its common folk, there is no more informative or vivid source than the travel accounts of Frederick Law Olmsted, *A Journey in the Seaboard Slave States,* 2 vols. (New York, 1856), and *A Journey in the Back Country* (New York, 1860).

Index

DATE DUE

DEC 18			
5-9-	02		
GAYLORD			PRINTED IN U.S.A.